Real Quick

A Celebration of the West Indies Pace Quartets

Real Quick

A Celebration of the West Indies Pace Quartets

Michele Savidge and Alastair McLellan
Foreword by Viv Richards OBE

BLANDFORD

For the McLellans,
the Johnsons
and the Savidges

A Blandford Book
First published in the UK by Blandford
A Cassell Imprint
Cassell plc, Wellington House,
125 Strand, London WC2R 0BB

Distributed in Australia by Capricorn Link (Australia) Pty Ltd
2/13 Carrington Road, Castle Hill, NSW 2154

British Library Cataloguing-in-Publication Data
A catalogue entry for this title is available from the British Library

ISBN 0-7137-2486-2

Typeset by Method Limited, Epping, Essex

Printed and Bound in Great Britain by Hartnolls Ltd, Bodmin

'. . . and if your stumps are found half way down the ground,
that means the West Indians are back in town.'

(Team song for the 1984 West Indian touring party. Arrangement
by Phil Ramocon, lyrics by Lance Percival. Blue Mountain Music)

'Now they're making restrictions and laws to spoil our beauty
But in the end, we shall prevail
This is just not cricket –
This thing goes beyond the boundary.
It's up to you and me to make sure that they fail.
Soon we must take a side
Or be lost in the rubble
In a divided world
There won't be no islands, no more.
Are we doomed forever to be at somebody's mercy?
Here's the key that can open the mighty door.
RALLY ROUND THE WEST INDIES . . .'

('Rally Round the West Indies', David Rudder, London Records)

Contents

Acknowledgements		9
Foreword by Viv Richards OBE		11
Introduction		13
1	Fast bowling: a West Indian tradition	17
2	The birth of the pace quartet	40
3	Pace like fire – 1979–94	58
4	The fast bowler as athlete	77
5	The art, craft and psychology of fast bowling	92
6	The team machine	103
7	Answering the threat	117
8	Nasty, brutish and short(-pitched)	148
9	Setting the record straight	179
10	Biographical notes and playing records	192
	Bibliography	204
	Index	206

Acknowledgements

THE West Indies pace quartet has dominated Test cricket since 1976. This unparalleled run of success has raised high passions. Nearly every cricket follower has a theory about why they have succeeded and the acceptability of their methods. We, of course, have developed our own beliefs while researching this book, but many of them are based on lengthy conversations with those who have been involved in international cricket during the period in which the pace quartets have ruled supreme.

Special thanks are due to Michael Holding and the West Indies physiotherapist Dennis Waight for their time and insight. Thanks also to Tony Cozier for his comments, and the wealth of information found in his writing over many years. Viv Richards not only wrote the foreword, but also spared a good deal of his time to speak about the subject with characteristic passion.

Of the batsmen who have had to face down the fast men, Graham Gooch gave us a fascinating insight into what it takes to succeed at the highest level. His one-time opening partner Tim Curtis gave, as usual, a highly perceptive analysis of the problems faced by a Test match débutant against the West Indies, while John Emburey told us how it feels to be a tail-ender facing up to Malcolm Marshall or Joel Garner. Mike Gatting and Tom Moody were also good enough to give us a brief taste of their experiences in the 'fast lane'.

Bob Willis, Vanburn Holder and Imran Khan all gave us the sort of perceptive analysis of the West Indian pace men that only other fast bowlers of similar class can provide.

C.L.R. James's *Beyond a Boundary* and Michael Manley's *History of West Indies Cricket* provided inspiration, as well as giving us an appreciation of the 'West Indian way', both on and off the cricket field.

We are also indebted to all West Indies cricketers – bowlers, batsmen and wicketkeepers – for the delight they have given to so many, for so long, a fact rarely appreciated by those in cricket's 'establishment'.

Alastair says: thanks to all at Thomas Telford for cutting me the slack to write this book and chipping in with many good suggestions. Amanda, as always, helped me keep things in proportion and on course.

Michele says: having a two-year-old daughter around is not conducive to the process of writing a book and I would have never met the deadline without the support of my own 'team machine'. So thanks to: my husband Michael Johnson for his (usually) constructive criticism of the manuscript and for keeping Lucy away from the computer; my parents Bill and Joan Savidge at Mission Control for reading the first draft and a great deal more; Jackie Whittaker for inestimable help with the aforementioned daughter; James and Ruth Ramsden for perceptive comments and moral support; and Michael Herd at the London *Evening Standard* for instilling me with, I hope, a good sense of journalistic discipline.

Foreword

by Viv Richards OBE
Former captain of the West Indies

The West Indies pace quartets are one of the glories of the modern game. They have taken the team to the pinnacle of achievement in Test cricket through sheer hard graft and professionalism, often raising their game to defeat the odds and keep us on top for the last 15 years.

In the Caribbean, the West Indies cricket team has been a focus of regional pride that is not found in any other aspect of life. Cricket is the only thing which binds the islands together – and together we are world champions. As such, cricket in the West Indies can often seem like a matter of life and death.

The pace quartet was not an accident or a freak of history. Clive Lloyd, my predecessor as captain of the West Indies, had the vision to spot a trend in West Indian cricket. Nobody else saw it and it took a great deal of foresight. He should receive credit, not blame, for that. Where would we be – and where would cricket be – without that vision?

His vision, which I and Richie Richardson followed, did not just involve the creation of a pace quartet. As you will read in this book, the 'team machine' played their part too. We have such pride in our performance and our athleticism – a fast bowler is nothing without the appropriate training, as our physiotherapist Dennis Waight reveals in this book. But our approach is also founded on professionalism and discipline, and any member of the team who neglects that will not be in it for long.

We started to play with four quicks after our 1975–6 tour to Australia when we lost by five Tests to one. The pace quartet was our response to ensure that we would never have to endure such humiliation again.

Yet, despite our achievements, the quartet has been continually maligned as a negative force by many in the cricketing establishment and much of the Press.

There are those in cricket's establishment who think we have been at the top for too long and they have attempted to devise all manner of means to curb our armoury with the absurd one-bouncer-an-over rule as well as over-rates stipulations. There are many reasons for the legislation, and envy and racism are among them: believe it or not, there are people involved in cricket today, in the late twentieth century, who think we have no right to be competing on the same stage as them – *let alone beating them at their own game!*

This book is a long overdue celebration of the skills of the West Indies pace quartet. I am sure it will redress the balance of the appalling criticism that not only the quicks, but the entire team, have had to endure for the best part of the past 20 years.

Introduction
Questions and answers

Q Why did two white English cricket writers decide to write a book about West Indian fast bowlers?

A To set the record straight.

Q What's the problem?

A Well, read this … 'Until we can breed 7 ft monsters willing to break bones and shatter faces, we cannot compete against these threatening West Indians. Even the umpires seem be scared that the devilish-looking Richards might put a voodoo sign on them!'

Letter to *Wisden Cricket Monthly*, June 1990

IMAGINE a similar letter being written and being published about Don Bradman's all-conquering Australian team which crushed England 4–0 during the 1948 Test series. That side's bowling was based around the pace attack of Lindwall, Miller and Johnston. Lindwall's nickname was 'Killer' and Miller's short-pitched bowling used to give England's No. 1 batsman Len Hutton vivid nightmares (as well as more than a few bruises). Under the rules at the time, a new ball could be taken every 55 overs and, in between the fast bowlers' assaults, the medium-pacer Toshack bowled a purely negative line designed to keep the batsmen from scoring. It was a series distinguished by English batsmen ducking bouncers and remaining scoreless for overs on end. Although the Australian method of attack was described by Jack Fingleton as 'bitter and calculating', the 1948 team which inflicted this ordeal on England is regarded as perhaps the greatest ever.

Yet the West Indies team which has dominated world cricket for the past two decades by relying on very similar tactics to Bradman's champions has been the most vilified and maligned in sporting history. And the major source of this sporting defamation has been the English (and Australian) press, as well as those charged with the administration of the game in those countries. By word and action they have accused the West Indies fast bowlers of basing their game on ugliness and brutality.

In fact, a Test batsman can consider himself unlucky if he receives an injury serious enough to force him to retire from the crease before he has faced 3,703 deliveries from the West Indies pace quartet. Roughly translated, this means that he would have to play more than 40 games against the Caribbean side to stand a better than average chance of being badly injured. A batsman is in considerably more danger of serious injury driving home after the game than he is facing the Windies pace quartet. Looked at another way, on average the Windies quartet prevent an opposition Test player from batting at the rate of less than one a series. It is hardly a great competitive advantage or a 'reign of terror', is it?

We believe that the West Indies cricket team, and particularly the pace quartet, is one of the glories of the modern game and hope that this book will do a little to balance the scales of justice. This book is a celebration of West Indian fast bowling, but it is also an apology to the West Indies pace men, their team-mates and their supporters for the slurs that they have had to bear from our countrymen for the past 20 years.

What is there to celebrate?

The West Indians play the game as it is meant to be played. Their exuberance in victory and despair in defeat knows few bounds. Unlike the sportsmen and women of many national teams, West Indians believe representing their country is a privilege which demands commitment. Because of this they care about their performance and do not mind who knows it. Not for them the cynicism of the old lag or the cocksure vulgarity of England's or Australia's younger players; they are still sensitive to the elation and deep depression they felt on first entering the game. Because of this it is the West Indian cricketer who is closest to the Golden Age amateur. And it is the 20-odd world-class fast bowlers who have made up the West Indies' pace attack for the past two decades who are the heart of this Caribbean crusade. There is nothing half-hearted, nothing jaded about the West Indies pace attack. It is elemental, a force of nature, a highly charged, emotional expression of a culture's sporting skills and craving for recognition.

But isn't it discipline rather than exuberance that has made the quartet such a force?

The Windies pace attack *is* disciplined, but it is not the world-weary professionalism possessed by most other successful teams. It is a successful channelling of cricketing talent which does nothing to weaken or lessen its impact. In the mid-1970s, the West Indies finally learned to maximize the strengths of their ebullient approach to the game while eradicating the weaknesses. They also no longer conformed to the stereotype of the brilliant but flawed 'calypso cricketer' and this was when they first learned of the prejudice which has cast a shadow over their unparalleled success in Test cricket ever since.

Why 'Real Quick'?

'Real quick' is the ultimate praise a West Indian crowd can bestow on a fast bowler. It distinguishes bowlers from those who are merely 'quick'. We also believe the Windies fast bowlers are *real* quick, in that they are the genuine article: fast bowlers with speed and skill to rank alongside any of the game's greats. Despite the heavy criticism they have received, they have remained true to the West Indian way of playing cricket and in doing so have produced the greatest concentration of fast-bowling talent in cricket history.

The greatest?

Over the past 20 years, a collection of tropical islands (plus Guyana) with a combined population only half that of London has produced five of the greatest fast bowlers ever: Andy Roberts, Michael Holding, Joel Garner, Malcolm Marshall and Curtly Ambrose; five more who in any other era would have been hailed as the best of their generation: Ian Bishop, Wayne Daniel, Sylvester Clarke, Colin Croft and Courtney Walsh; and an almost endless supply of high-quality pace men to act as 'support' bowlers, including Patrick Patterson, Winston Davis, Tony Gray, and Kenny and Winston Benjamin.

Why do they deserve this praise?

One fact stands out above all others: the West Indies (largely thanks to the fast bowlers we've just named) have not lost a Test series since 1980. They have played all the major Test nations, both home and away, on a variety of wickets, against teams as powerful as Greg Chappell's and Allan Border's Australians and Imran Khan's Pakistan side. And yet, to date, no team has been able to overcome the Windies pace quartet over the length of a five-match series. It is the greatest success story in Test cricket history and the fast bowlers wrote most of the finest chapters.

1 | Fast bowling: a West Indian tradition

All West Indians who come to the game try to bowl fast as a matter of course; to train a West Indian slow bowler you must begin with his grandfather.

Neville Cardus, 1934

1928–39 – The pioneers

The phenomenon of West Indian fast bowling was well in place before the 1970s: even in the 1920s, when the conventional wisdom of Test cricket meant that you played one out-and-out fast bowler, a fast-medium seamer and two spinners, the West Indies were fielding three truly quick bowlers in most matches. On the 1923 tour of England, before the West Indians had gained Test status, they fielded a trio of fast bowlers – George John, George Francis and Learie Constantine – which, had John not been already 40 years of age, would have surpassed the infamous pairing of Australians Gregory and MacDonald in ferocity.

In 1928, during their inaugural Test series against England, Francis and Constantine were joined by Herman Griffith, forming what *Wisden* described as 'the strongest combination of fast bowlers in any Test side'. Five years later, the 35-year-old Francis had been replaced by Manny Martindale. Finally the West Indies won their first Test rubber at home in the Caribbean during 1935 with the fastest trio of all: Martindale, Constantine and Les Hylton.

In this way the West Indies' policy of fielding their best bowlers, regardless of type, was established early, although this time it did not bring them conspicuous success. Of the 22 Tests, all but five against England, the West Indies won only four and lost 13. But this was not the fault of the fast bowlers, as their records show:

West Indian fast bowlers 1928–39

	Test matches	Wickets	Average	Strike rate*
E.A. Martindale	10	37	21.72	43
L.G. Hylton	6	16	26.12	60
H.C. Griffith	13	44	28.25	61
L.N. Constantine	18	58	30.10	62
G.N. Francis	10	23	33.17	70

* average balls per wicket

These figures lose only a little in comparison to England's and Australia's leading fast bowlers of the age, who of course had the twin advantages of playing more matches and picking up cheap wickets against second-rate Test sides such as India, South Africa, New Zealand and, of course, the pre-war West Indies. The performances of the West Indian fast bowlers were further hampered by the fact that Griffith and Hylton were both 34 when they made their Test débuts while Francis was 30, as well as by the generally poor quality of pre-war West Indian slip fielding.

English and Australian fast bowlers 1926–48

England	Test matches	Wickets	Average	Strike rate
W.E. Bowes	15	68	22.33	54
W. Voce	27	98	27.88	65
H. Larwood	21	78	28.35	64
K. Farnes	15	60	28.65	65
G.O.B. Allen	25	81	29.37	54
Australia				
E.L. McCormick	12	36	29.97	58
T.W. Wall	18	56	35.89	86

Fast bowling in the late 1920s and 1930s was a thankless task. Lovingly prepared wickets produced a paradise for batsmen, led by arch-dominator Don Bradman, and only bad weather could turn the tables. Even then, uncovered run-ups meant that fast bowlers often could not exploit the 'sticky' wickets. It was the worst possible time for a Test side based on fast bowling to make its début.

During the West Indies' only series against Australia before World War 2, the Australians won the first four matches by an innings. But when the sides came to Sydney for the last Test and found themselves playing on a less than perfect wicket, the Windies showed what they could do. After declaring at 350 for 6, the West Indies dismissed a batting line-up including Woodfull, Ponsford, Bradman and McCabe for 224 and then, after running up 124 for 5, did it again, this time for 220 (Bradman bowled Griffith 0). All three West Indian fast bowlers played their part, Francis bowling 35 overs and taking 4 for 80, Griffith 26 overs and 5 balls, 5 for 81 and Constantine 27 overs, 3 for 78.

But the Windies' greatest hour in the pre-war period came during England's 1935 tour of the Caribbean. England had left many of their best bowlers at home, but the batsmen in the party included Wally Hammond, Maurice Leyland, Les Ames and Patsy Hendren. Despite this batting power, the West Indian fast bowlers, admittedly assisted by often uneven matting wickets, were simply too good. Hendren topped the batting averages with just 202 runs at 28.85, Ames scored 164 at 27.33 and Hammond (second only to Bradman as a destroyer of bowling in the immediate pre-war period) 175 at 25.00. Leyland, who had scored 478 runs at an average of 68 against Australia in the previous English summer, collected just 36 runs in three tests.

In a scenario which was going to become familiar during English tours of the Caribbean from 1980 onwards, the wickets were shared evenly between the Windies fast bowlers. Martindale displayed Marshall-like irresistibility, taking 19 wickets for 12.57; Constantine had his most successful series with 15 wickets at 13.13 and Hylton provided valuable support with 13 wickets at 19.30. Largely through their efforts the West Indies won the series 2–1.

But who were these first generation West Indian fast bowlers, and what allowed them to enter the Test scene and immediately begin to compete with their counterparts from the established international sides? The answer is that even before West Indian cricket received international recognition, it had 'naturally' established a tradition of pace bowling which encouraged youngsters to emulate the feats of their fast bowling heroes.

The greatest of these was George John. He was the first of the early West Indian fast bowlers to be acknowledged outside the Caribbean and some would say the best. John's performance on the 1923 tour of England was one of the reasons why the West Indies were granted Test status five years later. That a 40-year-old fast bowler could come to England and take 49 wickets at 19.51 in first-class cricket was a strong indication of the potential of West Indian fast bowling.

And great potential there certainly was. Constantine claimed that, during the second decade of the twentieth century, Stingo, a local club in Port of Spain, Trinidad, 'included no less than seven bowlers who were in the international class'. One of these seven was the 'huge, dark and powerful' George John. Born in 1883, he was, according to Constantine, 'in a different class – a class by himself in the West Indies ... [he] could bowl as fast as Gregory and Larwood'.

Writing in the early 1960s, C.L.R. James describes John as 'about five feet ten, with a chest, shoulders and legs on him all power and proportion. He ran about fifteen yards, a quick step or two first, a long loping stride that increased until near the crease he leapt into the air and delivered, his arm high'. He continues, 'Statham is a splendid bowler and Trueman is a very fine one. But a fast bowler in the sense that John was a fast bowler I have seen only one – Tyson in 1954'. Yet, despite believing that John was 'hostility itself', James claimed that the fast bowler never bowled a bouncer, preferring 'to defeat you first of all by pace and sheer pace'.

John provided a world-class standard to which other West Indian fast bowlers could aspire. His batting equivalent was George Headley who inspired and set the standard for the immediate pre-war generation of West Indian batsmen. But whereas Headley was usually a one-man act in the batting line-up, from the West Indians' inauguration into Test cricket until the start of World War 2, there was always a pack of fast bowlers hammering at the selectors' door. And for that they could thank George John.

If the West Indies had made their Test début in 1923, when they were an arguably stronger side, John would no doubt have opened the bowling. But by the time the Windies took the field for their first Test he had retired. Instead, it was the 30-year-old George Francis who opened the bowling. Although the Bajan was to to play Test cricket for five more years, he was already past his best by 1928. Following very much in John's footsteps by bowling fast and concentrating on the stumps, he took 82 first-class wickets at 15.58 on the 1923 tour of England. Three years later he took 9 for 56 against a powerful Marylebone Cricket Club (MCC) team touring the Caribbean. Constantine, who toured with him in both 1923 and 1928, described him as 'a very quiet fellow. A great bowler. He skittled out famous English county players, always looking rather apologetic himself.'

Herman Griffith was the stock bowler in the West Indies' original Test attack. More fast-medium than truly quick (although James claimed he could be almost as quick as John on occasions), he bowled sharp outswingers. Francis was controversially chosen ahead of Griffith for the 1923 tour. This caused considerable debate in the West Indies, as Griffith, who was four years older, had already established a reputation as a high-class bowler, while Francis was considered by most as little more than a 'net bowler'. But Griffith got the opportunity to prove that he was Francis's equal by beating his fellow Bajan's wicket tally on the 1928 tour.

Constantine described the short but stocky Griffith as being 'never flustered, keeping a good length even after punishment, as likely to take two or three wickets after twenty overs as during the first five minutes of play'. These attributes were perfectly demonstrated during the first great exhibition of West Indian fast-bowling talent in Test cricket.

The third Test of the 1928 tour of England saw the West Indians dismissed for 238 and the home side reach 284 for 1. Hobbs and Ernest

Tyldesley had already added 129 for the second wicket when Griffith was reintroduced to the attack. Almost immediately Tyldesley was caught by Constantine off Griffith for 73. Next to the wicket was England's young batting star Wally Hammond, but he did not last long, caught Small, bowled Griffith 3. With the score still on 305, Griffith bowled Leyland for a duck. Francis dismissed Jack Hobbs for 159 and Griffith completed his spell by having Hendren caught for 14 and Chapman for 5. Griffith had ensnared the cream of English batting, which six months later was to demolish the Australian bowling attack in four consecutive Test matches, for just 21 runs.

In his seminal history of West Indian cricket, former Jamaican prime minister Michael Manley rates Manny Martindale sixth in the pantheon of great Caribbean fast bowlers, behind Holding, Marshall, Garner, Roberts and Hall, and ahead of fearsome rivals such as Charlie Griffith and Colin Croft. Martindale was the most successful of the pre-war West Indian fast bowlers and arguably the quickest. His record of taking a wicket every 43 balls was unparalleled among other fast bowlers of the age. This performance was particularly praiseworthy, given that Martindale took just 4 wickets during the 1939 three-Test series against England. By that time age had drawn the sting of his pace, but in the two Test series in which he was at his peak (1933 and 1934–5), Martindale was the West Indies' leading bowler.

Martindale did not appear particularly threatening, standing only 5 ft 9 in. But his run-up was long and climaxed in a classic side-on delivery. He bowled a wicked inswinger and of the 33 Test wickets he captured between 1933 and 1935, 14 were bowled or lbw. His fiercest exhibition of bowling came in the final Test of the 1935 series. In a scenario which has become all too familiar to England cricket supporters over the past 15 years, the West Indies declared late on the second day for 535. Martindale delivered the first ball to the English captain Bob Wyatt, bowling at 'a terrific pace'. Later in the over, Wyatt attempted to duck a short ball which failed to lift and had his jaw broken. Martindale then had Wyatt's fellow opener Townsend caught by Christiani for 8 and, with the score on 26, dismissed both Paine and Holmes. Constantine chipped in with Hammond's wicket and the close of play saw England 27 for 4 with their captain in hospital. Martindale went on to record his best Test performance (33 overs, 6 maidens, 84 runs, 7 wickets) as the West Indies won by an innings and 161 runs.

Jamaican Les Hylton is more widely remembered as the only Test cricketer to receive the death penalty. But before he was hanged in 1955, for the murder of his wife, Hylton had established a minor position within the West Indian fast-bowling fraternity. Again it was in the 1935 series that Hylton was the most effective, forming with Martindale and Constantine a quick-bowling trio rated by some ahead of England's threesome of Allen, Farnes and Bowes.

Hylton made a sensational start to his Test career, opening the bowling with Martindale on a weather-damaged pitch at the Kensington Oval in Bridgetown, Barbados. In 7 overs and 3 balls, Hylton took 3 wickets, including that of Wally Hammond, for just 8 runs. Unfortunately for the West Indies, he could not match Martindale's hostility in the second innings as England chased only 75 to win. Martindale captured 5 wickets for only 22 runs, but his partner lost his normal tight control of length and swing, and went for 6 runs an over as England rushed to victory by 4 wickets.

However, Hylton got his revenge in the very next Test. This time, bowling for much of the match with Constantine, he took 5 wickets for 80 runs and played a major part in the West Indies' 217-run victory.

The final member of the Windies pre-war fast-bowling line-up towers above the rest for as many reasons as he had talents. Learie Constantine was of course a brilliant all-round cricketer, but he was also an author with a style as lively as his fielding, a barrister, diplomat and politician. He was knighted in 1962 and, after being given a life peerage seven years later, became the first black man to take a seat in the House of Lords. He played an important part in achieving independence for Trinidad and Tobago, but perhaps even more significantly his patronage enabled C.L.R. James to raise the issue of self-determination in the Caribbean to a level which made it inevitable.

Constantine made a name for himself, not only in international cricket, but also with Nelson in the Lancashire Leagues. He was the ultimate league professional, helping his side win the championship in eight out of ten seasons. This performance, as well as considerable dignity and humour, of the first black man many Lancastrians had ever seen, also helped to break down centuries of racial prejudice.

Constantine had a level of self-belief which has perhaps only ever been equalled in a cricketer by Bradman and Ian Botham. It is this which makes him the true father of modern West Indian fast bowling. It was he who first expressed the mantra of today's West Indies fast-bowling quartet that – regardless of the score their batsmen put up – the bowlers could dismiss the opposition for less. And it was also Constantine who first had the confidence regularly to bowl short at the white men who were his Test opponents.

Unlike most of the West Indies pre-war fast bowlers, Constantine came from a middle-class background. His father, Leburn, was a plantation foreman and a good enough cricketer to be part of the two West Indian touring parties sent to England before World War 1. His son was brought up in relative comfort and, after leaving school at 15, became a solicitor's clerk. Not for him the indignity of eking out a living as a member of the ground staff at a white man's club, the only option open to many promising young West Indian cricketers at the time. Constantine's cricket was allowed to develop unrestrained, whereas those providing bowling practice for their white employers knew that bowling a bouncer was a quick route to immediate unemployment. It is not suggested that no other pre-war West Indian fast bowler ever bowled a bouncer, but it was Constantine who pioneered the tactical use of the short-pitched bowling which has become such an established part of the modern quartet's arsenal.

Constantine was a stocky but long-limbed man. His bowling style expressed his natural exuberance, a high, leaping action followed a long, bounding run. A typically ornate description from a West Indian newspaper summed up the overall impression, claiming that Constantine's bowling was 'always productive of some rare feat which makes spectators want to sit up and laugh themselves crying'.

During the 1923 tour of England, Constantine noted how the Warwickshire fast bowler Edward Hewetson, bowling round the wicket, had used short-pitched bowling to upset West Indian batsman Percy Tarilton. The West Indian all-rounder, who among his other talents was a fast learner, took note. When Constantine returned to the West Indies, he experimented with this new tactic in the Caribbean's intercolonial tournament. It was not a great success, but Constantine went on practising.

When the 1928 England tour came around, Constantine was ready to try out his new tactic on English batsmen. The crunch came at Old Trafford in the second Test. After the West Indies had been bowled out for 206, two decisive stands put England in a commanding position. Jack Hobbs and Herbert Sutcliffe put on 119 for the first wicket, and then Wally Hammond and Douglas Jardine added 120 for the fourth. The frustrated Constantine banged the ball in short to try to disturb the batsmen's concentration. It did not do him a lot of good, his 25 overs costing 89 runs for just 1 wicket. But Hammond, Jardine and, surprisingly, even Hobbs (who, remember, had faced Gregory and MacDonald) complained in the press about the fierceness of Constantine's short-pitched bowling. The West Indies team, on the other hand, said nothing when Larwood gave their batsmen a similar going-over in the first and third Tests.

There was even more for the English batsmen to complain about when a rather elderly, but nevertheless strong, England side toured the Caribbean in 1930. On a flat Bridgetown wicket, Constantine once again banged the ball in short as England ran up 467 in reply to the Windies' 369. Andrew Sandham made 152 (he was to score a world record 325 in the fourth Test) and Hendren made 80, but Constantine unnerved all the English batsmen except the younger and more fleet-of-foot Ames.

Before the next Test in Trinidad, Constantine was approached by the England team manager and told to cut back on the short-pitched bowling. Amazingly Constantine agreed, and watched with a mixture of wry amusement and anger as England's opening bowler Voce thudded them down into the middle of the pitch. Voce took 11 wickets for 149 runs in the match and Constantine 6 for 207. England won the match by 167 runs.

Constantine had had enough of this nonsense by the time the third Test started in Georgetown, Guyana (at that time British Guiana). After the

West Indies had scored 471, he steamed in to take 4 for 35 as England slumped to 145 all out. In the final innings of the match, as England tried to hold out for a draw, Constantine bowled 40 overs and took 5 for 87 as the Windies won a few minutes before the close of play.

When Constantine returned with the West Indies for the 1933 tour of England, the controversy over short-pitched bowling had been raised immeasurably. In the preceding winter, England had recaptured the Ashes as Larwood and Voce used persistent short-pitched bowling to packed leg-side fields to reduce drastically the effectiveness of Australia's main asset: Don Bradman. In England itself, without the benefit of television coverage, the majority view of 'Bodyline' bowling, as it became known for obvious reasons, was that England had won fairly and squarely, and that the 'whining' Australians were simply bad losers. On a contemporary newsreel, Australian wicketkeeper Wally Oldfield is shown receiving a fierce blow on the head from a short-pitched ball. The commentary tells the viewer that 'the unlucky bowler is Larwood'.

Despite this uncontroversial view of the tour, there was considerable tension in England as the West Indians arrived. Would England bowl Bodyline at the Windies – surely there was no need – and would the Caribbean team, especially Constantine, retaliate? This tension was made manifest when, in the match between the MCC and the touring side in late May, the openers Joe Hulme and Jack Hearne fended off bouncer after bouncer from Constantine and Martindale. When Patsy Hendren came to the wicket he was wearing a cap padded with thick rubber, and two extra peaks to guard the temples and ears.

The first Test was an anti-climax as Constantine was unavailable, Larwood injured (he was never to play for England again) and Voce out of form. But this was only postponing the inevitable, and during the second Test at Old Trafford matters came to a head. The wicket was very slow and unsuitable for short-pitched bowling. Constantine was therefore surprised to hear his captain, George Grant, a white man, order him and Martindale to bowl Bodyline. The two West Indies pace men roasted the English batsmen and one ball from Martindale split Hammond's chin. But, with the wicket getting slower by the minute, Douglas Jardine – England captain and Bodyline mastermind – saved the day with a resolute 127.

After the match it was strongly rumoured that the English cricketing authorities had requested that Grant adopt Bodyline tactics so that they might see for themselves what all the fuss was about. By all accounts they were horrified and Bodyline was banned soon after.

It is ironic that the originator of modern West Indian fast bowling should have played such a significant part in ending the most dangerous and destructive form of the craft. But his more enduring legacy is that his every action demonstrated that the black man had every right to do anything the white man did. True, among other things, that meant propelling a hard leather ball towards another man's head at over 90 m.p.h., but that was part of the game as it had been played since the legalization of overarm bowling. More important, Constantine's use of tactical short-pitched bowling was part of the process which showed that those who were equals on the field should be equal off it.

1940–59 – The lost generation

The years lost to World War 2 caused a major hiccup in the Caribbean's production of world-class fast bowlers. The seven-year interruption in Test cricket effectively cancelled out a generation of West Indian fast bowling talent and the lack of any role models for young cricketers to follow meant that the Caribbean side were without a top-flight quick bowler until 1957.

The 11 years following World War 2 saw the only extended period when the West Indies team was without at least two very good fast bowlers, normally its strongest resource. Ironically, it was also during this period that the West Indies drew level with the world's two leading cricket powers, England and Australia, driven forward by a combination of awesome batting talent and bewitching spin bowling.

Not that this was evident from the first two series played by the Windies after the end of the war. During England's 1947–8 tour of the Caribbean and a visit to India a year later, the West Indies fielded four different fast bowlers. Between them they took 53 wickets in nine Tests. Three of the quartet continued to play for the Windies during the triumphant 1950 tour of England and the hugely disappointing tour of Australia in the English winter of 1951–2. But the six Tests in which they appeared during these two series yielded just 11 wickets for the four quick men. And then, nothing.

The problem was age. The four fast bowlers – Prior Jones, 'Foffie' Williams, John Trim and Hines Johnson – were all over 30 when they made their post-war débuts (Williams had played one Test against England on the 1939 tour). They were still skilful and quick enough to make sure that the West Indies won their first two series after the war, but after that age quickly dulled their talents.

The clearest example of the quality of this generation of West Indian fast bowling was Hophnie Hobah Hines Johnson. He made his début in the fourth Test against England in 1948 and, as if to make up for lost time, Johnson threw himself at the English batsmen. After an opening stand of 129 between Hutton and Robertson, Johnson dismissed both openers and Ken Cranston before returning to capture the last two English wickets. In England's second innings he once again took 5 wickets to finish with match figures of 65 overs and 5 balls, 24 maidens, 96 runs and 10 wickets.

Astoundingly, he was passed over for the 1948–9 tour of India, but when he returned, at the age of 39, to take part in the 1950 series against England he was still fast enough to unsettle Len Hutton and, together with Worrell, reduce England to 25 for 4 on the first day of the third Test. But Johnson was becoming injury-prone and his two Tests in England brought him just 3 wickets for 142 runs. He, of all the Windies post-war fast bowlers, must have sighed for what might have been.

The most capped West Indian fast bowler in the five years after the war was Prior Jones. It was he who bowled the first ball for the West Indies in Test cricket after the enforced break, as well as playing throughout the five-Test series against India. Hailing, like Constantine, from Trinidad, Jones was an accomplished fast bowler who had mastered the art of cutting the ball both ways.

His début against England was successful; he took 4 wickets for 54 runs as the touring side were dismissed for 253. However, West Indian Test selection of fast bowlers in this period was notoriously erratic and Jones did not play again until the first Test of the Indian tour. On good batting wickets, four of the five Tests were drawn. Jones played his part in the fourth Test victory, but his most important contribution came during the fifth Test.

Set 361 to win in 6½ hours, a stand of 139 for the fourth wicket between Modi and Hazare saw the Indians closing in on the target with wickets to spare. That they finished just 6 runs short with two wickets standing was largely thanks to Jones. In the boiling Bombay heat he sent down 41 overs, a third more than any other West Indian bowler, gave away only 85 runs and took 5 wickets, including that of Hazare for 122. It was his control, bowling to tightly packed leg-side fields, that enabled the West Indies to secure their 1–0 victory in the inaugural series against India.

Jones was no more than a bit-part player in the 1950 tour of England. Despite his heroics in India, Johnson was the number one West Indian bowler and Jones only played in the second and fourth Tests because the 39-year-old was unfit. By the time the 1951–2 Australian tour started, Jones was back as the Windies' first-choice fast bowler following Johnson's retirement. But at this stage the West Indian bowling attack was firmly based on the spin of Ramadhin and Valentine, and he only got a single, and final, game.

Ironically, the West Indians were defeated 4–1 in this series, largely because in Lindwall, Miller and Johnston the Australians had a fearsome and high-class pace attack. Lindwall, for example, took 21 wickets during the series and once roasted the West Indies' leading batsman, Everton Weekes, by bowling him 15 bouncers in six overs.

After the Australian tour, Jones returned to Trinidad to relive past glories in a house he rented from one of the founding fathers of West Indian cricket (and manager of England's Bodyline tour), Plum Warner.

Foffie Williams, who according to Gary Sobers bowled as fast as Martindale, had made his début alongside Gerry Gomez in the second Test of the 1939 tour of England. Neither had made an impact on the game. When the war ended, Williams was 33 and he was clinging on to his Test place by his fingernails. He did not disgrace himself in the first three Tests of the first series against England, but with the younger Jones and Trim now on the scene he knew his days were numbered.

Williams still had time to make his own small mark on the Test scene. Coming in at No. 7 in the second innings of the first Test, he decided to take the attack to off-spinner Jim Laker. Laker was in his first Test and had taken 7 wickets for 103 in the first innings, including that of Williams for 2. This time the script was different. Laker's first two balls to Williams were driven for six, while the third and fourth balls both went for four. Williams reached his 50 in only 30 minutes, a record at the time for the West Indies, and eventually made 72 in 63 minutes.

When the 1948 MCC touring party arrived in Guyana to take on the local side, the 32-year-old John Trim caused a sensation by snapping up nine English wickets. A few days later he was stepping on to the same Georgetown field, this time as a West Indies player.

He was given the considerable advantage of a rain-damaged pitch and bowled tightly in his opening spell. However, the medium-pacer Goddard and the leg spinner Ferguson soon took over, reducing England to 110 for 8. Trim then returned and snapped up the last two wickets, finishing with the analysis of 10 overs, 6 maidens, 6 runs and 2 wickets. Trim was dropped for the next Test in favour of Johnson, but made a highly successful return to the West Indian side during the fourth Test against India in 1949. After the Caribbean side had notched up 582, Trim, together with Gerry Gomez and Jones, dismissed India for 245 and 144. Trim was the leading wicket taker with 7 for 76.

Trim played in the next Test, taking another three wickets, but was again dropped from the side, this time until the fourth Test of the West Indies' 1951–2 tour of Australia. Opening the bowling with Gomez, Trim was a revelation, dismissing both Morris and Miller, and finishing with 5 for 34 off 12 overs. However, his fortunes then declined as he was run out for 0 twice in the match and, when in the final innings Australia were set 260 to win, went wicketless as the host side squeezed home by 1 wicket.

And so ended John Trim's highly unusual Test career. Match figures of 3 for 44 in his first Test were followed by his exclusion from the side for four consecutive Tests. When he returned, he captured 10 for 188 in two matches, but then was not selected for seven matches. His final hurrah in Australia gave him the highly impressive Test career figures of 18 wickets at 16.16.

Trim died in 1960 at the age of 45, surprisingly young for this powerfully built, deep-chested man. He left behind a family of 13 children.

The career figures for the leading West Indian fast bowlers of the immediate post-war period were:

West Indian fast bowlers 1939–52

	Test matches	Wickets	Average	Strike rate
J. Trim	4	18	16.16	44
H.H.H. Johnson	3	13	18.30	61
E.A.V. Williams	4	9	26.77	88
P.E. Jones	9	25	30.04	74

During the mid-1950s, the West Indies picked fast bowlers almost out of habit rather than necessity. As well as Ramadhin and Valentine, they had four good quality, medium-pace, seam-bowling all-rounders in Jerry Goddard (33 wickets in 27 Tests), Gerry Gomez (58 in 29), Denis Atkinson (47 in 22) and the left-arm Frank Worrell (69 in 51). There was also the flowering genius of Gary Sobers, who would soon add aggressive left-arm pace to his slow bowling, masterful batting and eye-catching close fielding.

The flag of West Indian fast bowling was kept flying by Frank King, Tom Dewdney and then the fearsome Roy Gilchrist. Their Test records are:

West Indian fast bowlers 1953–9

	Test matches	Wickets	Average	Strike rate
R. Gilchrist	13	57	26.68	57
D.T. Dewdney	9	21	38.42	78
F.M. King	14	29	39.96	99

Until Gilchrist and Dewdney teamed up for the 1957–8 series against Pakistan, six consecutive rubbers passed with the West Indies normally fielding only one fast bowler.

The first of these was Frank King. Before his début, most West Indian fast bowlers had tended to be relatively short, stocky men with powerful hips and shoulders. King, on the other hand, was tall and slim, and 'glided up to the crease like a ballet dancer' with a long flowing run-up that ended in an elegant bowling action. He can be seen as a prototype for the modern West Indian fast bowlers such as Michael Holding, Courtney Walsh and Curtly Ambrose.

King made his début at the age of 26 during the home series against India in 1952–3. For a débutant he made a considerable impact, playing throughout the five-match series and finishing with 17 wickets at 28.24 as the Windies won the series 1–0. His greatest hour came during the drawn third Test. After Worrell and Gomez had reduced India to 117 for 3, King worked his way through the Indian middle order to take 5 for 74 from 31 overs. He also broke the left hand of Indian wicketkeeper Maka, forcing him out of the game.

However, the West Indies' hopes that they had unearthed another Martindale were to come to little. During the next nine Test matches, King was to take just another 12 wickets at the very poor average of 56.58.

King was replaced as the number one West Indian fast bowler by Tom Dewdney half-way through the 1954–5 home series against Australia. Dewdney was from Jamaica, a large man who relied more on movement and accuracy than pace to take wickets. The 21-year-old had a baptism of fire during his first Test. On a beautiful batting pitch in Barbados, the West Indies had done well to reduce Australia to 233 for 5, Dewdney taking 2 wickets. But then Keith Miller and Ron Archer added 206 for the sixth wicket, before Ray Lindwall weighed in with 118. The Australians finished with 668 and Dewdney had figures of 33 overs, 5 maidens, 4 for 125.

Dewdney continued to play for the West Indies for another three years, but only once had any real impact on a Test match. This was the fourth Test during the 1955–6 series in New Zealand. The Jamaican fast bowler took 5 for 21 as the home side were bowled out for 255; the West Indies, however, only managed a combined total of 222 in their two innings.

Dewdney is perhaps best known for being the third occupant of the car driven by Gary Sobers that crashed into a cattle truck during an early morning run to London on 6 September 1959. Sobers and Dewdney both survived, but Collie Smith, the brilliant young West Indian all-rounder, was killed.

The West Indies' next fast bowler was also from Jamaica, but he would prove a world away in terms of talent and controversy. Roy Gilchrist rushed to the wicket and bowled with a side-on action that was all shoulders and hips. Although a relatively short man, he was the West Indies' fastest bowler since Martindale and all agreed that he had the talent to equal his illustrious predecessor.

The 23-year-old Gilchrist made his début against England in the first Test of the 1957 series in England. He played in the first four Tests and although he was not a great success, there was a general consensus that he was already the fastest bowler in the world.

When Pakistan arrived in the West Indies during January 1958, Gilchrist began to turn his promise into achievement. On a wicket where the West Indies had just hit 579 for 9 declared, Gilchrist and Collie Smith dismissed Pakistan for just 106. The West Indies' reward for this achievement was to field for over two days while Pakistan, following on, ran up 657 for 8 (Hanif Mohammad 337). But there was to be no resisting Gilchrist in the second Test in which he took 7 wickets as the West Indies won by 120 runs. In the fourth Test, Gilchrist took a further 6 wickets and the West Indies celebrated the discovery of a great fast bowler along with the series victory.

At the end of the same year, Gilchrist travelled with the West Indian touring party to India. This time he had a new opening partner, a brilliant young Barbadian fast bowler called Wes Hall, and the Indians did not know what had hit them. In the first Test, Gilchrist took 6 wickets and Hall 4, but the Indians saved the game. In the second Test, Gilchrist was injured but Hall took 11 wickets and the West Indies won by 203 runs. Gilchrist was back for the third Test and took 9 wickets (Hall 6) as the West Indies won by an innings and 336 runs. The shell-shocked Indian batsmen collapsed again to Hall and Gilchrist in the fourth Test, but managed to rediscover enough backbone to save the fifth.

Gilchrist's figures for the series were 198 overs, 73 maidens, 26 wickets at 16.11. It seemed that the West Indies, with Hall taking 30 wickets in the series, now had a fast-bowling attack equal to any they had had before the war. But reaching that goal would have to wait another year. The fifth Test against India was to be Gilchrist's last.

Gilchrist had heard that Swaranjit Singh, an Indian batsman, had been bad-mouthing him. The two met in a match prior to the series and Gilchrist gave him a roasting, banging in bouncer after bouncer and sending down 90 m.p.h. beamers aimed at the batsman's head. Gilchrist refused to apologize for these deliveries, for, as Sobers commented at the time, 'Gillie meant it'.

Singh and the West Indian captain Gerry Alexander had been at Cambridge together, a fact which only heightened the tension between Gilchrist and his skipper. When Alexander told Gilchrist to stop bowling beamers, the fast bowler ignored him and the West Indian skipper decided he should be sent home. Alexander relented, but the disagreements continued and Gilchrist was dispatched at the end of the Indian series, while the rest of the team travelled on to Pakistan, where they lost a three-match rubber 2–1.

Gilchrist was the 22nd child of a Jamaican factory worker and was a hero to his working-class countrymen. He was 'discovered' playing in a village cricket match and brought by a patron to Kingston, who gave him a job, and considerable guidance in what to do on and off the field. Later he pledged similar allegiance to Frank Worrell. On the Indian tour he was removed from both good influences, Worrell not making the trip, and nobody knew how to control him.

C.L.R. James, who perceived that the middle-class (white and light-skinned black) establishment that ran West Indian cricket did not understand the emotions of the working-class majority which was increasingly providing most of the West Indian players, took up Gilchrist's case. He suggested that Worrell should be sent to extract an apology from Gilchrist and that, if this was forthcoming, the fast bowler should be given a second chance. But the West Indian cricketing authorities were adamant that Gilchrist was now beyond the pale and so the Test career of one of the Windies' finest fast bowlers was ended. Gilchrist continued to play league cricket in England, taking hatfuls of wickets, bruising bodies aplenty and never being far from controversy.

The West Indian cricket establishment's reaction to the Gilchrist affair only served to strengthen James's belief that a change was needed to ensure that the West Indies had a truly representative cricket team. His campaign, waged through the pages of *The Nation* newspaper, finally succeeded in 1959 when Frank Worrell was appointed as the first black captain of the West Indies Test team.

1960–9 – Hall and Griffith

With Gilchrist out of the picture the West Indian selectors had to find a partner for Hall. This scouting exercise took just over a year, and involved two false starts with Chester Watson and Charlie Stayers.

Watson was 20 years old when he was picked to partner Hall in the 1960 home series against England. At 6 ft 1 in, he capped an 11-pace run-up with a smooth and lively action. He was not as fast as Hall – few were – but could get the ball to rise sharply from the pitch. Watson proved a willing work-horse and he gave the English batsmen a regular going-over with the short ball, but he lacked penetration.

Two years later, India arrived in the Caribbean to face Hall, Watson and a new fast bowler, Charlie Stayers. The Windies won the series 5–0, but Stayers contributed little. His place was usurped by Lester King who took 7 wickets in the fifth Test and then had to wait another six years for his only other Test appearance.

But the debate about the relative merits of King, Stayers and Watson was made academic at the start of the 1963 series in England. Bajan fast bowler Charlie Griffith, who made an unspectacular début against England in the 1960 series, re-emerged transformed. Now 24, he had filled out and his huge, stocky frame meant he could produce considerable pace from a relatively short run-up. Hall had found a partner worthy of him and West Indian fast bowling was finally reborn.

West Indian fast bowlers 1960–9

	Test matches	Wickets	Average	Strike rate
W.W. Hall	48	192	26.38	54
C.C. Griffith	28	94	28.54	60
C.D. Watson	7	19	38.10	77
S.C. Stayers	4	9	40.44	71

Hall and Griffith re-established West Indian pace bowling as a potent and consistent threat by opening the bowling for the Caribbean side throughout the 1960s. By the time they finally ran out of steam during the 1968–9 tour to Australia they had made fast bowling once again the strongest component of West Indian cricket. On their retirement, at least four high-quality fast bowlers rose to take their place and this generation of West Indian cricketers spawned in turn the greatest explosion of fast-bowling talent the world has known.

As we have already seen, Hall made his début at the age of 21 against India. He played throughout both the Indian and Pakistani series, taking 46 wickets and immediately establishing himself as a world-class bowler.

Hall is reckoned by many to be the greatest fast bowler the West Indies have ever produced. His average is considerably higher than that of, say, Malcolm Marshall or Joel Garner, but his supporters argue that the batting sides of England and Australia (though not the other Test sides) were stronger during his Test career. His strike rate of 54, however, is the equal of the modern generation of West Indian fast bowlers.

But these comparisons are academic. What really mattered about Wes Hall was that he was the archetypal West Indian fast bowler. Standing 6 ft 3 in, with a solid but lithe frame, he raced across the turf in 33 giant raking strides to deliver the ball with a beautiful side-on action which ran seamlessly into a sweeping follow-through that took him yards out on to the off-side. The batsmen watching Hall run in would have noticed something else too: a gold chain swinging hypnotically in time to the surging run and, as he bowled, flying up and often over his neck. As a fast bowler Hall seemed an ideal made flesh.

A delivery from Hall was timed at 91 m.p.h. in the early 1960s, but as well as pace and movement, Hall's greatest attribute was stamina. If his captain wanted him to, he would bowl all day. This was most famously demonstrated on the last day of the Lord's Test in 1963.

England were chasing 234 to win and had reached 116 for 3 at the end of the fourth day. Hall had two of the wickets and had also broken Cowdrey's arm with a short ball. Start of play on the fifth day was delayed by rain and it was not until 2.20 p.m. that Hall resumed the attack. England batsman Brian Close was playing the innings of a lifetime and, when the score reached 203 for 5, it seemed that England would pull off a famous victory. But then Hall had Fred Titmus caught by McMorris and dismissed Freddie Trueman with the very next ball.

Griffith, who had also been bowling for most of the day, had Close caught behind for 70 soon after. But when Hall began his last over, after bowling for more than three hours with only the 20-minute tea interval offering any respite, England needed eight runs to win with all-rounder David Allen and pace bowler Derek Shackleton at the wicket. The first three balls produced two runs and off the fourth Allen was run out. Cowdrey, his arm in plaster, heroically returned to the wicket. But Shackleton was facing and somehow managed to block Hall's final two deliveries as they thundered towards his off-stump. The match was drawn and Hall left the field, shoulders slumped with exhaustion, with the figures of 40 overs, 9 maidens, 4 wickets for 93.

After the 1958–9 tour of the sub-continent, Hall returned to the Caribbean to prepare for the 1960 home series against England. His partnership with Watson was not the equal of the Hall–Griffith partnership, but it was fierce enough for the duo to be warned for intimidatory bowling by umpires Lloyd and Lee Kow. At the end of the series, he was once again the West Indies' leading wicket-taker.

When the Windies arrived in Australia for the 1960–1 tour, Watson's career was on the wane and Hall was to be his side's only fast bowler in four of the five Tests. However, in the first Test he was magnificent. In a scenario uncannily similar to the Lord's Test two years later, Australia needed only 233 to win in their final innings and failed to do so largely through Hall's efforts. This time the greater part of Hall's contribution came in the early part of the innings as he dismissed Simpson, Harvey, O'Neill and Favell to leave Australia 57 for 5 (McDonald being bowled by Worrell). But at 92 for 6, Benaud and Davidson embarked on the most famous partnership in Australian–West Indies cricket and, as they passed the 200 mark, the match looked won. But Worrell recalled Hall who almost immediately had Benaud caught behind for 52. So tightly did the giant paceman bowl in the game's concluding overs that three Australian batsmen ran themselves out in a desperate bid for victory. The scores finished level, producing Test cricket's first tie, and Hall had figures of 17 overs and 7 balls, 3 maidens, 5 for 63.

In the next Test, Hall took another six wickets, but the strain of carrying the pace attack got to him and the last three Tests brought him just six more scalps.

With hindsight it seems that the West Indies captain took advantage of Hall's willingness to bowl. The fierce workload he had to carry at the start of his Test career often meant that Hall's effectiveness would decline as a series unfolded. This was demonstrated again when Australia toured the West Indies in 1964–5. Hall produced a match-winning 9 for 105 (from 43 overs) in the first Test, then bowled another 35 overs in Australia's first innings in the second Test as the visitors ran up 516. In the final three Tests he took only 5 wickets.

Time after time, Hall would demonstrate the ability to force his giant frame through marathon spells. In the first innings of the second Test against England in 1966, Hall bowled 36 overs and took 4 for 106. In the very next game, he repeated the performance, bowling 34 overs in the first innings and taking 4 for 105.

Charlie Griffith could not have been more different from his opening partner. They shared the same home island, but little else. Hall was treated with affection as well as respect by most of his opponents; Griffith's achievements on the other hand were often viewed with great suspicion.

The genesis for this attitude arose from Griffith's explosive impact on the

1963 series against England. When the 21-year-old Griffith made his début against England in the last Test of the 1960 series in the Caribbean he was viewed by the English team as a 'rather ordinary medium pacer'. His 24 overs in the match cost 102 runs for just 1 wicket.

He certainly exuded menace. Although an inch shorter than Hall, Griffith was much stockier with a heavily furrowed brow and, on the field at least, was completely unsmiling. But his shambling run-up and open-chested action was an anti-climax. Imagine the shock then of the English Test players who competed against Griffith in the county games before the 1963 Test series in seeing the Bajan transformed. Not only was his run-up considerably longer, but he had added yards to his pace and was now as great a threat to both a batsman's wicket and, particularly, his physical well-being as Hall. There could only be one answer, they concluded: Griffith must have become a chucker.

The impression was reinforced by two of Griffith's strengths. Even with a low arm action, he was able to get the ball to rise steeply and, without any noticeable extra effort, Griffith was able suddenly to produce a ball 20 m.p.h. faster than his normal delivery. These extra-quick deliveries were usually bouncers or yorkers and therefore often resulted in broken wickets or bones.

Griffith had already been no-balled for throwing by West Indian umpire Cortez Jordan during a match between India and Barbados in March 1962. Earlier in the same game, Indian captain Nari Contractor had ducked into a ball from Griffith. Sobers remembered the point of impact as 'the sound of eggshells cracking'. Hit on the back of the head and bleeding heavily from the nose, Contractor hovered between life and death, receiving pint after pint of new blood, much donated by the West Indian players. That he survived was considered a miracle.

The controversy over Griffith's action came to a head during the Australians' 1964–5 tour of the West Indies. Hours of film were taken of Griffith's bowling and most observers concluded that, with some deliveries, his arm did appear to bend as it swung upwards towards the delivery point. However, few could agree whether it stayed bent long enough to be constituted illegal. The Australian captain Bobby Simpson certainly believed that Griffith threw many of his deliveries and expressed his opinions in more than one newspaper.

His predecessor as Australian captain, Richie Benaud, later stated that Griffith had attempted to alter his bowling action in time for the 1966 tour of England. This, however, did not prevent the Bajan fast bowler being no-balled by former Kent batsman Arthur Fagg during the tourists' game with Lancashire.

Griffith was a figure made for controversy, but he was also a personality beset by contradictions. The image of a giant (very) black man who cheated at cricket and liked to smash white men's skulls pandered to the racism that was abroad in the cricketing world, particularly in England where spurious concerns over immigration were raising the temperature. But when the *Daily Mail* conducted a poll of the UK's favourite cricketers in 1966, Griffith was voted into ninth place, ahead of his opening partner Hall.

Griffith obviously showed different sides of his character to different people. Compare these two views of the Bajan fast bowler:

> Charlie was quiet, inclined to be moody, and was suspicious – partly as a result of the throwing controversy, I imagine – of anyone white.
>
> (Trevor Bailey, *From Larwood to Lillee*)
>
> Griffith was the same as ever, a very big, very strong, very kind, very reserved, in fact very modest man.
>
> (C.L.R. James reports on the departure of the 1963 West Indian touring party)

Bailey does admit, however, that Griffith mellowed with age and became 'great fun'.

Griffith was never more effective than on his first tour of England during 1963. After a quiet start, taking only one wicket in the first Test, he produced amazing performances during the next four games.

Charlie Griffith v. England 1963

Old Trafford	30 overs	8 maidens	48 runs	1 wicket
Lord's	56 overs	13 maidens	150 runs	8 wickets
Edgbaston	49 overs	12 maidens	103 runs	5 wickets
Headingley	39 overs	10 maidens	81 runs	9 wickets
Oval	50 overs	11 maidens	137 runs	9 wickets

Against a batting line-up including Ted Dexter, Ken Barrington, John Edrich and Colin Cowdrey, Griffith's performance has a claim on being the best ever by a West Indian fast bowler over the length of one series. His origins as a fast-medium bowler meant that he knew how to cut back his pace and move the ball around, a valuable attribute in England where conditions make this kind of bowling particularly effective. And when Griffith's ability to move the ball was combined with his fierce changes in pace, he was very often unplayable.

Griffith was never such a force again, but he became a valuable foil to Hall and, particularly, to Gary Sobers whose left-arm medium-pace bowling reached the very highest level during the 1960s. His contribution is demonstrated by the fact that of the 23 Test matches in which Hall and Griffith played together, the West Indians won 10, drew 9 and lost only 4: at the time the most successful run in Caribbean cricket history.

The Hall–Griffith partnership was destroyed in a blaze of Australian batting talent during the fifth Test of the 1968–9 away series. As Australia ran up 619 (Walters 242, Lawry 151), Hall finished with 36 overs for 157 and Griffith 37 for 175. The hunters had finally become the quarry. But the very next Test, against New Zealand two weeks later, saw a new West Indian fast bowler capture six wickets as the Windies won by five wickets. Hall and Griffith's example would not be squandered, there would be no repetition of the post-war slump in fast-bowling talent: the conveyor belt had started rolling.

1970–5 – The dress rehearsal

Between the retirement of Hall and Griffith, and the emergence of the modern fast-bowling quartet, the Windies remained well stocked with fast-bowling talent. The players and their Test records are as follows:

West Indian fast bowlers 1970–9*

	Test matches	Wickets	Average	Strike rate
J.N. Shepherd	5	19	25.21	76
K.D. Boyce	21	60	30.01	58
V.A. Holder	40	109	33.27	83
R.M. Edwards	5	18	34.77	73
G.C. Shillingford	7	15	35.80	79
B.D. Julien	24	50	37.36	91
U.G. Dowe	4	12	44.41	85

* Only those who made their début before 1975 and who had completed their Test careers by 1979 are included

Most of these bowlers were more fast-medium than fast, although some, particularly Vanburn Holder, were capable of very quick spells. England batsman Frank Hayes, for example, remembers that bowlers such as Holder, Boyce and Julien bowled 'a yard quicker' in Test cricket than they did when competing on the county circuit. These three bowlers in particular kept the torch burning until the arrival of true speedsters, such as Andy Roberts, as well as winning more than a few Test matches.

As Hall and Griffith declined, another Bajan fast bowler had a brief moment of glory. Richard Edwards was already 28 when he made his début in the second Test of the 1968–9 series in Australia. He had been kept out of the Windies side by his two fellow countrymen, but was now given his chance. His first two Tests saw Australia score 510 and 547, winning by a mile each time, and he was dropped. He was reinstated for the three-Test series against New Zealand and found the conditions (and the strength of the batting line-up) much more to his liking. In the first two games of the series, Edwards captured 13 wickets and looked to have established himself in the side. But he was not picked in the tour party due to travel to England in May 1969 and retired from the game a year later.

The reason that Edwards was passed over for the trip was the rise of two younger fast bowlers. Vanburn Holder and John Shepherd (24 and 26 years old, respectively) were two of the new breed of promising West Indian cricketers to opt for a career in English county cricket as overseas internationals. Shepherd had joined Kent in 1966 and was to play a significant part in the county's domination of English cricket's one-day and first-class competitions during the 1970s. Holder, who signed with Worcestershire in 1968, was to team up with New Zealand opener Glenn Turner to bring the county its first championship for nine years in 1974.

The registration of overseas players by English counties was to start a trend which would see almost all of the West Indies' modern fast-bowling stars establish their reputation in county cricket.

During the 1969 series the young West Indian fast bowlers had to work hard to dismiss the Englishmen. During the first Test, Holder was quick but ineffectual, while Shepherd on the other hand put in a performance of which Hall would have been proud. Bowling for much of the time in tandem with Gibbs, Shepherd pounded through 59 overs and took 5 wickets for 104. Unfortunately it was not enough to stop England winning by 10 wickets.

In the next Test, Sobers (who was now leading the pace attack), Holder and Shepherd were joined by Grayson Shillingford to form the first West Indian pace quartet, if one considerably slower and less skilful than those to come from the West Indies after 1976. The 25-year-old Dominican fast-medium pacer had a good début, taking 4 wickets for 83 runs. Shepherd bowled another 43 overs in the first innings of the match, finishing with 3 for 74.

In the third Test, it was Holder's turn to come good, capturing 4 wickets for 48 runs in the first innings as England were dismissed for 223. Shepherd completed a highly successful first series by bowling another 24 overs and taking 3 for 43. But he was injured in the field and his absence was one of the reasons why England were able to set the West Indies a target of 303 which proved 30 runs too many.

Next, the three young West Indian fast bowlers were pitched against India's famous spin trio of Bedi, Prasanna and Venkataraghavan. In a series dominated by the bat (and won by India 1–0) they came off second best. Shillingford was preferred to Shepherd for the first three Tests and did nothing, while Holder took only 6 wickets in three Tests.

The third Test of the series against India saw the début of perhaps the best of the early 1970s generation of West Indies fast bowlers. The 27-year-old Keith Boyce was from Barbados: a lively fast-medium pace bowler,

37

brilliant fielder and hard-hitting batsman. His bowling could be expensive, but his strike rate was that of a Test match opening bowler. Boyce spent 12 seasons with Essex and became one of the best-loved overseas players. His Test début, however, was relatively inauspicious and he was dropped from the West Indian side immediately afterwards.

His replacement, the 21-year-old Jamaican Uton Dowe, was perhaps the fastest bowler to play for the West Indies between Hall and Roberts, but apart from speed he had little else to recommend him. He started well, dismissing Sunil Gavaskar for 1 (the Indian batsman's previous scores in the series being 65, 67 not out, 116 and 64 not out), and went on to take 4 wickets for 69. But in the last three innings of the series, Gavaskar had his revenge, scoring 117 not out, 124 and 220. Dowe took 3 more wickets, but they cost him 176 runs.

Over the next year, the Windies trusted their attack to spin bowling, hoping to maximize the threat of their one world-class bowler, Lance Gibbs. During the 1971–2 series against New Zealand and the 1972–3 series against Australia, the West Indies experimented with five different opening bowling partnerships. The period was one of stagnation for the West Indies (which brought eight draws and two defeats), but it did allow them to conclude that Shillingford and Dowe were not up to Test standard and that, when it came to the choice of an all-rounder, Boyce's more dynamic approach was to be preferred to Shepherd's steadiness.

The West Indies rediscovered the right fast-bowling combination on the 1973 tour of England. To the opening partnership of Boyce and Holder was added the left-arm pace of Bernard Julien. The 23-year-old from Trinidad was not as quick as Boyce or Holder and often proved very expensive, but his left-arm deliveries provided another alternative for the West Indies skippers. He was also an even better batsman than Boyce and a fine fielder.

The first Test against England during the 1973 tour saw the first great performance by a West Indies fast bowler since the heyday of Hall and Griffith. Boyce took 11 wickets for 147 runs, at the time the second-best match figures for a West Indian, as the Windies beat the home side by 158 runs. Boyce also smashed 72 runs in the Windies' first innings.

Holder returned for the second Test to make up a four-man pace attack with Boyce, Julien and Sobers. However, the impact of this new approach had to wait until the third match. After the West Indies had scored 652 for 8 wickets, Holder and Boyce ripped through the home side to dismiss England for 233. In the second innings, Julien joined with Boyce to bundle the Englishmen out for 193. The Windies had won by an innings, and a strategy was beginning to take shape.

But the realization of the plan was put on the back burner for the first two Tests of the return series against England in the following spring. Boyce and Julien played four Tests apiece, but Holder played only one as England drew a series in the Caribbean for the last time to date. The series does, however, have an important place in the development of modern West Indian fast bowling. The third Test saw the début of Andy Roberts, the first Antiguan to play Test cricket, and destined to be one of the greatest fast bowlers of all time.

In the English winter of 1974, the West Indies travelled to India under their new captain Clive Lloyd with four fast or fast-medium bowlers: Roberts, Holder, Boyce and Julien. The scene was set for a return match between the West Indian pace men and the Indian spinners; one extreme against another. Despite the spin-assisting wickets of the Indian sub-continent, the Windies won the series 3–2, with the prototype pace quartet triumphant.

West Indian fast bowlers v. India 1974–5

	Matches	Wickets	Average
A.M.E. Roberts	5	32	18.28
V.A. Holder	4	17	18.53
B.D. Julien	4	9	27.78
K.D. Boyce	3	6	41.00

Boyce had been disappointing, true, but the result of this series told the West Indian selectors that four fast bowlers used together were likely to be successful regardless of the local conditions. It was a lesson rammed home by the Australian fast bowlers a year later and one that the West Indies team has not forgotten to this day.

2 | The birth of the pace quartet

How Clive Lloyd forged a team out of his side humiliated by Lillee and Thomson is one of the modern epics of our time.
Tim Hector, editor, *The Outlet* newspaper, Antigua

CLIVE LLOYD's development of a four-strong pace attack during the late 1970s was the defining moment of modern Test cricket. It provided the foundation of an unprecedented period of dominance by the Caribbean side: the greatest shift in international cricket's balance of power since Australia rose to challenge England in the 1880s.

Lloyd had experimented with the idea of a pace quartet during the 1974–5 series against India, but it was not until the West Indies' World Cup victory over Australia in 1975 and their subsequent humiliation Down Under later the same year that the idea began to develop real substance. During the 1975–6 series, the Australian pace-bowling attack of Dennis Lillee, Jeff Thomson, Max Walker and Gary Gilmour shattered West Indian morale, technique and bones as Clive Lloyd's side crashed to defeat, five Tests to one. It was this series defeat (the worst in West Indian cricket history), together with the arrival of Packer cricket, which goes a long way towards explaining why the West Indian four-pronged pace attack came to be born.

The first Test on the 1975–6 tour was held at Brisbane's Gabba ground and saw Australia post a convincing victory by 8 wickets, with Gordon Greenidge out for a pair and Greg Chappell becoming the third Australian captain to make 100 in his first Test innings as skipper. Both Dennis Lillee and Gary Gilmour took 6 wickets in the match.

In the second Test at Perth, the West Indies appeared to have put that first Test débâcle behind them, beating Australia by an innings and 87 runs, with more than a day and a half to spare. Michael Holding, in the third over of the second day, bowled Ian Chappell, Jeff Thomson and Ashley Mallett in seven balls and the Australian first innings closed at 329. West Indies opener Roy Fredericks hit 169 and put on a first wicket stand of 91 with Bernard Julien, who had never opened in his life before. Lloyd scored 149, despite having been painfully hit on the body three times in one Thomson over, and the West Indies reached a total of 585 before bowling out Australia for 169.

So, with the score at 1–1 after two Tests, the series looked set for a close-ly fought tussle. But, in spite of their impressive second Test victory, the West Indies came completely unstuck in the rest of the series. Australia won the third Test in Melbourne by 8 wickets, the fourth in Sydney by 7 wickets, the fifth in Adelaide by 190 runs and the sixth in Melbourne by 165 runs.

After the fifth Test, Australian commentator Keith Stackpole asserted: 'When the West Indies conquer their contradictions they will surely be a great side ... When they're bad, they're very, very bad but when they're good they're stupendous.' That criticism was taken fully on board by Lloyd who knew he had to eradicate his side's propensity to capitulate under pressure and build on its 'stupendous' qualities.

The painful lesson at the hands of a rip-roaring Australian fast-bowling attack sowed the seed of a plan in Lloyd's mind. Former West Indies cap-tain Viv Richards recalls that Lloyd first gave voice to his thoughts over a drink: 'Clive and I were having a few beers and he said, "Smokey, if we can get two more fast bowlers [Michael Holding and Andy Roberts were already playing], we could really do something. We could make it a much better contest. I think we could be as aggressive as they are." And Clive was right,' says Richards. 'He started something and I kept it going – and it's still working. I tried my best to maintain it, and although I didn't have the same quality [of fast bowlers], we were still able to maintain that presence.'

Richards acknowledges the influence of the West Indies' defeat during the 1975–6 series on the creation of the pace quartet, but is adamant that the Windies' motives were not ones of revenge. 'I never saw any devil in terms of how I felt towards the fast-bowling department, but we did learn our lesson from Lillee and Thommo,' he says.

Make no mistake, Lillee and Thomson were fierce in 1975–6. Ashis Nandy in *The Tao of Cricket* wrote:

> In 1975–76 in Australia, the gifted West Indian batsman Vivian Richards, constantly facing a nearly homicidal barrage of fast bowl-ing from Dennis Lillee and Jeff Thomson, began to show a 'neur-otic' loss of self-confidence. Even though many considered him the world's greatest batsman, no one felt that the cricketing culture which produced such a breakdown in one like Richards needed to be re-examined. It was Richards who was duly put under psychiatric care so that he could emerge 'healthy' and 'normal' and as insensi-tive as Lillee and Thomson about the fate of his fellow cricketers facing the West Indian battery of fast bowlers.

Richards, who during his career and since has spoken vehemently against what he has perceived to be anti-West Indies press coverage, believes that many commentators have now conveniently forgotten the barrage of short-pitched bowling the West Indies had to cope with in 1975–6: 'That [the bowling of Lillee and Thomson in 1975–6] is why sometimes I found it rather absurd when people would tell you that our bowling was brutal. Some of these people were reporting cricket in 1975–76 and must have seen what we went through.'

If the seed of the West Indies fast-bowling quartet was sown in Australia, the idea fully blossomed in Lloyd's and Richards's minds in the same country during Kerry Packer's World Series Cricket. The detractors of West Indian pace bowling are often the same people as the detractors of Packer cricket – and it is he they can partly thank (or blame) for the Caribbean production line of the greatest fast-bowling artists.

The Packer 'Circus', as we shall see later in this chapter, shaped the competitiveness of the successful West Indians of the 1980s.

Richards maintains: 'I would like my runs in Packer cricket to be made first-class. It was the toughest, hardest, meanest cricket ever played in terms of sheer strength and competitiveness. It was winner takes all. And Packer had the best fast bowlers in the world there.

'It really fuelled my attitude to the rest of my career. It was so competitive out there.

'Of course, even though you loved the sport, you were attracted to the money. There was a new dimension: you were paid a good salary for the first time in your life. And you felt that you had to go out there and do the business. I think that created the competitive edge in every team and held me in good stead for the future. Everyone went on and became tougher individuals after that.

'In 1975–76, we became hard.'

While Packer cricket shaped the competitive spirit of the West Indians, it also became fundamental in binding them together as a collective unit. To understand that transformation, it is necessary to have some comprehension of West Indian politics in a wider sense during the last 20 years.

The West Indies are made up of a number of independent island states, with individual currencies and economies, separate governments and different aspirations. In cricketing terms, islanders were, and in some cases still are, more avid supporters of their island's cricketers than collectively of the West Indies.

According to Tony Cozier, the doyen of West Indies cricket reporting: 'For an abundance of reasons, most founded in history and geography, insular bickering is never far below the surface of West Indies cricket and success on the field is no antidote.'

Vanburn Holder stresses the fact that there was a lot of pressure on the selectors to pick 'home' players. 'If a certain player wasn't picked, an island would say, "We're going to ban the Test, we're not going to watch it." That attitude wasn't good for the team, because you have to play your best side, whether that's five or six from Barbados, three from Jamaica, it doesn't matter as long as it's the best side.

'But I think when Clive became captain he had a lot more say than some others before him and he often got what he wanted.'

The fact that West Indies cricket was able increasingly to appease these hugely patriotic peoples and bind the team together for the sake of success is one of the most striking features of Lloyd's reign.

Overcoming insularity was one of Lloyd's main aims. He believed that cricket is the instrument of Caribbean cohesion. 'It is the musical instrument on which we orchestrate our emotions; from the extreme of wild enthusiasm to the depths of despair,' he has said. Echoing Vanburn Holder's words, Lloyd said that the Windies Test side had often suffered from insularity, the call for arithmetical representations from each territory, prejudice and a lack of confidence that selection methods would guarantee that the best talent emerged. He maintains that Sir Frank Worrell took the West Indies a long way up the road towards a solution to these problems and considers that his goal was a continuation of Worrell's work.

From a heartfelt Caribbean perspective, Tim Hector, editor of *The Outlet*, Antigua's independent newspaper, is sure that Lloyd succeeded: 'The more those island nations, separate and fragmented as mini-states, became peripheral in politics and economics, the more from 1977 West Indies cricket teams became the champions of world cricket. That, to put it mildly, is phenomenal.

'While the West Indies in the imaginative literary field reflected or refracted the "dereliction", the "splintering and fragmentation", the "diminished man", West Indian cricket embodied a "wholeness and coherence", a sense of regionalism so striking, that it can only be viewed as the Regional State in embryo, or in full bloom in cricket if you prefer.'

Michael Holding puts much of the development of regionalism, as opposed to insularity, down to World Series Cricket: 'The Packer "Circus" made a huge difference to our entire attitude, team spirit and morale. When we were banned from international cricket, we bonded together: all the island rubbish went out, we were a group of banned cricketers and we had to stick together. And that is where the team spirit came from,' says Holding. 'There was never any competition between us – it was all for the West Indies.'

The West Indies had been frequently criticized for buckling under pressure and it was this development of team spirit that became fundamental to their later success. As an example of this failure in temperament you need look no further than the fourth Test of that unhappy Australian tour in 1975–6. Australian captain Greg Chappell was given not out caught at the wicket, a decision which sparked an uninhibited show of dissent from the West Indians. Holding (the disappointed bowler) cried tears of frustration, saying, 'I'm not bowling another ball. I'm done!', while Lance Gibbs and Lloyd told him that this was part and parcel of cricket, and he had to get on with it.

But after the setbacks they encountered in Australia, the West Indies toughened up and learnt, as Richards says, to conduct themselves professionally, as well as showing themselves to be good team players. Lloyd thought that his main aim as captain was to produce a stable team that would be full of confidence and discipline. 'The "high fives" during practice was started by Clive,' says Richards. 'All that camaraderie came after we won the World Cup against Australia in England in 1975. All the bowlers were encouraged all the time, even if they got you out in the nets!'

But Tim Hector takes Richards's and Holding's argument a giant leap further, believing that West Indian cricket is the Caribbean's response to US cultural imperialism, which came with American economic dominance over the islands.

He believes that three people are responsible for the establishment of West Indian cricket as both cultural resistance and the embodiment of the Caribbean Regional State: Clive Lloyd, Viv Richards and Richie Richardson.

'Those who bewail the current preoccupation with US television and therefore US basketball', says Hector, 'miss the point by a mile – or more than that … The point is, given the US economic dominance, basketball inevitably came. The key point is that despite the US's enormous power, and in spite of its tremendous, even overwhelming, impact, cricket brought by the British, and West Indianized in the West Indian humanizing process, soared and continues to soar, in response to American cultural dominance.'

So Clive Lloyd is honoured not only for the overwhelming contribution he made to West Indian cricket with his legacy of a fast-bowling quartet, but also for his contribution to Caribbean independence. He is a towering figure in West Indian history.

As an astute thinker, Lloyd was well aware of the legacy he himself inherited. The captains immediately before him – Worrell, Rohan Kanhai and Gary Sobers – provided Lloyd with a sense of purpose but, more important, the knowledge that he had much to do to lead West Indies cricket to the heights which Worrell had visualized.

John Arlott said of Lloyd that the key to his captaincy lay in the fact that he was a thinking man. 'Under Sobers, whom he idolized as a player,' said Arlott, 'Lloyd had observed all the generally attributed West Indian weaknesses. It was said that they did not fight back, that they lost relaxedly; that they would throw their wickets away through obsession with attack; that they were hook-happy; that their out cricket was too casual; that their bowling was not tight.

'He observed all those shortcomings and their effect and, while for most of the time he felt himself too junior to say anything in criticism, he made mental notes.'

Tim Hector further believes: 'How Lloyd forged a team out of his side humiliated by Lillee and Thomson is one of the modern epics of our time.

The meteoric climb back, from the nadir to the apogee of world cricket, and the maintenance of that development, when all around him in politics and economics were succumbing to structural adjustment, either self-imposed or [International Monetary Fund] IMF-imposed, must at the very least involve a style and type of leadership hitherto unknown, and not easily surpassed.'

Vanburn Holder believes that Lloyd had something of an advantage over previous captains of the West Indies. 'A lot of the players were playing in English county cricket,' he says, 'which added to the professionalism.'

Lloyd's professional approach helped him to restore morale after that Australian rout, which Vanburn Holder for one claimed was so psychologically damaging. 'It was one of my first tours away and I must admit that I'd had enough after a while. Our bowlers did their job well, especially in the second Test in Perth, and then we got hammered, destroyed. And that shattered me. We were a better side than that.'

Lloyd of course inspired Viv Richards, his successor as captain. And Richards, despite his monumental individual performances, says he gained the greatest satisfaction during his career through what the West Indies achieved as a unit. 'We're a team made up of so many different islands, cultures and beliefs and to have achieved the way we have, that has given me the most pleasure.

'People in England don't realize that cricket is the *only* thing which binds the islands together. In David Rudder's song "Rally Round the West Indies", there is a line – "This one goes beyond the boundary" – which says it all.'

There is overwhelming evidence then that political considerations have a great bearing in understanding how and why the pace quartet came into being. Lloyd was the right man, in a political context, and in the right place, to pick the team up after their humiliation in Australia in 1975–6 and subsequently to bind them together during the Packer series. The fact that the side felt that their achievement in winning the inaugural World Cup in 1975 was not recognized further helped his cause.

Lloyd has gone on record as saying that he was 'disgusted' at the lukewarm reception from the West Indies Cricket Board after they had won the World Cup. Team members received only the £350 fee which had been agreed before the competition. And if Packer cricket did nothing else, it sharpened up the minds of the board in terms of how their players should be remunerated. Lloyd has said that the board was virtually broke when he took over the captaincy. Overseas tours were very important in financial terms for the board – winning them even more so – but players believed they were poorly rewarded for their efforts.

The 1975–6 Australian tour after the West Indies' World Cup victory had all the makings of a titanic contest with the mouthwatering prospect of the new world champions confronting Ian Chappell's beaten finalists on antipodean soil. But, as we have seen, the Australian attack of Lillee and

Thomson, backed up by Walker and Gilmour, humbled the tourists. Lloyd's view was summed up by Trevor McDonald in his biography of the Guyanese captain:

> We had a whole lot of problems, but the main one was that our batsmen were frequently exposed to Lillee and Thomson, still fresh and raring to go with a relatively new ball. Our players all round were put under constant pressure by sheer pace on some very quick wickets. And many of us were hit.
>
> I had a double dose. I got hit on the jaw by Lillee in Perth and by Thomson in Sydney. Julien's thumb was broken, just when we felt he might help solve the problem about our opening batsmen; Kallicharran's nose was cracked by Lillee in Perth and everyone at some stage during the tour felt the discomfort and the pain of a cricket ball being sent down at more than 90 miles an hour. But that's the game. It's tough. There's no rule against bowling fast. Batsmen must cope to survive.

Lloyd refused to become bitter about the defeat; there was never any question of attaching blame, of saying they shouldn't have bowled like that. Lloyd took it, literally, on the chin and instead of bellyaching about it, consolidated his plans to beat the world.

Fresh from their Australian battering, the West Indies travelled home to play four Tests against India and, as we shall see, it was during this series that world cricket changed irrevocably.

Both sides were tired, with the Indians arriving from a drawn series in New Zealand. Both teams resembled weary warriors, India's Sunil Gavaskar having been hit in the face by a short-pitched delivery during a game in New Zealand and having had no match practice before the first Test in Barbados.

The West Indies were struggling with both physical and psychological 'injuries'. Alvin Kallicharran was still suffering from his broken nose, inflicted during what he described as 'in every sense a horrible tour'. Andy Roberts played in the first two Tests but then succumbed to the pressure of having to play eight Test matches, and a great number of other important and hard-fought games, in just over three months. Opener Gordon Greenidge was absent injured and the West Indies were forced to use Lawrence Rowe as an opener with Viv Richards, the unfit Kallicharran and Lloyd to follow.

Lloyd planned to build his bowling attack around Roberts, Holding and Bernard Julien, supported by leg-spinner David Holford, as well as off-spinners R.R. Jumadeen and A.L. Padmore, and left-armer Inshan Ali. Holder and young fast bowler Wayne Daniel were held in reserve.

The Indian spin-dominated attack was led by the captain Bishan Bedi, supported by Prasanna and Chandrasekhar, but Prasanna broke down in the first Test, thus making way for Venkataraghavan. In the first Test at Bridgetown, Barbados, Holford took 5 for 23 as the Indians were bowled out for 177 and, in reply, the West Indies declared at 488 for 9. Holding and Roberts took 5 second innings wickets between them, and spinners Jumadeen and Holford the rest as the Indians lost by an innings and 97 runs.

The second Test at Port of Spain, Trinidad, was drawn with the West Indies making 241, India declaring at 402 for 5 – Gavaskar and Patel both recording centuries – and the West Indies making a second innings total of 215 for 8.

The third Test should have been played at Bourda in Guyana, but as that ground was under water it had to be staged again at Port of Spain, Trinidad. Lloyd was very unhappy about that as he thought the Indians, after their creditable performance in the second Test, stood a more than fair chance of winning there: and he was right.

The West Indies made 359, with 177 from Richards. On a slow wicket, Holding shouldered the burden of the West Indies attack as an exhausted Roberts had retired from the series. His performance provided a taster of what was to come. On a lifeless pitch, he bowled 26.4 overs (3 maidens), at a cost of 65 runs for 6 wickets. India were all out for 228 and the Windies had a lead of 131. The Windies declared their second innings at 271 for 6, setting a target of 402 for India. Only once before in history had a side made more than 400 runs to win a Test match in the fourth innings. But centuries from Gavaskar and Viswanath (combined with Holding's exhaustion) helped India to victory by 6 wickets.

The series was set at 1–1 but Lloyd felt the third Test defeat keenly and his plan for an all-out pace attack became clear in his mind – and in the minds of the West Indies Cricket Board. In his biography of Lloyd, Trevor McDonald recounts: 'Lloyd believed the spinners had let him down. In the West Indies dressing room he called the three spin bowlers (Ali, Padmore and Jumadeen) to him and asked with a distinct sarcastic edge to his voice: "Gentlemen, I gave you 400 runs to bowl at and you failed to bowl out the opposition. How many runs must I give you in future to make sure that you get the wickets?" Nobody ventured a reply.' Lloyd's misplaced reliance on his spinners to bowl his side to victory had come unstuck and it was not something he ever cared to repeat.

For the final Test of the series at Sabina Park, Jamaica, the West Indies dropped Ali and Padmore, and brought in Wayne Daniel to join Holding, Holder and Julien. But the match became something of a farce with India declaring their first innings at 306 for 6 because Patel, Viswanath and Gaekwad had been put out of the match with injuries.

Gaekwad's injury was caused by Holding when the batsman ducked, assuming that a delivery of great speed would lift: it didn't. He had been hit over the ear, batting bravely for 81, and had to be hospitalized for several days. Viswanath suffered a broken left hand when he was caught at leg slip off Holding. Patel had gone down the wicket planning to hit Holder out of the ground, but was hit in the mouth as the ball flew from a top edge. Bedi had seen enough and declared to ensure that neither he nor Chandrasekhar would have to face the bowling. Holding, at breakneck speed on an unpleasant pitch, had taken 4 for 82 in 28 overs. In their first innings, the West Indies made 391 all out.

But the story of the match, and the first chapter of *the* story of modern cricket history, really began to unfold in India's second innings. Viswanath and Patel, both hurt in the first innings, did not appear and Gaekwad was in hospital – all three were absent hurt. So, when Holding beat Gavaskar for pace, having him caught by Julien for 2, India were, for practical purposes, 2 runs for 4 wickets. Bedi decided that, for the second time in the match, neither he nor Chandrasekhar would face the West Indian quicks and the innings was closed on 97, with 5 wickets down. The Windies were invited to make 13 runs to win the match, and this they did, taking the series 2–1. India's extraordinary second innings scorecard looked like this:

India second innings, fourth Test, Jamaica 21–25 April 1976

S.M. Gavaskar	c Julien b Holding	2
D.B. Vengsarkar	lbw b Jumadeen	21
M. Amarnath	st Murray b Jumadeen	60
Madan Lal	b Holding	8
S. Venkataraghavan	b Holding	0
S.M.H. Kirmani	not out	0
A.D. Gaekwad	*absent hurt*	–
G.R. Viswanath	*absent hurt*	–
B.P. Patel	*absent hurt*	–
B.S. Bedi	*absent hurt*	–
B.S. Chandrasekhar	*absent hurt*	–
(nb 6)		**97**

On the rest day the Indian manager Polly Umrigar had called the match a 'war' and accused Michael Holding of intimidatory bowling. After the match Bedi insisted that India's second innings should be recorded as completed with five marked 'absent hurt', as he and Chandrasekhar had injured their hands while in the field. This advice was duly taken and the resulting scorecard, as Bedi no doubt wished, told an over-exaggerated story of carnage.

Lloyd has since confessed to having some sympathy with the Indians, but remains unrepentant, while Vanburn Holder says now that he really felt sorry for the Indian batsmen as the bowling was so quick. But he is quite sure, even with his retrospective experience as a first-class umpire in England since 1992, that the injuries were not caused by intimidatory bowling. 'It's only intimidatory if it's overdone,' he says. 'It wasn't then.'

After the watershed Indian series, Lloyd prepared for an England tour with two fast bowlers on hand in Michael Holding and Andy Roberts who had all the hallmarks of greatness. In Australia, Holding was faster than Jeff Thomson, who was clearly the fastest of the Australians. The lithe Jamaican was timed at 97 m.p.h., and that was before he had really developed his athletic prowess.

But it was England captain Tony Greig who became responsible for firing up the West Indians to some supreme performances during the 1976 tour of England. After the Australian tour, Greig said: 'They [the West Indies] seemed unable to retain their concentration over a long period. The short ball must be hooked and the well-up ball must be driven. There is little room in this repertoire for defence.'

And even before a ball had been bowled in anger in England, Greig, interviewed on BBC television, said: 'I like to think that people are building these West Indians up, because I'm not really sure that they're as good as everyone thinks they are. Sure they've got a couple of fast bowlers, but really I don't think we're going to run into anything any more sensational than Thomson and Lillee and so really I'm not worried about them. You must remember the West Indians – these guys – if they get on top they're magnificent cricketers. But if they're down, they grovel. And I intend with Closey [Brian Close] and a few others, to make them grovel.'

As Trevor McDonald pointed out in his authorized autobiography of Viv Richards: 'It had perhaps never occurred to Tony Greig that for the South African captain of an English team to publicly threaten to make the West Indies *grovel* was probably the closest any cricketer ever came to making a formal declaration of war.' And in McDonald's biography of Clive Lloyd, the skipper said: 'Quite simply we were angry. We decided that it was important for us to show Tony Greig and all the other detractors of West Indian cricket that the grovelling days were over. We were in the process of building a side of character and we set out to tell Greig's side just that.'

And it was Holding who, in the summer of 1976, shoved those provocative words of Tony Greig back down his throat.

The West Indies, with their four-pronged attack of Roberts, Holding, Daniel and Holder surrounded by allegations of intimidatory bowling, had won the series against England 2–0 by the time they reached August's final Test at The Oval. It was in England's two innings that the next page of a story that had begun at Port of Spain was turned, giving a further hint of what the next 20 years would bring.

Holding bowled with unbridled pace on a featherbed Oval pitch to take 14 wickets in the match, including clean bowling Tony Greig in both innings, the first of those dismissals prompting a pitch invasion by West

Indian supporters still smarting from the England captain's pre-series inanities. Inspired by Clive Lloyd's positive captaincy which saw him keep an attacking field throughout the innings – even though he was criticized for relying on pace on a pitch which looked ideal for spin – Holding produced some of the fastest bowling ever seen in England.

The West Indies turned in a total of 687 for 8 declared, which included a breathtaking 291 by Richards (incidentally taking his Test runs total for the calendar year to 1710). In reply, Dennis Amiss, making 203, was the only England batsman capable of weathering Holding's storm. By the close of England's innings at 435, Holding had returned figures of 8 wickets for 92 runs off 33 overs. In the second innings, he bowled 20.4 overs, taking 6 wickets for 57 runs.

England's fast bowler Bob Willis, who played in that Oval Test taking 1 wicket, said: 'Michael Holding gave the finest display of fast bowling I have ever seen. Having bowled on the pitch I know what I'm speaking about when I say there was nothing there to help the pace bowlers. But Michael managed to make it seem perfect for speed.'

Some years later, Holding remarked that had he been older in 1976 he might not have gone steaming in on such a slow pitch and it was just his youthful enthusiasm that got the better of him. But his performance also typifies the attitude of his captain Clive Lloyd who, despite conditions which may have appeared hopeless to fast bowlers, would maintain pace, pace and pace again. His commitment to the real quicks was alive and kicking whatever the circumstances.

So 1976 was a watershed for West Indian cricket and its key players. Lloyd picked up his bruised soldiers from the morass of defeat in Australia, dusted them down and made them believe in themselves. Vanburn Holder, who took three wickets in the Oval Test, says: 'Too many times before Clive took over we weren't really together as a team; we might have won but we weren't really a team even when the great man [Sobers] was captain. We weren't pulling together.'

But they did pull together in England and despite what must have been huge temptation, Lloyd did not publicly, verbally remind Tony Greig of his comments. Viv Richards and Michael Holding picked up the gauntlet and let their cricket do the talking.

The following winter, Pakistan, led by Mushtaq Mohammad, and including a young Imran Khan and Javed Miandad, toured the Caribbean. The West Indies were without Lawrence Rowe, and Holding and Daniel were both injured. But, as has happened many times since, two awesome quick bowlers without any Test experience were given their first chance at international level and almost immediately began to make their mark on cricket history. The two bowlers were Colin Croft of Guyana and Joel Garner from Barbados. Their arrival marked the completion of Lloyd's dream of a bowling attack consisting of four genuinely ('real') quick bowlers.

It was the second Test at Port of Spain, Trinidad, that marked Croft out as an extraordinary bowler. He took 8 for 29 in 18.5 overs as Pakistan were bowled out for 180. The pitch was not all that helpful to the quicks; it was just honest-to-goodness straight speed that did for them.

Croft finished the series, which the West Indies won 2–1, with 33 wickets at an average of 20.48, Garner with 25 wickets at 27.52. Roberts took 19 wickets, but at an expensive average of 40.15. And as there was no worthy successor to Lance Gibbs on the horizon, so the dearth of West Indian spin bowling merely helped to add depth to Lloyd's consolidation of a pace quartet.

The West Indies were due nearly a year's rest before they played their next series, against Australia in the Caribbean. But long before the Aussies arrived, a crisis arose which was to shake not only the West Indies Cricket Board but cricket boards throughout the world. Early in the spring of 1977 one of the best-kept secrets in sporting history was revealed when Australian media magnate Kerry Packer announced that he had signed up 35 of the world's leading players on three-year contracts. World Series Cricket (WSC) or the 'Packer Circus', as it became known, involved an annual cycle of six five-day Test matches, six one-day matches and six three-day round-robin matches. Prize money, which was additional to contracts worth between $16,500 and $35,000 a year, totalled A$100,000. The contracts were exclusive, not allowing the players to play in other games which clashed with Packer's fixtures.

The Australian WSC contingent numbered 18, including the Chappell brothers, Ross Edwards, Ian Redpath and David Hookes, Rodney Marsh, Dennis Lillee, Jeff Thomson (who later resigned), Gary Gilmour and Max Walker.

The West Indies team was signed *en masse*. Lloyd, Richards, Roberts and Holding were the first to be approached, but Roy Fredericks, Greenidge, Collis King, Julien, Garner, Rowe, Deryck Murray, Holford, Kallicharran, Croft, Haynes and Richard Austin were all soon on board.

The players signed up to form an awesome Rest of the World side including Asif Iqbal, Imran Khan, Majid Khan, Mushtaq Mohammad (Pakistan); Tony Greig, Alan Knott, Derek Underwood and John Snow (England); Graeme Pollock, Barry Richards, Eddie Barlow and Mike Procter (South Africa).

The shock felt by cricket's establishment at the news that this deal had been carried on behind their backs was huge and cries of 'It's just not cricket' echoed around the oldest institutions in the game. Greig was instantly dismissed from his post as captain of England and Mike Brearley appointed in his place. Kerry Packer, who had arrived in England, denied allegations of a 'pirate Test series', saying it was to be a 'Super Test series' with the world's finest cricketers playing against each other. He also claimed that he had personally contacted each country's cricket boards. The West Indies board denied that it had ever received such a communication.

Ian Wooldridge in the *Daily Mail* wrote: 'Far from being a shock development, I suggest that the only surprise about what happened was that it was so long delayed. If the game's administrators failed to see it coming, then they are low in perception.'

They *had* failed to see it coming, so we can draw our own conclusions about their perceptiveness.

From the players' point of view, there was no doubt that the money was extremely attractive. And from the West Indies players' point of view – representing one of international cricket's poor relations – even more so. Added to that was the fact that Packer had signed the West Indies *as a team*, which gave the players a great deal of self-respect.

Kerry Packer had seemed to suggest that he might be cricket's long-term saviour. But what Packer really wanted – rather more than securing a rosy future for the good of the game – was exclusive rights to televising cricket in Australia. At a meeting of the International Cricket Conference (ICC) in London, Packer demanded exclusive television rights in Australia when the agreement with the Australian Broadcasting Commission ran out in early 1979. The ICC refused to agree to that demand and the talks broke up.

After the meeting, Packer told reporters: 'I am only in the arena because of my disagreement with the Australian Cricket Board. Had I got those TV rights, I was prepared to withdraw from the scene and leave the running of cricket to the board. I will now take no steps to help anyone, every man for himself and the devil take the hindmost ... I have never wanted to control cricket, but I wanted and I would have expected to get exclusive rights when the current TV contracts ran out. I said I would go back under the control of the Australian board, have shorter tours and withdraw from the scene completely if our network could have these rights and the players were not victimized.'

Some Packer players had proclaimed him as cricket's Messiah but those comments after the ICC meeting made it clear to some that the Australian's interest in the game was not as altruistic as it might have first appeared.

The ICC laid down five conditions which decreed they should determine programmes, dates and venues of international cricket. Packer dismissed these and added that he had now signed a total of 51 players, including England's leading batsman, Dennis Amiss.

On 26 July 1977 the ICC's meeting decided on three resolutions which would apply sanctions against players who defied their cricket boards. They decreed that any cricketer who took part in a match not approved by the international governing body would not be eligible for selection for a Test match, unless an express application was made to and approval granted by the local authority. They also warned against participation in non-approved games between 1 October 1977 and 31 March 1979, a period which covered the proposed Packer series.

Allan Rae of the West Indies Cricket Board expressed the board members' concern, saying that they were keen to avoid a confrontation with the players, were concerned about any infringement of the players' rights and were conscious of the problems concerning the pay of their players.

As the cricket world watched increasingly open-mouthed, Pakistan's Zaheer Abbas and the West Indies' Alvin Kallicharran withdrew from Packer cricket on the advice of their agent, while Bob Woolmer of England joined up, even after the Test and County Cricket Board (TCCB) declared that any player barred from Test selection would not be eligible for county selection.

Packer brought a case for an injunction and damages against David Lord, the agent of Zaheer and Kallicharran, and the ICC. A temporary injunction restraining Lord was granted pending the outcome, and the hearing began on 26 September 1977 and lasted for 31 days. The judge declared that the declarations of the ICC on 14 June were 'ultra vires and null and void'. That applied too to the new rules announced by the TCCB concerning non-selection, and Packer emerged triumphant.

The following February the ICC decided not to appeal as it 'would not be in the best interests of cricket', and Kent and Hampshire went back on their decision of not engaging any Packer players, saying that they would treat them as eligible for 1978 and following seasons.

Meanwhile, the West Indies board, in common with their peers, faced a dilemma over selection for Australia's tour to the Caribbean in March and April 1978. The Australian board would not pick any Packer player for a Test which meant it would in practice field only a second XI. The West Indies board decided to pick its best players, including those contracted to Packer. But although Deryck Murray, the wicketkeeper and vice-captain, was picked for the first Test, he was stripped of his role as vice-captain. The board said at the time and has said since that it did not demote Murray, aged 34, as an act of victimization, but because he was getting older and it had to find a replacement. To be fair, Murray's replacement as vice-captain was Richards, himself contracted to Packer.

The first two Tests were won easily by the West Indies within three days with the pace bowlers undoing the Australians, led by Bobby Simpson, who had come out of retirement for the series. Roberts, Croft and Garner – Holding was injured – were simply too much for the Aussies in the first two Tests.

But for the third Test in Guyana, the selectors dropped Desmond Haynes (who had made over 60 in the first and second Tests), Deryck Murray and Richard Austin. All three were Packer players.

The board argued that it had to begin to establish players for the tour to India in 1978 for which the Packer players would not be available because of their World Series contracts. Apparently Haynes and Austin had given assurances over their availability for India, but afterwards both players, so it was said, went back on their promise by signing with Packer.

Lloyd immediately resigned as captain after the selectors' decision and said he would not play under the circumstances of 'gross victimization'. Then all the West Indies players contracted to Packer followed their mentor and quit the team in support.

So the West Indies also fielded what amounted to a second XI at the third Test in Guyana which Australia won by three wickets. The West Indies managed to win the fourth Test in Trinidad by 198 runs to lead the series 3–1, but the fifth Test, played in front of a tiny crowd, was characterized by crowd trouble and ended in a draw.

With the cream of the West Indies otherwise engaged, the West Indies' official side – or second XI – toured India, who had their first XI available, and Sri Lanka in 1978–9. Against India, the West Indies lost one Test and drew five. Perhaps the most significant player to emerge on this tour, certainly for our purposes, was Malcolm Marshall from Barbados. Although he took only 3 wickets for 265 runs there was no doubt that he was 'real quick'.

On the other side of the world and in another world in a cricket sense, Packer's West Indians were making their presence very much felt during World Series Cricket's 1977–8 season. The first two Super Tests were won by the West Indian XI, although they lost the next to the WSC Australian XI. The fourth Super Test was played between the Australians and a World XI which contained five West Indians – Fredericks, Richards, Lloyd, Roberts and Garner. The World XI won by 4 wickets, following up their victory by again beating the Australians (this time by an innings and 73 runs) in the fifth 'Test' at Perth. In the last match, the Australian XI regained some ground by defeating the World XI. After a second Super Test series in 1978–9, in which the World XI finished with three wins and one defeat, Packer's 'Circus' came to the Caribbean.

The West Indies won the first 'Test' at Kingston, Jamaica, by 369 runs. A significant event was that Lawrence Rowe, a shining star in World Series Cricket, was struck on the left temple by a delivery from Lillee and suffered a fracture, in spite of wearing a helmet: a piece of protective equipment which had, for the first time, become a necessity for many batsmen in nearly all games featuring international fast bowlers. The second 'Test' in Barbados was drawn, Australia won the third in Trinidad and the last two games, in Guyana and Antigua, were both drawn.

As the Packer series concluded in the Caribbean, the second World Cup (scheduled to take place in England in June and July) – and all the lucre that promised – was imminent. Almost without warning the Australian Cricket Board announced that exclusive broadcasting rights for ten years had been granted to Packer's Channel 9 as soon as the agreement with the Australian Broadcasting Corporation ended at the beginning of 1981. Packer had won hands down.

However, the West Indians involved with Packer had not emerged as triumphant. They were quickly reconciled with the West Indian board, but, as Andrew Caro, WSC's former managing director, said in 1979, they too often seemed sensitive and unsure, both on and off the field. 'Very often they seemed to suspect the motives of the management, the nature of the pitches, the decisions of the umpires and the comments of the press.'

In the second Super Test series, it is fair to say that the West Indies players did not perform to their ability. Viv Richards in the first series, for example, played nine innings, had a top score of 177, a total of 725 runs and an average of 90.6. The next year in Australia, Richards reached 50 only once in all of the eight Super Tests played. Joel Garner said that there was a feeling of depression in the dressing room in that second series and he believed the players were affected 'by a kind of guilt. We felt we had done something wrong. We had a lot of confidence in WSC; but even with the greatest confidence and a full appreciation of the principle that lay behind what we were doing, we remained at heart West Indian players. I felt this meant that we should be playing West Indies Test cricket.'

Caro thought that there was 'a disturbing separateness about the West Indian team. They needed greater care and understanding, and they should have been encouraged to become more involved both in the general atmosphere of World Series Cricket and in the Australian way of life. While it is fine to try to generate a sense of team spirit, it is also essential to join in the overall social activities. Those who hid behind their racial and political principles should have been made aware of their position as visitors.'

That is a derogatory view and Caro appeared to have little idea of the problems with which Lloyd was constantly wrestling. Former Australian captain Greg Chappell believed that WSC was the making of the West Indies: 'They had always been good front runners. Their only weakness had been that they were a bit impetuous, they couldn't pull out of a dive. But living together for two years made them believe in themselves. WSC matured them.'

It was fundamental to Lloyd's strategy that he foster team spirit, first and foremost, not become part of some social whirligig that would not benefit his team's drive for togetherness. If he had to do that at the expense of the desires of WSC administrators, then so be it. It appears from Garner's words that the team was still together, but had lost sight of their cause. But with the luxurious benefit of hindsight, it is quite clear that Lloyd extracted a positive experience for the majority of his players, not just in terms of overcoming the demon of insularity, but also in financial terms and in creating a fitness ethic that stood his side in good stead for the next decade and a half.

Caro supposed that one of the reasons the West Indies did not play with their customary brilliance in WSC 1978–9 was that they were no longer as keen on victory as they had been in the first series. He said: 'It is plainly ridiculous that such brilliant cricketers, from such a group of poor countries, where an average labouring wage is A$28.00 per week, be denied the opportunity of earning a tour wage of A$500.00 a week with World Series Cricket. The attainment of this enormous financial security may have diminished their hungry need to succeed. If so, let us hope that it is a temporary aberration.'

However, rather than diminishing 'their hungry need to succeed', the second series of WSC was a period of consolidation off the field for the West Indies side. For really the first time in their history they were learning about playing as a collective unit and for the first time in their careers they were embarking on intensive physical conditioning. The West Indies in fact gained more positively from their WSC experiences than any other cricketing nation involved with Packer. Lloyd had established his base point: 'The basic thing I had to get right was making the players happy in what they were doing.'

Furthermore, Lloyd strengthened his position as his side's guru. Tony Cozier believes that Lloyd's personality was similar to Worrell's. 'Fairly untypically for a West Indian, Lloyd is calm and collected. And, like Worrell, there was a bit of a generation gap, although not to the extent that there was with Worrell. But Lloyd was almost a legendary figure who had made his reputation so the players tended to look up to him. He was fortunate that he came along at the right time and that Packer cricket came too so that the players could become more together.'

That togetherness, so lacking in the past, gave Lloyd the bedrock from which he was able to build. Without the 'all for one, one for all' mentality that he had engendered, the West Indies would have achieved nothing in comparison with the dizzy heights they have scaled since the late 1970s.

Now Lloyd can safely say: 'Winning plays a great part in our cricketing structure because it keeps us together as islands, and at the same time makes us a very happy people.'

However, it is still not entirely a rosy picture; would that it were. Inter-island rivalry reared its head as recently as 1994 when only 10 days after Brian Lara's record-breaking innings in the Antigua Test in April, the Trinidad and Tobago Cricket Board of Control (TTCBC) issued a statement expressing 'its grave concern at what is perceived to be an organized and calculated plot by a privileged few to deny Trinidad and Tobago and its cricketers their just due'.

The board did not identify 'the privileged few', but listed its complaints as 'a well orchestrated regional plan to exclude Phil Simmons from Test cricket, now and in the future', the omission of wicketkeeper David Williams and young leg spinner Didanth Ramnarino from representative matches against England, 'the previous criticisms which were designed to force his [Williams's] exclusion from the international stage' and the 'unexplainable selection' of Curtly Ambrose before Lara as Player of the Series.

Tony Cozier said at the time that, even by West Indian standards, this was a remarkable piece of xenophobia, and the reaction was predictably swift and damning.

The West Indies Cricket Board of Control (WICBC) held its annual general meeting in St Vincent two weeks after the TTCBC's statement had been issued and the affair prompted lengthy discussion. But, after the meeting, the WICBC dismissed the complaints as 'totally without merit' and 'ill-considered', and said they conveyed disunity and, in the process, rendered immense damage to the board's image.

'In the circumstances, the board feels compelled to express its displeasure at the statement of the TTCBC and urges it to be mindful of the grave dangers of promoting divisiveness in West Indies cricket,' it added in a press statement.

The board made it clear that such divisiveness must be stamped on as soon as it rears its ugly head. Dissent does no credit to the efforts of Clive Lloyd and his predecessors, and threatens the very power which the West Indies have, against tougher odds than are faced by any other cricketing country, striven to maintain for so long.

But these issues were not at the forefront of Clive Lloyd's mind in 1979. His main priority was to prove that a Test bowling attack based around four fast bowlers could be consistently successful. The next 15 years were to prove his theory, beyond even Lloyd's wildest dreams.

3 | Pace like fire – 1979–94

Testing the theory – 1979–81

The West Indies selectors lost no time in putting their theories into practice, with the Packer schism finally healed over and, for the Windies, a
number of valuable lessons learnt. The West Indian squad of 14 for the 1979
World Cup, which they went on to win, included no fewer than five out-
and-out fast bowlers and no specialist spinner. The original fast-bowling
quartet was Andy Roberts, who had then played in 27 Tests and was 28
years old, Michael Holding (13 Tests, age 25), Joel Garner (seven Tests, 26)
and Colin Croft (seven Tests, 26). The reserve was the 21-year-old
Malcolm Marshall, who had played just three Test matches.

The quartet, who were to play their first Test together in Australia in
December of that year and 11 times in total, were perhaps the most perfectly balanced of all the West Indian pace-bowling combinations. Roberts
was the tactician, the experienced international cricketer whose time in
county cricket and in the Packer circus had taught him most of the fast-
bowling tricks there were to know. Roberts had the talent to use this knowledge and, of course, brought along some tricks of his own, including the
infamous two-speed bouncer. Roberts would devise a plan to dismiss each
batsman, and use different body actions and grips, as well as sheer speed, to
execute it.

Although Holding was far from being an unintelligent bowler, he had
much less need to exercise his mind to defeat batsmen: his main weapon
was sheer speed through the air. That was why he was able to cancel out any
negative influence of a benign batting pitch, most famously during the Oval
Test of 1976.

Whereas Roberts shouldered his way to the wicket in a way reminiscent
of Charlie Griffith, Holding brought back memories of Wes Hall. But
where Hall was a wave rushing to the shore, Holding was like a cheetah
charging at its prey. Many have complained of the long run-ups used by
West Indian fast bowlers, saying they are unnecessary, time-wasting and
monotonous, yet nobody but a Philistine would say that Holding's
approach to the wicket was not a thing of beauty.

Those who seek to denigrate the achievements of modern West Indian
fast bowlers often point to their physical attributes, height and strength, as

if to suggest that these give them some unfair advantage and remove the need to use skill to succeed at Test level. For these people, Joel Garner was the number one target. At 6 ft 8 in he towered over even his fast-bowling colleagues. Since he was blessed with long arms as well as height, the ball would flash down at the batsman from well over 8 ft. Even good length balls would leap up at the batsman's ribs, a factor which often made run-scoring almost impossible. But Garner's physique was as much a hindrance as a help. Unlike most tall fast bowlers, Australia's Bruce Reid for example, Garner has a solid build. While this is useful in warding off the type of stress injuries which dogged Reid's career, it made fast bowling an act of sheer hard work. Unlike the 6 ft 7 in Curtly Ambrose for example, Garner's approach to the wicket often seemed laboured and his bowling action seemed to require the kind of effort needed to get a jumbo jet off the runway.

With so much effort going into each delivery, Garner might have been forgiven for sometimes struggling with line and/or length. In fact only Ambrose challenges Garner for accuracy among the leading fast bowlers of the modern age.

Where Garner's strength was his accuracy and bounce, Colin Croft relied on discomfort and uncertainty. After an angled run-up to the wicket the heavily muscled Croft would suddenly swerve sharply to the left. His left foot would splay out towards the off-side and the chest-on action this produced resulted in the ball being delivered a yard wide of the stumps, slanting in towards the batsman's legs.

Batsmen were faced with the task of working out how to face very quick deliveries being directed at them from a straightish mid-off with a confusing, windmilling action. Effectively this meant that, if batsmen did not adjust their stance, employing conventional strokes would often mean playing across the line. Many thought the answer was to play forward, thereby reducing the sharpness of the angle, but Croft was fond of the bouncer and batsmen often found the ball homing in on their left armpit.

Although Holding was widely acknowledged as the fastest of this paticular quartet, many batsmen believed Croft was the more difficult to face. Mike Gatting, for example, makes the point that because of Holding's 'lovely action', you could 'see the ball all the way through'. With Croft, he says, 'you never knew where the bloody thing was coming from'. However, England's Frank Hayes, who scored a century on his Test début against the West Indies, claims that Holding's smoothness caused its own problems. At Old Trafford during the 1976 series, Hayes claimed that Holding bowled him 'the fastest ball he ever faced'. The delivery was 'a foot wide of the off stump, but it was a daunting experience realizing that the ball was in the keeper's gloves with little, if any, reaction on my part. It was Michael Holding's first-ever ball to me, and the combination of naked pace and the languid simplicity of his action confused my senses and prevented reflex action'. Holding took 7 wickets for 41 runs during this match, which England lost by 425 runs. Unlike the great majority of his colleagues in the pace quartet, Croft would never help a batsman that he had hit and his 'meanness' can be judged by the fact that his team-mates believed he would 'bowl a bouncer at his grandmother'. But Croft was not an unthinking thug (he became a pilot after his cricket career finished) and he often planned his assaults with considerable cunning. The end result of this highly discomfiting form of attack was a strike rate which few other fast bowlers could equal.

There was much greater variety in the West Indies' original fast-bowling quartet than in many of the collections of fast-medium trundlers, and spinners with flat trajectories and little spin, which have made up many supposedly more 'balanced' Test teams.

The fact that Roberts, Holding, Garner and Croft were all in their mid-twenties meant that they had time to gel as a unit, and develop strategies which made the most of their talents and provided mutual support. At Test level, this learning process began during the 1979–80 series in Australia.

The series was an unconventional and highly charged one for a number of reasons. Not only had the West Indies arrived in Australia openly declaring their intentions by selecting five fast bowlers, but they were facing many of the same players who had inflicted that 5–1 defeat on them four years earlier. In particular Lillee and Thomson, two of the greatest inspirations for the pace-bowling quartet, were still there, this time joined by Australia's bowling find of the Packer period, Rodney Hogg. The series also marked the return of players such as Greg Chappell and Rod Marsh to the Australian Test team after their involvement with the Packer circus. Hopes were high among Australian supporters that they would help re-establish Australia as the world's leading cricketing power, a position they had held immediately prior to the Packer coup.

The Tests against the West Indies were interspersed with three Test matches against England. It was a highly unusual arrangement, with England refusing to put the Ashes at stake, and has not been repeated. Australia had little trouble in beating England, world champions by default during the Packer period, but against the West Indies the balance of power had shifted.

The first game between Australia and the West Indies was inconclusive. The pace-bowling quartet, which delivered all but five overs in Australia's first innings, dismissed the home side for 268. Garner returned the best figures, taking 4 wickets for 55 runs off 22 overs. But after the West Indies had scored 441, Australia saved the game by running up 448 for 6 wickets, Australian captain Chappell making 124, Kim Hughes 130 not out and débutant opener Bruce Laird 75 to follow his first innings 92. Roberts took 1 wicket for 70 runs, Holding 1 for 94, Croft 1 for 106 and Garner 2 for 75 from 41 overs. But this was the calm before the storm.

The second match, at Melbourne where the West Indies had suffered seven consecutive defeats, followed the same script for its first half. Australia made 156 with Holding taking 4 wickets for 40 runs, Croft 3 for 27 and Garner 3 for 33. But this time Australia could not hold out. Again Laird and Hughes provided some resistance, but once the young opener was dismissed by Holding, Croft and Garner swept away the tail, and the West Indies won by 10 wickets.

For the third match, Australia brought back the captain's brother, veteran campaigner Ian Chappell. However, it did little good as Australia scored 203 and 165 (Ian Chappell 2 and 4), and the West Indies won by 408 runs. The one-day world champions had also secured the Test crown. The decision of the West Indies selectors to rely purely on pace had been totally justified as the averages for the series show.

West Indies fast bowlers v. Australia 1979–80

	Overs	M	Runs	Wkts	Av
J. Garner	127.4	34	301	14	21.50
M.A. Holding	111	24	319	14	22.79
C.E.H. Croft	121.3	20	378	16	23.63
A.M.E. Roberts	112	20	296	11	26.91

All four bowlers had been a success individually but, more important, they had worked together as a unit, sharing the workload evenly and maintaining a consistent pressure on the strong Australian batting line-up.

After such a *tour de force*, the West Indies fast bowlers were expected to demolish their next opponents, New Zealand. But a stubborn performance by the New Zealand team during the first Test underlined the fact that the West Indies fast bowlers had yet fully to develop the maturity which would later allow them to recover so many seemingly lost positions.

Roberts was injured and the West Indies chose to field off-spinner Parry in his place. The lack of Roberts's experience was crucial. Richard Hadlee used the low bounce offered by the helpful pitch to take 5 wickets (four of them lbw) for 34 runs. The West Indies were bowled out for 140 and, when New Zealand replied, wasteful short-pitched bowling by Holding, Croft and Garner allowed the home side to pass their opponents' score with only four wickets down. When New Zealand were finally dismissed for 249, only two wickets had fallen to lbw decisions and both of those were won by Parry. In defence of himself and his colleagues, Garner points out that the West Indies had just finished a long tour of Australia, where 'a good length' was a yard or two shorter than in New Zealand.

In the West Indies' second innings Hadlee took another 6 wickets (three lbw) and New Zealand were faced with making 104 to win. As they were to do many times over the next 14 years, the West Indies fast bowlers raised their game in a moment of crisis. Holding tore in and dismissed John

Wright and Bruce Edgar before the score had reached 30. John Parker came in at No. 4 and, before he had scored, Holding thought he had him caught behind. But the appeal was turned down and the fast bowler's frustration at what he saw as incompetent umpiring boiled over. His aborted victory celebrations had taken him level with the stumps at the batsman's end and, with one graceful swing of his right leg, he sent all three stumps sailing through the air.

Croft and Garner then worked their way steadily through the New Zealand middle order, reducing the home side to 54 for 7. But Hadlee and Cairns edged the score on to 73 before Garner bowled the great New Zealand all-rounder. Croft then appealed for a catch behind off the edge of Cairns's bat, but again the decision (which the West Indies believed was clear-cut) was turned down. Finally Holding did have Cairns taken by Murray, but the last wicket pair of Troup and Boock somehow nudged and nicked the winning runs.

From that point, Holding claims that 'for me, my tour was as good as over' and, in disgust at what he saw as unforgivably poor umpiring, he stopped appealing. Roberts returned for the second Test, but still the umpiring problems persisted. After New Zealand had reached 53 for 3 in reply to the West Indies' 228, Kiwi captain Geoff Howarth put his team in command by scoring 147. The Windies, however, claimed that he was incorrectly given not out on numerous occasions during his innings and with Howarth on 99 not out during tea on the third day, the West Indies stayed in the dressing room for an extra 12 minutes debating whether they should resume the game. On the next match day, after another appeal was turned down, Croft barged umpire Goodall from his feet during his run-up. The West Indies only managed to save the game thanks to a powerhouse batting performance in the second innings from Greenidge, Haynes, Rowe and King, but the series was rapidly disintegrating into farce.

The rain-hit third Test ended with New Zealand on 73 for 4, after being set 180 to win by the West Indies. This draw meant that New Zealand clinched the rubber, the last series defeat for the West Indies to date. It was suggested by some commentators that the New Zealand umpires' apparent dislike of giving caught behind decisions was due to the unfamiliarity with constant high-speed bowling. Whatever the correct explanation, it is unfortunately hopelessly disguised by recrimination and bad feeling. What was clear to the West Indian fast bowlers (and their captain) was that to lose their 'cool' was to surrender the initiative. And despite some very high-pressure situations, the West Indian fast-bowling quartets have almost never again allowed the wheels to come off as they did in New Zealand.

The Windies team did not appear to have recovered its momentum by the time it reached England a couple of months after finishing the tour to New Zealand. The Caribbean side won the first Test by 2 wickets, thanks to Roberts's 8 wickets and Garner's 7, but the remaining four Tests were drawn, with England having the upper hand in two games. In terms of the development of the pace quartet, the series was notable only for the return to the Windies Test side of Marshall, whom a year later Geoff Boycott was describing as 'the best of the West Indies Test bowlers in terms of accuracy and variation'.

Marshall, who to date has played in more Tests and taken more wickets than any other West Indian specialist bowler, was the least imposing of all the modern West Indian fast bowlers. He is only 5 ft 11 in, and with a relatively slim and apparently unathletic build, so that inexperienced Test batsmen must have let out a sigh of relief when they saw him replacing Croft or Garner. But it did not take long for the Bajan to show that he was just as deadly as his giant team-mates. Marshall raced to the wicket as if in a fury and his curving run ended in an explosive open-chested delivery. His lack of height meant that any short-pitched ball tended to 'skid through', producing countless mistimed strokes, while his command of swing and seam allowed him to make the most of prevailing conditions. Marshall was also the fiercest competitor in the West Indies pace quartet and it was largely his example which meant that the foursome's initial success did not disappear through complacency.

The Windies series in Pakistan followed much the same pattern as the rubber against England, the Caribbean side winning a close-fought four-match series 1–0. However, both Holding and Roberts were being rested, with Sylvester Clarke returning to the side to keep the quartet intact.

Clarke was another Bajan who had been drafted into the West Indian side during the Packer schism. Clarke was similar to Marshall in technique but, unfortunately, closer to Croft in temperament. His lack of Marshall's dedication and intelligence kept him on the fringes of the West Indian side and eventually he did the 'unthinkable' and joined a 'rebel' tour to the apartheid state of South Africa. However, the unhappy course of Clarke's life should not conceal the fact that he was a very fast, very awkward and highly skilled quick bowler. On the tour of Pakistan, for example, he opened the bowling ahead of Garner and Marshall. Clarke also played for Surrey in the English County Championship for nearly a decade and when the world's 22 best players were being assembled for the MCC's bicentenary match in 1987, both Graham Gooch and Mike Gatting claimed that Clarke should have been picked.

Despite Clarke's success in Pakistan (he took 14 wickets) the first-choice quartet – Roberts, Holding, Croft, Garner – was restored for England's 1981 tour of the Caribbean and the Windies recaptured their form of a year before. With the Caribbean sun on their backs, the pace quartet swept the Windies to decisive victories in the first two Tests, the final two games being saved through a combination of bad weather and some heroic rearguard actions from Gooch, Boycott and Gower.

It was a good way for the West Indies to end the first phase of their quest for world domination. In 17 months they had played 19 Tests, winning 6, drawing 12 and losing only 1. The record of the West Indies' pace bowlers over the period was:

	Matches	Overs	Maidens	Runs	Wkts	Average
J. Garner	18	704.2	214	1402	74	18.95
C. Croft	17	616.3	130	1713	76	22.54
M. Holding	15	558.1	139	1502	58	25.90
A. Roberts	11	393.2	86	1005	33	30.45
M. Marshall	9	292	56	819	31	26.42
S. Clarke	4	98	24	242	14	17.29
Total					**286**	**23.36**

This level of performance is now expected from West Indian fast bowlers but at the time it was unprecedented. In England, Australia, New Zealand, Pakistan and the West Indies, in all types of playing conditions, the Caribbean fast bowlers had taken on all-comers and (usually) triumphed. During this period, the West Indies destroyed one of cricket's most enduring myths: that different playing conditions demanded different types of bowlers to exploit them. There was no doubt in the West Indies selectors' minds that 'pace conquers all'. And whenever one of the front-line fast bowlers was unavailable, the West Indies were able to substitute him with an up-and-coming quick who performed just as well as the player he had replaced. Roberts might have been reaching the end of his career, but Marshall was already making strong claims for the role of the team's fast-bowling strategist.

But if the ecstatic West Indian supporters and their shell-shocked rivals believed that they had experienced some short-lived golden age, they were very much mistaken. Over the next five years, the West Indies were to become one of the best Test sides ever, and their cutting edge was to be provided by the pace quartet.

The peak – 1982–6

The most dominant period in West Indies Test cricket started with a sharp reminder that the greatest fast bowler of the age was not yet a West Indian. In a match full of heroic performances, the first Test of the 1981–2 series against Australia kicked off at Melbourne in late December. Kim Hughes scored a brilliant undefeated century, but Holding with 5 for 45 was simply too quick for Hughes's team-mates and the Australians were all out for 198. But for once the West Indies got a taste of their own medicine and Dennis Lillee's 7 for 83 had them crashing to 201 all out. In the second innings, Australia reached 184 for 3 before Holding began a spell of bowling even more devastating than his first innings performance. Defeating batsmen by pure pace, he bowled Border, Hughes and Alderman, had Wellham lbw, and Marsh and Lillee caught behind. Holding finished with 6 wickets and the West Indies had to score 220 to win a great Test match. At 150 for 6, with Murray and Roberts at the wicket, the match appeared evenly balanced. But Lillee was destined to have the last word, trapping Roberts, Holding and Garner all lbw, and winning the game for Australia with match figures of 53.4 overs, 11 maidens, 127 runs, 10 wickets.

The second Test was drawn, but crucially Lillee broke down during the third Test (only bowling nine overs) and the West Indies won the match with Holding taking 8 wickets. This short series against Australia marked the high point of Holding's career. He took 24 wickets in three Tests at an average of just 14.33 and, with Lillee's retirement following the third Test, was unchallenged as the world's most widely admired fast bowler.

After just three Tests in 1982, the West Indies played a five-match home series against India during February–May 1983, winning 2–0. The fifth Test saw Garner (who had only taken seven wickets in the first four games) replaced by Winston Davis. The giant paceman was playing county cricket for Somerset during the English summer and the workload was beginning to wear him down. Davis was seen as a possible long-term replacement. Tall, with a whippy action, the St Vincent fast bowler promised to follow Garner in combining pace with a consistent line and awkward bounce. Figures of 53 overs and 4 wickets at 43.75 in the drawn fourth Test proved at least that he had stamina.

In the English summer of 1983, the West Indies suffered an unexpected and devastating defeat by India in the final of the third one-day World Cup. But the team had little time to regroup before they prepared for their sternest test yet: a six-match away series against their World Cup conquerors. How would the pace men perform on Indian wickets and how would they cope with the task of playing six Tests in just two months? The West Indies were also without the out-of-favour Garner, while both Croft and Clarke had opted for the lure of the krugerrand. The side also contained Andy Roberts, who was now a shadow of the bowler who had once terrorized the world's leading batsmen.

Malcolm Marshall suddenly found himself the main strike bowler (along with Holding), while Davis, Wayne Daniel and a young Antiguan, Eldine Baptiste, provided the support. Baptiste was more in the mould of Boyce or Julien than the 1980s vintage of West Indian bowling talent, a hard-hitting all-rounder and useful fast-medium pace bowler. He owed his place in the Test side to the lobbying of fellow countryman Viv Richards and concerns over the length of the West Indian tail. Daniel had fallen out of favour with the West Indian selectors after the 1976 tour of England, and only owed his place to the unavailability of Croft and Clarke. However, the burly Bajan pace man was to help Middlesex win a hatful of trophies and he would have doubtless played over 50 Test matches if he had been born in any other part of the world.

The ability of the pace quartet to overcome almost any handicap placed on them was demonstrated during the first Test. After the West Indies had scored 454 on a typical Indian featherbed, Marshall had Gavaskar caught behind for a duck and soon reduced the home side to 18 for 4. The lack of high-class support for Holding and Marshall was highlighted when Binny and Madan Lal were able to put on 117 for the ninth wicket, but India were still forced to follow on 247 behind. Again Marshall ripped out both Indian openers before they had made double figures and the home side never recovered, finally being dismissed for 164.

Daniel replaced Baptiste for the second Test and rewarded the selectors with six wickets, but the game was drawn. During the third Test in Ahmedabad, Daniel did even better and had a rare chance to show a Test crowd why he was so feared in English domestic cricket. Daniel took 5 wickets for just 39 runs as India were dismissed for 241, some 40 runs behind the Windies' first innings score. In the West Indies' second innings, Indian all-rounder Kapil Dev turned in one the great modern fast-bowling performances. He bowled throughout the innings and took 9 wickets for 83 runs from 30 bone-shaking overs. After such heroics, he could have reasonably expected the Indian batsmen to have a good stab at making the 242 runs required to win the match. But again the pace quartet raised their game at exactly the right time. India were dismissed for just 103: Holding took 4 for 30, Davis 3 for 21, Marshall 2 for 23, Daniel 1 for 11.

The fourth Test was another high-scoring draw and for the fifth, Andy Roberts returned for Daniel. It was a good move, Roberts taking 3 for 56 from 24 overs as India once more under-achieved with 241. The West Indies established a lead of 136 and did not need to bat again. Marshall emulated Kapil Dev by bowling right through an innings as India were dismissed for just 90, the Bajan fast bowler taking 6 for 37. The sixth Test saw Gavaskar re-establish his reputation as a great player of West Indian pace bowling with an undefeated double century, but the game was drawn and the West Indians had won the series 3–0. The achievement of the West Indian fast bowlers on the dry and dusty Indian wickets is best shown by comparing their performance to that of the home side's spinners.

West Indian fast bowlers v. India 1983

	M	Wkts	Av	BPW	Runs/100 balls
M.D. Marshall	6	33	18.81	40.18	46.83
M.A. Holding	6	30	22.10	44.77	49.36
W.W. Daniel	3	14	23.71	42.00	56.46
A.M.E. Roberts	2	5	29.60	66.80	44.31
W.W. Davis	6	14	40.14	76.50	52.47

Indian spin bowlers v. West Indies 1983

	M	Wkts	Av	BPW	Runs/100 balls
Maninder Singh	4	10	33.40	92.10	58.31
N. Yadav	3	9	37.55	74.77	50.22
R. Shastri	6	12	47.25	105.75	44.68
K. Azad	2	2	73.50	153.00	48.04

Not only were the West Indian fast bowlers much more penetrative, they were also able to compete on equal terms with the Indian bowlers in terms of economy, in the past always the spinners' main strength. In the most alien environment imaginable to a West Indian fast bowler, the quartet had shown they could compete on every level and in every way.

When 1984 dawned the West Indian pace quartet were about to reach their peak. Over the next three years, the West Indies were to play 27 Tests, win 19 of them and lose only two. The 27 games included two periods in which the West Indies won every Test they played, one stretch lasting 11 games, the other seven. The West Indies' record during the 27-match sequence, starting with the 1984 home series against Australia and ending with the series in Pakistan during October–November 1986, went as follows: D D W W W W W W W W W W W D L D D W W W W W W W L W D.

It was England and Australia who suffered the full brunt of this show of power, as the Windies' record against the different opponents during this period shows.

West Indies Test record 1984–6

Opponents	P	W	D	L
Australia	10	6	3	1
England	10	10	0	0
New Zealand	4	2	2	0
Pakistan	3	1	1	1
Total	27	19	6	2

Of the 19 victories, six were by an innings and 10 by at least either eight wickets or 200 runs. What is more, in the six drawn Tests during this period, the Windies were on course for victory in five. And yet this record was achieved despite the fact that the West Indies only scored an average of 481 runs per match. It is not that Richards, Greenidge and co. under-achieved, simply that the pace quartet quickly turned most matches into non-contests.

West Indies pace bowlers 1984–6*

	M	W	Av	BPW	Runs/100 balls
M.D. Marshall	25	143	18.92	41.81	45.24
J. Garner	24	116	20.41	46.77	43.63
M.A. Holding	17	68	21.18	43.85	38.23
C.A. Walsh	10	32	25.16	56.59	44.45
E.A. Baptiste	8	14	29.93	80.14	37.34
B.P. Patterson	6	22	23.95	40.68	58.89
W.W. Davis	4	14	24.64	51.21	48.12
A.H. Gray	3	14	16.21	42.43	38.22
W.W. Daniel	2	7	28.14	54.00	52.12
M.A. Small	2	4	38.25	67.50	56.67

* ranked by number of appearances

The West Indies rarely had a settled pace quartet, as can be seen from the fact that they had to use no fewer than 10 fast bowlers during the 27 games. However, all this did was to reveal just how deep the Windies' fast-bowling resources had become. Of the seven fast bowlers who joined Marshall, Garner and Holding during this mid-1980s period, only Milton Small proved a disappointment. The other six all entered Test cricket and all produced performances which left their bowling average at the end of the 27-match period under 30, the benchmark of a successful international bowler.

The greatest find of the period was Courtney Walsh. The 6 ft 5 in Jamaican made his début during the 1984–5 series against Australia. Another of the growing legion of West Indian fast bowlers with an open-chested action, Walsh quickly slotted into the stock bowler's role within the quartet. His stamina, accuracy and skill at bowling fast with a ball 30 overs old provided the replacement for Garner that the West Indian selectors had been looking for. Unfortunately Walsh's success meant there was no regular place for Tony Gray. He came from Trinidad and was six months younger than Walsh, but looked uncannily similar: tall and almost unbelievably thin for an international athlete. He was a similar type of bowler to Walsh, relying on accuracy rather than pure pace. However, competition from Walsh and injury problems meant that Gray was never able to fulfil his potential as a Test bowler.

Just as Garner's retirement meant that the West Indies had to find a new stock bowler, so Holding's decision to call it quits in the mid-1980s left the Windies' selectors with the problem of locating a new strike bowler. He duly arrived in time for the first Test of England's 1986 tour of the Caribbean. Jamaican-born Patrick Patterson was a fearsome sight for a batsman. He charged to the wicket and bowled with a high kicking action, a terrifying scowl on his face. And he was fast: very, very, *very* fast. He made his début on his home ground of Kingston, and took advantage of an under-prepared wicket to terrify the English batsmen and pick up seven of their wickets. He was immediately acknowledged as the fastest bowler in the world, but as the series continued it became clear that Patterson possessed few other talents. He has drifted in and out of the Windies side, doing well on bouncy Australian pitches, but struggling in conditions where a bowler needs more than sheer speed to defeat Test batsmen.

However, the West Indies' three main strike bowlers gave their (mostly) younger colleagues an easy introduction into Test cricket. Marshall, Holding and Garner took a wicket on average every seven overs. And during that time only an average of 19 runs would be scored. This sort of performance would be difficult for opponents to cope with if it came from just one bowler; coming from three it was simply irresistible.

Despite the dominance of fast bowling in the West Indies team during this period, it is interesting that the side's most used stock bowler was an off-spinner. Roger Harper had made his début during the 1983–4 tour of India, making little impact. But with the start of the 1984 series against Australia, he became a regular and successful member of the West Indian team. Two things, apart from his highly economical bowling, helped him maintain his place: his fielding, which was brilliant even by West Indian standards, and the decision by the West Indian selectors to play five bowlers. They were encouraged to order this change in strategy by three factors: the strength of the West Indies batting line-up; the arrival of Jeffrey Dujon, a wicketkeeper who was also a high-class batsman; and the fact that bowlers such as Baptiste and Harper were genuine all-rounders. Harper's bowling record during the mid-1980s was:

	M	W	Av	BPW	Runs/100 balls
R.A. Harper	17	39	25.00	69.15	36.15

Yet despite this performance, Harper has only played six more Test matches in which he took just six more wickets. He developed the dreaded 'yips' – his run-up and bowling action falling to pieces – and the West Indies Test side doesn't carry passengers. This was a pity in more ways than one. Harper was a very exciting cricketer and his continued presence might have added a greater amount of light and shade to the Windies' hugely impressive, but sometimes overly methodical, bowling attack. Harper was also an intelligent man and a natural leader who might have challenged Richardson for the West Indian captaincy had he stayed in the side.

Overhauling the machine 1987–91

At the end of three years' unquestioned dominance, the start of 1987 saw the West Indies side in a state of transition. The series in New Zealand during February and March marked the end of the careers of Garner and Holding. There was much talk of 'an end of an era' and of the Windies losing their grip on the unofficial title of world champions. The three-match series against New Zealand was drawn 1–1, with the home side holding the upper hand in the drawn first Test, and the experts began to question whether the new generation of West Indian fast bowlers could match the performance of Roberts, Holding and Garner.

For a while it appeared they could not. After a relatively long lay-off from international cricket, the West Indies travelled to India in November 1987. The injured Marshall was left at home, and Walsh was given the responsibility of leading a comparatively inexperienced quartet completed by Patterson, Winston Davis and the uncapped Winston Benjamin. Spinners Harper and Butts were also chosen. The first Test was won by the visitors, with Patrick Patterson terrifying the Indian batsmen on a helpful wicket. The second match was drawn, with the Windies in the stronger position. During the third match Patterson, Walsh and Davis could not overcome one of Calcutta's notorious flat tracks: India totalled 565, and Walsh and Davis went for nearly five runs an over. The trend of the series was completed in the fourth and final match, which India won by 255 runs on a spinners' wicket in Madras. Débutant leg-spinner Hirwani took 16 wickets and the Windies fast bowlers could not equal that performance. At the end of the series Walsh (heroically shouldering his new responsibilities) had bowled well, Patterson had been effective in patches, but there were still serious question marks over Davis and (mainly through lack of opportunity) Benjamin.

Nor did the introduction of a new fast bowler to the West Indian side, the giant Curtly Ambrose, appear to provide the answer to the West Indies' problems. The home series against Pakistan in early 1988 started disastrously. Marshall was still injured, while Ambrose replaced Davis but with little impact. For once, it was the West Indian batsmen who were on the receiving end of high-class fast bowling. Pakistan captain Imran Khan took 11 wickets and his side came home by nine wickets.

Imran took another nine wickets in the second Test, but Marshall returned to great effect and the game finished with Pakistan 30 runs away from victory, but with only one wicket remaining. The third game was just as nail-biting, with the West Indies set 265 to win, after Marshall had taken nine wickets. They made the runs (and drew the series) but lost eight wickets in doing so. Even this would have been beyond them if the injury-hit Imran, after bowling heroically for most of the series, had been able to send down more than six overs. The West Indies had drawn three consecutive series and the pace quartet no longer appeared to be the unconquerable force it had been in the early 1980s.

With the past year in mind, it was an uncertain West Indian side that arrived in England in May 1988. The fast bowlers – Marshall, Patterson, Ambrose, Walsh and Benjamin – were all more or less known quantities, but time was well overdue for them to start operating successfully as a unit if the Windies were to continue with the strategy of fielding a pace quartet. After the drawn first Test, the crunch came in the second match at Lord's after the Windies had totalled only 209 in their first innings. It was a below par score on a good wicket, and the West Indies were in severe danger of losing the initiative to a poor and troubled England side.

Faced with this crisis, Marshall turned in one of the greatest performances of a glittering career. He took 6 wickets for just 32 runs in 18 overs and, well supported by Walsh and Ambrose, played the major part in dismissing England for 165, the last eight wickets disappearing for 53 runs. Given this example, the West Indian fast bowlers never looked back. The Caribbean side won the next three Tests against England and the first three Tests of the following series against Australia. The West Indies were back on top and the pace quartet was in command.

Marshall, of course, dominated in a way that no other bowler had previously done within a Windies pace quartet, taking 52 wickets at 17.90 during the two victorious series against England and Australia. But he was not let down by the other members of the quartet, Benjamin taking 12 wickets at 12.58, Ambrose 48 at 20.90 and Walsh 29 at 31.45. Only Patterson continued to disappoint, his 16 wickets costing over 40 runs.

Of the two new recruits to the West Indian hall of fast-bowling fame, one was something of a pretender. Winston Benjamin was (like his fellow Antiguan Baptiste) much closer to the 1970s-style West Indian pace-bowling all-rounder. But Benjamin was a class act, who (like Holder and Boyce) knew how to trick a batsman into making mistakes. One of his favourite stunts was to begin to walk back to his mark, suddenly turn round and come in off a short run. Often the delivery would be a bouncer, sometimes (the double bluff) a slower ball.

Curtly Ambrose also came from Antigua, but there the comparisons end. Ambrose looked like an even taller, skinnier version of Walsh. But it was three other predecessors who appeared to influence his bowling style. In Rod Marsh's words, Ambrose had 'Garner's height, Holding's rhythm and Roberts's temperament'. The combined effect has made Ambrose the most feared and respected fast bowler on the planet. He is possibly the most accurate truly fast bowler to have lived and is capable of spells in which he snatches half a dozen Test match wickets in the space of a few overs. On these occasions he has a Botham-like irresistibility. Batsmen appear to become mesmerized by his right hand which wags from side to side, like a cobra's head, before sweeping down to deliver the ball from well over 8 ft.

Despite the victory over England, the Windies' comeback was not yet complete. When the West Indies returned to the Caribbean for a series against India they found a fourth world-beater ready to join the proven spearheads of Marshall, Walsh and Ambrose. Ian Bishop was tall, strong and every bit the replacement for Michael Holding that most West Indians (including Holding himself) thought he was. He toured England in 1988 with the West Indian side, but was now a world away from the skinny youngster who had bowled with little effect in games against the counties. His rangy frame was now packed with muscle, and in his first Test, many observers argued that he was the fastest of the Windies pace men and, next to Ambrose, the most accurate. He joined Marshall, Ambrose and Walsh in the second Test against India and immediately impressed, taking 6 wickets for 87 during the visitors' first innings. He finished the series with 16 wickets at 23.12 and became an automatic choice for the West Indian side.

During the series against India, Walsh became the target of some controversy, when the Indian players started 'whispering' about his action. Walsh's bowling arm certainly whips over his shoulder in a way that some might mistake for throwing, but the issue has never been raised again, inside or outside the West Indies.

Despite injuries to Marshall, Walsh and Ambrose, the pace quartet narrowly beat a resurgent English side in early 1991. To fill the gaps created by the injuries, the Caribbean selectors unusually did not blood new fast-bowling talent, but called up two 30-year-old medium-pacers. Eldine Baptiste and Ezra Moseley (who had been banned since the early 1980s for touring South Africa) did a steady, if unspectacular, job, but their selection showed clearly that the Windies were now depending on relatively few players when it came to maintaining their pace-bowling strategy. The fast-bowling resources were not as deep as they had been in the 1980s, but (as was demonstrated by the arrival of Ambrose and Bishop) the West Indies were still able to give the pace quartet new impetus whenever it was necessary.

In late 1990, Marshall, Ambrose, Walsh and Bishop (the best West Indies pace quartet since Holding, Roberts, Garner and Croft) then took part in a battle royal with the Pakistani trio of Imran Khan, Waqar Younis and Wasim Akram. It was the first time that the West Indian batsmen had faced this quantity and quality of pace bowling from Test match opponents. During the three-match rubber in Pakistan, the Windies batsmen never passed 300 and on three occasions were dismissed for less than 200. Haynes made only 198 runs at 33, Richardson 162 at 32.40, Greenidge 58 at 9.66 and Dujon 30 at 6.00.

The first Test was won by Pakistan with Waqar taking 8 wickets and Wasim 6. The Windies fast bowlers hit back in the next game as the Caribbean side levelled the series. Bishop led the way with 6 wickets, but Marshall and Ambrose collected 4 each and Walsh 3. All was set up perfectly for the decider at Lahore in early December and the game lived up to its billing. Imran decided, for the first time in the series, that he was fit enough to open the bowling, and removed both Greenidge and Haynes in

6 overs. Thanks to a brilliant 134 from Hooper, the Windies reached 294. This looked to be a match-winning score when Pakistan made only 122. The runs came from 50 overs, but this bland statistic conceals two wonderful bowling performances from Ambrose and Bishop. Ambrose bowled 20 overs, conceded only 35 runs and took 5 wickets. This was matched by Bishop who stayed on for 19.2 overs and captured the other 5 Pakistani wickets for 41.

In the Windies' second innings Waqar opened the bowling and dismissed Greenidge for 1. Then, after Imran had removed Richardson and the débutant Lara, Wasim ripped through the West Indian tail, taking 5 wickets for 28 runs off 9 overs. Pakistan were set the seemingly impossible target of 346, a task that seemed even steeper when Ambrose dismissed Aamer Malik for a duck before Pakistan had knocked one run off their target. The West Indies bowlers threw themselves into the attack and the Pakistan wickets fell consistently: Ramiz Raja for 41; Shoaib Mohammad for 49; Salim Malik for a duck; Masood Anwar for 37. At 187 for 6 the match looked all over, but then Imran and Wasim came together, and began to turn the game around. When stumps were drawn on the final day, Pakistan were 242 for 6 with Imran on 58 and Wasim 21. One hundred and four runs to make, four wickets to fall: the fairest end for a pulsating and a highly competitive series. It was perhaps the best example of how a series totally dominated by pace bowling could be constantly exciting.

The Windies returned to the Caribbean to take on a powerful Australian side. Bishop developed the back injury that has dogged his career, but ironically the Windies were able to field the same quartet for the entire series, one of the few times this has proved possible during a five-match rubber. Patterson was the bowler chosen to replace Bishop and, for once, his no-frills pace bowling proved more successful than that of the more skilful Ambrose and Walsh. The West Indies won the series 3–1 thanks to the consistent performance of all four fast bowlers, and the batting of Richardson, Logie, Haynes and Greenidge.

The series was a bad-tempered one, dominated by short-pitched bowling from both sides. It was the first half of the fourth Test which was the most uncomfortable for the batsmen on both sides and also again underlined how the Windies fast bowlers could dig their side out of almost any hole. Both sides went into the game at Bridgetown, Barbados with batting line-ups creaking with talent. The West Indies' first seven read Greenidge, Haynes, Richardson, Hooper, Richards, Logie and Dujon, while the Australian batting line-up of Taylor, Marsh, Boon, Border, Jones, and Mark and Steve Waugh was perhaps even stronger. Much good it did either side as the pace bowlers ran riot on a bouncy pitch. The West Indies batted first, and McDermott and Hughes took 4 wickets each as the home side slumped to 149 all out. In reply, the Australians looked to be getting on top when they reached 95 for 3. But Marshall dismissed Border and Jones, and Patterson accounted for Steve Waugh. Then Walsh, bowling for the first time in the innings, took the last four Australian wickets for 14 runs off 5.1 overs. The West Indies had a lead of 13 and, as is often the case with the West Indies' opponents when they see an apparently overwhelming advantage swept away in a few hours, Australia had their earlier confidence torn to pieces. In their second innings the West Indies made 536 (Greenidge 226) and Australia lost by 343 runs.

On the bouncy West Indian pitches, the loss of Bishop was not too much of a handicap, but it became more of a problem on the following tour to England. Led from the front by Graham Gooch, the home side drew the series 2–2.

With Marshall finally acknowledging that age had caught up with him, the West Indies were facing another period of transition comparative to the one they had overcome in 1987–8. They were to encounter similar problems in reasserting their ascendancy.

Fast forward into the future – 1992–4

The West Indies' next game was an historic one, South Africa's first since the lifting of the apartheid-inspired ban. South Africa went into the one-off game at Bridgetown with four pace bowlers and, during most of the match, it was they and not the Windies quartet who posed the greater threat. Bishop was still injured and the West Indies chose the uncapped Antiguan Kenny Benjamin to replace Marshall.

The West Indies made 262 in their first innings and South Africa replied with 345. South Africa's lead of 83 might have been even greater had not débutant all-rounder Jimmy Adams taken 4 wickets with his gentle left-arm spin. The West Indies scored 283 and South Africa reached 122 for 2, only 79 runs from a famous victory, at the end of the fourth day. This was the West Indies' tightest corner yet, and Richardson opened the attack on the fifth day with his two most experienced bowlers Ambrose and Walsh. It was a wise move. Walsh led the way, dismissing both overnight batsmen Kepler Wessels and Peter Kirsten almost immediately. With their two most experienced players gone, the rookie South African side crumbled to 148 all out. During the morning session, Walsh bowled 11 overs, 7 of which were maidens, and took 4 wickets for 8 runs. Ambrose took the other 3 wickets and finished with the amazing match figures of 60 overs, 26 maidens, 8 wickets for 81 runs.

Despite this victory, and Bishop's return, the West Indies were no more than slight favourites when they arrived in Australia during November 1992. Australia quickly showed that those odds would have to be recalculated. During the first Test the West Indies were set 231 runs to win, but immediately slumped to 9 for 4 and finished the game struggling at 133 for 8. During the second Test at Melbourne, Australia drove home their advantage. Leg-spinner Shane Warne took 7 wickets for 52 runs and the home side was victorious by 139 runs. The third game was a high-scoring draw lit up by Brian Lara's scintillating 277. With Australia one up with two to play, the fourth game at the Adelaide Oval looked as though it would see the end of the West Indies' 13-year record of not having lost a series. On a wicket which gave considerable help to the pace bowlers the West Indies made 252 and 146. Australia made 213 in their first innings and were set 186 runs to win. At 102 for 8 it seemed that the West Indies had done enough, but a gutsy partnership between débutant batsman Julian Langer and No. 10 Tim May took Australia to 144. After Langer was caught behind off Bishop the game took a final twist. Craig McDermott displayed that his 'iron man' training had given him mental as well as physical toughness. He and May took the score to 184, two runs away from victory and writing their names in the history books. Instead it was Walsh who seized the pen. A bouncer rocketed past McDermott's bat, the Windies appealed and McDermott was given out. The Windies could breathe again. And, as had been seen time and again in individual matches involving the West Indies, once the fast bowlers had recovered an apparently losing position they would never relax their grip. It also proved to be the story of this series.

Ambrose had taken 10 wickets for 120 runs in the fourth Test, but his finest hour was yet to come. The fifth Test was at Perth, the fastest pitch in the world, and Ambrose was unplayable. Australia reached 85 for 2 in the first innings when the giant Antiguan was brought back for his second spell of the match. In 32 balls he took 7 Australian wickets for just 1 run. Australia never recovered and lost the match by an innings and 25 runs within three days. The West Indies' record, by the margin of just one run, had been maintained.

The home series against Pakistan in 1993 was billed as a world championship clash. But the Windies, buoyed up by the victory over Australia, were just too good. Just as the Windies' morale was soaring, that of the Pakistanis was plummeting as they fought off mischievous drug allegations against captain and vice-captain (and main strike bowlers) Wasim and Waqar. The West Indies won the first Test within three days (making it the second three-day victory in a row), but not without the now traditional first innings scare. The Windies were bowled out for 127, but hit back by bundling out the Pakistanis for 140 and then scoring 382 in their second innings. The second match was won by 10 wickets and the third drawn with the Windies in the stronger position. The world championship had turned into a non-contest.

Bishop's back injury flared up again before the 1994 home series against England. This forced the Windies to rely on the two Benjamins (Kenny and Winston). Although capable of bowling a quicker ball, these two bowlers (along with another fringe player, Anderson Cummins) are no more than fast-medium. Many have interpreted this fact as evidence that the West

75

Indies' fast-bowling resources are finally drying up. 'Real quick' or not, Kenny Benjamin proved too good for most of the English batsmen, taking 22 wickets at 25.73 during the series. But the West Indies' success in the series was mainly based on Ambrose's genius and Walsh's success in taking the new ball, something which he had rarely done during his 10-year Test career.

4 | The fast bowler as athlete

A healthy body creates a healthy mind

Clive Lloyd

THE WEST INDIAN fast bowlers are athletes, in the purest sense of the word. That will cause raised eyebrows among some traditionalists, but again C.L.R. James proves our inspiration. During 1937, he wrote in the *Glasgow Herald* that: 'The splendid physique, trained and adapted to endurance and highly skilful performance, is not only the enjoyment of millions of modern people. All through the ages humanity has admired such men. That most intellectual of peoples, the Greeks, gave their athletes a high place, a thing our modern "high-brows" might remember.'

Clive Lloyd placed a great emphasis on athleticism and for one very good reason. 'Our fitness was paramount', he insists, 'because we had great cricketers who had to think through situations and in order to perform such a task you must be physically fit.'

Since Lloyd's captaincy, the West Indies teams have been trained to develop their athleticism and in so doing have raised cricket – and particularly fast bowling – to a new dimension. Michael Holding states: 'Once upon a time, fast bowling was looked upon as sheer brute force and ignorance. That is not so today.'

The West Indians have evolved from being 'mere' cricketers (most of whom are still not renowned for great levels of fitness when compared to other international sportsmen) to being athletes of the highest calibre. They reasoned that there is not a single top-level successful sportsman performing today who can rely on natural ability alone. This realization led to the belief that – with the stakes becoming ever higher amid the pressure of keeping your Test place – the work ethic needed to be as strong in international cricket as it had to be in any other great endeavour. The additional fact that latter-day cricketers face extra demands with the sheer volume of matches required of them has merely increased the necessity to sharpen up physically and stay on top of their game.

The forerunner of adopting a fitness ethic was of course Australia's Dennis Lillee who, by sheer hard work and application, overcame terrible injury. But the transformation in the West Indies team in general and the fast-bowling quartet in particular is due primarily to one man, another

77

Australian, who could be called the unsung hero of the West Indies' all-powerful team of the 1980s and 1990s.

Dennis Waight, a former Australian rugby league player and 'conditioner', joined the West Indies in 1977 during Kerry Packer's World Series Cricket when a friend asked him if he would like to work with the Rest of the World side.

When Waight joined the West Indies he knew exactly what he was dealing with. 'I'd seen the Tests the previous year when the Windies had their 5–1 hiding from the Aussies,' he says. 'I thought they had potential then and I thought it would be a challenge to see if I could bring it out. Better fitness and prevention of injuries was my aim so I signed with them on a three-month contract and that was 17 years ago.'

Viv Richards believes that Waight is owed enormous credit for maintaining the successful machine of four quick bowlers by creating a fitness ethic throughout the team. 'I never knew fast bowlers before who used to train that much in stamina or muscle-building to combat injuries,' says Richards. 'He really got the guys working. I was impressed with how he would have the fast bowlers training even when they weren't involved in a match. He concentrated on building muscles which are used constantly throughout your career and where fast bowlers are particularly vulnerable – backs, shoulders, knees.

'In the past, fast bowlers seemed to break down quite easily – and still do in other sides. Dennis helped to prevent injuries by keeping the guys totally focused and as a result our bowlers have not broken down as much as others. At first some guys were not convinced about Waight's approach because it is a lot of hard work, but someone like Michael Holding benefited from having him, having someone who knew exactly what he was dealing with. Dennis has played a very big part in our success.'

He has played as important a part in the psychological as in the physical preparation of the side. Tony Cozier believes: 'Waight's influence has been great in getting all the players together before a game.' In that sense, as Holding iterates, Waight's approach ideally complemented that of Clive Lloyd. It was Waight, for example, who led the 'warm-up' on the outfield before each game. And the constant 'high-fives', evident to anybody watching, are symptomatic of the team spirit engendered by these pre-match work-outs.

The fast bowlers in particular were, of course, well aware that the hard work ethic instilled by Waight would pay dividends, and perhaps one factor should not be overlooked as Joel Garner believed: 'In a team that could call on the number of fast bowlers that we had, it was dangerous, career-wise, to be injured.' That incentive is one of the reasons for the lack of complacency about fitness evident among the West Indies quicks. Even with the legacy of Packer cricket, the game at domestic level in the West Indies does not pay a fortune. Becoming a Test fast bowler, on the other hand, is, as

Holding points out, a 'good career move'. He explains that: 'The board helps with a pension scheme payable after the age of 35. But it is only for Test players. Red Stripe players don't get much money. So the incentive is there for Red Stripe players to try to move up to Test level, where the money is. If you don't play for the West Indies, you don't get any money out of cricket!'

While Waight's methods have inspired change in the preparation of every other Test-playing country, no other side, for various reasons which we will discuss later, has produced bowlers approaching the same calibre as the West Indies and no other side has been as relatively injury-free, bearing in mind the number of Tests and one-day internationals required of modern players.

For a start, stress fractures, it appears, are few and far between in the West Indies fast men; the bowlers suffer less wear and tear – especially when you bear in mind that they are bowling faster than any other bowlers in the world – and they can, if required, bowl longer spells.

Waight believes that is due to a number of factors. 'Flexibility and stretching have helped the bowlers a hell of a lot,' he says. 'Looking at the stress fractures in particular, we used to do a lot of strengthening of the lower back. Not over-strength work, but enough to balance it out.

'Then we did a lot of running – and *learning* to run.' Waight places a lot of emphasis on this, insisting that the West Indies fast bowlers have to *learn* to run first before concentrating on any other part of their game. Only by learning to approach the wicket in a smooth, controlled and stress-free way, does Waight believe that bowling rhythm can become second nature. That seems a simple enough approach, but Waight then goes on to explain his extraordinary method of educating the West Indies fast bowlers in the art of running.

'They have to learn to run into the wicket – *with their eyes closed*, floating, feeling comfortable.' The explanation conjures wonderful images of Holding, Marshall, Ambrose et al., trance-like, as they practise running in. Former Pakistan captain Imran Khan – no mean fast bowler himself of course with 382 Test wickets at 22.81 – believes that Holding's run-up was the best ever. 'He ran in like an athlete,' Imran says, 'and we all started running like him.'

But Waight explains that efficient run-ups do not all have to conform to the Holding model. 'Marshall's run-up, for example, was very different to Holding's. Although Malcolm's run-up was smooth, it was like a whippet's: there was nothing jerky. Short, quick, but smooth.

'If he closed his eyes, Malcolm could do it [run to the wicket] a million times, on and off, on and off, and there would be the same footmarks every time. That perfect balance in the run-up means there is less chance of injury.

'And then if you've got a nice, smooth run-up, you can develop the extra pace coming through. And if you've got a nice, good rotational arm speed then you consolidate that extra pace.'

Length of run-up is equally important as the fast bowler needs to be at high speed at the point of delivery. But the length of run-up should not be overdone. Alf Gover, the former Surrey and England fast bowler and doyen of cricketing coaching in England, recounts the tale of Winston Davis in his autobiography *The Long Run*.

> I . . . then took him to my outdoor nets; here I stood by the bowling crease and sent him to bowl off his full run. He went so far back I thought he was going home! He set off from the far distance approaching the crease like a four-minute miler but had no acceleration towards the crease. I gently pointed out to him that, although a fast bowler required an appreciable length of approach to the bowling crease, he was over-doing it by doubling the required length. I also pointed out that I could hardly recommend him to a county because with his inordinate length of run-up he would not last the course in three-day matches.

If Waight's approach to run-ups is novel, then his opinions on bowling actions will be seen by many as heretical. He is adamant that it is a mistake for bowlers to get too side-on in their bowling actions.

'If you get too side-on just before you deliver', he says, 'the front foot bangs down. I find that if you are more open-chested you seem to get less stress fractures.'

England's great fast bowler Fred Trueman of course has other ideas, believing that sideways-on is the right way, always was the right way and always will be.

But Waight is unequivocal: 'Most of our great quicks were all open-chested. Michael Holding looked side-on but when he delivered, his chest was coming round. It was the same with Croft, Garner, Roberts, Marshall and Ambrose.'

It is important to bear in mind that Waight has never worked on, altered or refined any of the West Indians' actual bowling actions. That is established well before they get to him. Marshall, for example, was almost completely open-chested at the point of delivery, a 'faulty' action in the eyes of many purists who cite the forerunner of the modern West Indian quicks, Wes Hall, as having the archetypal classical fast-bowling action, with his back foot landing parallel to the crease, the front foot pointing towards long leg. As for Colin Croft! Geoff Boycott said that Croft disproved most of the traditional rules for fast bowling. '"Deliver the ball from close to the stumps with a side-on action," they say. Well, Croft's feet are all over the place, his left foot is outside the return crease, his arms wave like windmills and his chest is square as he lets the ball go. A hundred Test wickets with that action? Try explaining that to youngsters in the nets.'

'The only real side-on bowler,' states Waight, 'and he came through the ranks just before I had a chance to work with him, was Ian Bishop and he has broken down. We did try and turn him around but it was too late.'

So, the gospel according to Waight is quite straightforward: forget most of the coaching manuals you've ever read. Practise learning to run into the wicket with your eyes closed and, once you've perfected that, deliver the ball open-chested. (What should not be beyond dispute in this argument, however, is that an up-and-coming quick bowler should not attempt to mix the two actions of sideways-on or open-chested. A mixed action will see a bowler trying to get side-on with the trunk of his body but with his feet pointing down the wicket, causing severe strain on the bowler's back.)

To look a little more closely at technique, most of the West Indian bowlers deliver with level shoulders and their right arm close to their head.

Many have different actions and run-ups, but they all follow certain basics. The position of the front (left) arm is deemed vital to a quick bowler if he is to bowl straight. It should be high and pulled back behind the bowler, and as the arm comes forward the bowler should drive it towards his target, then let it continue behind him. If the front arm veers away from the body it will take the bowler with it, affecting his accuracy. His bowling arm should follow the path of the front arm towards the batsman and finish across the bowler's body. The bowler's head should be as still as possible at the point of delivery: you can see the West Indian fast bowlers following the ball with their eyes down the pitch into their follow-through.

The West Indies quicks also possess a great deal of power in rotating their hips with good waist mobility. The right hip and foot are brought forward and through quickly to give impetus to the right shoulder and the right arm. Then the quickness of the hip action helps the bowler's right foot to land on the ground after he has released the ball. Finally, running at speed helps the right foot, right hip and right shoulder come forward – all while maintaining perfect balance of course.

The placement of the bowler's front foot determines the body action. For the inswinger, the toe points straight down the pitch while, for the outswinger, the toe points to the leg slip.

But where does the actual power for delivering the ball come from? Waight has his definitive answer. 'The power is in the quickness of the rotation, so the shoulder is the answer. If you watched Holding and Marshall, you saw they had a whippy arm, or what we call very quick rotational cuff. That's where the power and speed came from.' Holding concurs with this, saying that a fast arm action is vital to send the ball down as fast as you possibly can. He adds that when a quick bowler really wants to let one fly, he gets extra speed from his last few strides to gain a quicker rotation of his trunk on delivery.

So much for theory, what of the practice? Speed of delivery has become a benchmark for ranking the world's fast bowlers. The real first test of any merit was carried out in Perth by the University of Western Australia and the Department of Physical Education. It involved Dennis Lillee, Andy Roberts, Michael Holding and Jeff Thomson.

Thomson's delivery was clocked at 99.70 m.p.h. from the hand and at 80.73 m.p.h. as it reached the batsman. His speed of run-up was 11.20 m.p.h. Roberts and Holding were next fastest, followed by Lillee who recorded the fastest run-up: 20.86 m.p.h. The tests also rated the relative importance of the components of fast bowling. The final ranking placed arm action as the most important, followed by leg action and hip rotation, the efficiency of the run-up, trunk flexibility and shoulder girdle rotation, and finally hand action.

But what advice would Waight give to a young fast bowler who wants to bowl real quick? 'I would go to a nice flat piece of land, such as a football pitch, mark out a distance of say 40–45 metres, walk up to that mark, or jog up to that mark and then race back, trying to lift your legs and try to come through the line like Carl Lewis, with a pumping arm action.

'And just do that day after day after day, to get the run smooth. Don't run flat out, run at 75 to 80 per cent effort. Eventually, they will have got into such a rhythm that I'd then want them to do that with their eyes closed. Then they will know the split second when they should hit their mark and run through. Once you feel that comfort I believe you can then go out there and do whatever you want to do.'

But could Waight accomplish such results with cricketers from other nations or cultures? Isn't his very starting point with a West Indian youngster, because of his natural physique, an advantage? Waight is not sure. Former England captain Bob Willis, on the other hand, believes the West Indians are naturally more athletic, but one wonders what Waight could have done for him. Willis says: 'I had a particularly poor, physically demanding bowling action which took a lot out of me. I wasn't as good a physical specimen as Michael Holding.' Imran Khan concurs: 'The West Indians are natural athletes. You have to put it down to that.'

Waight counters: 'I wouldn't say that the West Indians are naturally more athletic. That could be a bit of a myth. But they have got a certain rhythm and timing which adds to the movement of the body. And it could be in-bred.'

In *A History of West Indies Cricket*, Michael Manley says that the Caribbean climatic conditions encourage a freedom, almost a spontaneity, of movement. 'These sons and daughters of the tropics are loose-limbed and athletic, relaxed and free-moving, because they spend so much of their time in the warm outdoors. By the same token, they do not take easily to the long grinding physical application which makes a marathon runner. Sprinting and fast bowling, on the other hand, come easily.'

In fact, all of the West Indian fast bowlers are masters of controlled sprinting in their run-ups, with their strides lengthening to the point where they release the ball. Rhythm is so essential to the accuracy of fast bowlers that it is little wonder Waight spends so long perfecting the run-up. Ambrose, for example – and bear in mind that he is 6 ft 7 in – arrives at the crease with his back foot landing sufficiently behind the bowling crease for his front foot not to overstep the popping crease without any loss of rhythm. And, as we shall see later, Waight preaches rhythm even at the expense of no-balling.

Waight used to believe that the lower part of the back was the important physical difference between West Indian and other fast bowlers. In the early 1990s, he said: 'Holding is lean but he has that good muscle definition where it counts. Whites don't have that type of build. Greenidge isn't a bowler but if you look at him you see how he has the little extra bump in the lower back ... I think it's their greatest asset.'

However, Waight is now not so sure that the West Indians have any inherited advantage even though most physiologists seem to agree that Afro-Caribbeans and black Americans have a tendency to athleticism, with denser bones which make them less injury-prone.

Today Waight says: 'Blacks seem to have a different curvature which could be a problem for the lower back although, interestingly, the fast bowlers don't seem to have it. All the Windies quicks are strong in the lower back.' (Although Malcolm Marshall discovered, as we shall see later, that he had a weak back which required special attention.) 'A huge man like Joel Garner – 6 ft 8 in and 16–17 stones – never had any problems with his back. He had a thick-set back and good rhythm.'

Waight continues: 'I find in the joints – especially legs, knees and elbows – that they seem to be more floating, more giveable. The joint seems to shift around a bit! If an orthopaedic surgeon tested the ligaments, they would wobble. Marshall's knee would float everywhere but there was nothing wrong with it, it was strong. So you would have to say that the movements are looser and that they have a little bit of give.'

Marshall suffered agonizing problems with his back early on in his Test career during the 1981–2 series in Australia and seriously believed he might never play cricket again. It was only the work put in by Edmund Sealey, chiropractor and physiotherapist to the Barbados athletics squad, that put him right. Marshall's back muscles were discovered to be weak and fast bowling only put those muscles under more strain. Sealey prescribed 100 sit-ups a day with other exercises to build up strength and stamina in his back, and Marshall was on the road to recovery. Marshall says Sealey saved his career, and before the start of every day's play and under super-vision by Waight prior to Tests, Marshall went through his list of exercises: his back never troubled him again.

Perhaps the most important difference between West Indian fast bowlers and those from other nations, according to Waight, is the amount of fast twitching fibres they possess. Here a brief physiological summary is

83

helpful. There are two types of fibres in the body: fast twitching and slow twitching. Fast muscle fibres, primarily those concerned with fine, rapid, precise movement such as those associated with fast bowling, have twitch durations as short as 7.5 milliseconds. Slow muscle fibres, principally those involved in strong and sustained movements (say taking part in a tug of war), have twitch durations of up to 100 milliseconds.

Waight believes, without doing a controlled scientific test, that most of the West Indies team, not just the fast bowlers, would have more fast twitching than slow twitching fibres.

'Fast twitching is an explosive fibre so they explode a little quicker. Slow twitchers are harder to define – but I do know that you can't coach a slow twitcher to become fast. On the other hand, you could help a fast twitcher to develop his slow twitching for endurance.'

All of this begs the inevitable question: can Dennis Waight's training methods make a fast bowler faster?

'I don't know,' he says, with a certain degree of modesty. 'I believe if you have very good flexibility, you will be a good mover for a start. But even if you look loose-limbed, it won't work if you don't do the stretching and flexibility exercises. I'm a great believer in static stretching, instead of ballistic stretching, which is the physical jerks stuff. Some people think that's wrong, but I've worked at it, I've planned it.

'We've built up to holding one stretch for one minute [hence the term "static stretch"]. That way you can control the stretch, learn to get the muscle long, educate the muscle to be long. No pain, no gain is not the answer. It is to educate it, not to hurt it but to get to the point where you say it feels like that's as far as you should go and then back off.

'You've also got to do strengthening work. I'm a great believer in isometrics [exercises which keep the muscle the same measure or length] so I use a lot of rubber bands. I think you can control the muscle or joint you are working on when you do slow strength work. And you don't bulk up as much as you do if you use weights. If you're too bulky, you can't bowl. Simple as that. You want strong muscles, but not bulkiness.'

Talking of bulky players brought up the subject of Ian Botham and other cricketers who have had problems in that department. Waight was coach at Somerset in the early 1980s and looked after Botham (as well as continuing his work with West Indian colleagues Viv Richards and Joel Garner) during that time.

'I never had a problem with Ian there,' says Waight. 'When he went on, he developed problems. Ian carried a lot of weight but when he was at Somerset he was fairly all right. But he'd put on a stone and a half every time he went on tour and I would just get him to stretch. For a big man, he ran up very gently and his legs were like iron, which protected his lower back. "Both" was exceptionally strong; in the same vein, Merv Hughes doesn't look fit but he would bowl all day. It's about strength and stamina.'

Waight does not impose dietary restrictions on the fast bowlers, although Michael Holding said that he wasn't too keen on them eating too much Chinese food – which, incidentally, is Curtly Ambrose's favoured form of nutrition. Waight would simply tell by looking at a bowler and his movements whether he had not been eating good food or had been eating too much good food!

'Flexibility would come down a fraction,' he says, 'so I just ask them to do a bit more work and watch what they're eating. But I'd rather they came to me at the start of a tour 7–8 lb overweight because two weeks will get rid of any surplus weight very easily. If they are at their ideal weight at the beginning of a tour it can be difficult to maintain that level for the entire series.'

Many have posed the question as to whether dietary differences could affect the production of fast bowlers. The issue is particularly alive in India and in *A Maidan View*, Mihir Bose wonders, 'Could a country that lived on rice and vegetables really produce fast bowlers to match those from countries that ate beef and pork? ... Is vegetarianism an enemy of fast bowling?' Bose concluded by saying that lack of proper diet does explain the poor standard of the Indian physique. 'However, this is because for many Indians their diet is simply inadequate, not because they are vegetarians. Part of the Indian problem was that they ceased to believe that they could produce a fast bowler, capable of challenging the West. However, Kapil Dev has proved, without doubt, that they can.'

As in all other aspects of Waight's work with the team, he preaches the values of balance and moderation, hence a balanced diet. 'They can eat anything in moderation. I'm not a great believer in "you can't eat this or that". The body requires fat after all.

'But being world champions helps because they have acquired an image so they want to look good, and they want to play well because that keeps the money coming in. They like looking after themselves because that makes them play better, feel better and gets them and the team better results.'

It is perhaps in the prevention of injuries to the fast bowlers that Waight has been of most value to the West Indies team, though even before he joined them it is notable, as Tony Cozier says, that West Indian fast bowlers rarely broke down. However, they did not have to play anywhere near the amount of cricket that is expected of their successors. By the very nature of their occupation, fast bowlers are more prone to breakdown than any other member of a cricket team, particularly in the modern era when the sheer volume of games only exacerbates potential problems. Pounding in, over after over, landing with huge force to put knees and lower back under constant pressure can ultimately take its toll.

But as we have seen earlier, Waight believes that balance and rhythm in the run-up and a more open-chested action will help to prevent injuries, while swimming, stretching and restrengthening more vulnerable areas will increase their stamina.

'I try to keep the bowlers going for a long time,' Waight says. 'But it doesn't come easily. It's hard work for me and for them. But the more they play, the more endurance they get. And the more rhythm they've got, the less it takes out of them: remember they've got to bowl 200 balls a day.'

Holding, the most obviously athletic of the West Indies quicks in the eyes of the layperson, believes that Waight improved his performance by as much as 30 per cent. And Holding was *not* an athlete before he took up cricket; he was not the 400 metre runner that many seem to believe he was. In fact, he didn't even get to represent his school as a runner.

'Before Dennis,' says Holding, 'most of us jogged a lot before the game and then went into the match. 'Dennis started a regime of a lot of running and stretching and as fast bowlers we did more stretching and exercises than anyone else. For instance, we were playing a State game in Adelaide; the captain won the toss and elected to bat so Dennis took us off on a short run – 45 minutes to one hour – as he figured we would not be bowling that day.

'We stayed fit for a longer period of time with his strengthening and stretching exercises which meant we pulled less muscles. But if we did get injured, we got better quicker.

'I personally had a few minor muscle injuries but no particular weak spot. In the latter stages of my career I had slight tears in the left hamstring because I had had a knee operation on my left leg and the hamstring got weaker after that. After a knee operation, the muscles tend to waste away so you have to do a lot more work on that leg to strengthen it.'

West Indian fast bowlers are not immune to injury – Marshall's back, Holding's hamstring and Bishop's long-term problems are just three instances among many that are testimony to that – and as Waight says there might be badly dug footholds, the bowlers might land at a bad angle which could cause pelvic tilt, but if the run-up is right, bearing in mind those factors that you cannot control, the chances of physical damage diminish.

In concentrating on good technique, Waight has ensured that, once a fast bowler comes to him, he will be assured of relatively pain-free, injury-free performance.

Former England captain and fast bowler Bob Willis, who played in five series against the West Indies, had injury problems – which might easily have defeated a lesser individual – throughout his career, especially at the beginning. 'I hardly played three Tests in a row before getting injured. I got myself physically fit and went through a spell from July/August 1976 until 1980 when I only missed one match through injury. But fast bowlers are going to get injured and have knee problems later in life and have hip problems simply by the nature of their work.

'I think everyone got fitter when Packer came along and the rewards for playing cricket improved. Packer particularly underlined the West Indians' capability for making a living out of playing cricket. Prior to that they had played a lot in Lancashire Leagues and the batsmen had a place as overseas cricketers playing in county cricket but then the emphasis moved to the fast bowlers. I think a couple of seasons ago, 80 per cent of the overseas players in the England county game were overseas fast bowlers.

'There have been West Indian bowlers who struggled with injury, Ian Bishop for one. But mostly they have good [as in low stress] run-ups and bowling actions.'

It seems that West Indian fast bowlers are destined to be just that because, as Waight explained earlier, of those fast twitch fibres. Work carried out at the Cricket Academy in Adelaide bears out Waight's theory. The academy, in conjunction with the Australian Institute of Sport, which has conducted a great deal of research into fast bowling, has pronounced that a fast bowler cannot be taught to be genuinely fast – they either are or they are not – but they can be coached, with subtlety, to be more effective and less injury-prone.

Alf Gover is equally sure that fast bowlers are born, not made. That said, Gover is responsible for adapting the technique of Andy Roberts at the beginning of his career, as he says in *The Long Run*: 'Andy Roberts had pace but his fault was a tendency to fall away towards the off-side field. This resulted in too many deliveries going down the leg side … To cure it, I placed two high stools on Andy's left-hand side at his delivery point, warning Andy that he could do himself harm if he continued to fall away. A couple of hard knocks did the trick and the good-humoured Andy soon had his body balance going over the front leg towards the batsman. Accuracy and away-swing were his rewards and his potential had improved 100 per cent.'

Formal 'coaching' is not a term too often heard among the West Indies team, while Waight adopts the stance of 'training' rather than 'coaching'. Rigid coaching, in an English sense, is looked upon with a rather disdainful eye in the Caribbean. Surrounded by the best exponents of their craft, they have tended to learn from each other. Joel Garner, for example, received tuition in the Barbados Cricket League from no less than Charlie Griffith and Gary Sobers. Griffith, believed Garner, 'appeared to have a driving desire to give young bowlers that aggressiveness and will to win that I felt, even at the time, was an attempt to pass on his legacy to another generation of Barbadian fast bowlers. During those sessions, Charlie gave me a feeling of pride in being a fast bowler. Renowned for a devastating yorker, he taught me how to bowl one that swung in the air.' How could anyone fail with such expert advice?

Quick bowlers are generally encouraged to bowl absolutely flat out, then given guidance on how to be more effective. Michael Holding believes that English coaches are far too preoccupied with fast bowlers bowling line and length, and there is obviously so much more to it than that! There also seems to be an unspoken fear among many in the West Indies that coaching could lead to the over-analysis of any perceived problem (whether real or not), which would cancel out natural ability. Former Wimbledon tennis champion, the late Arthur Ashe, once remarked: 'There is a syndrome in sports called "paralysis by analysis".' When exceptional fast bowlers emerge that has to be the last thing on anyone's mind. The Australian quick, Craig McDermott, has said: 'I don't believe in the coaching of quick bowlers. I prefer to learn through playing.'

McDermott of course was frequently over-bowled during the early part of his career, and this undermined both his health and effectiveness as a strike bowler. It is certainly the case that his career received a considerable set-back when Australian coach Bobby Simpson told him to cut down his pace and concentrate on bowling long, containing spells.

Once they're out on the field, the West Indies quicks are on their own, leaving Waight in the pavilion to observe and to be on hand in the event of any trouble. And while the side's fast bowlers, as we have seen, are the least injury-prone of their kind because of their physical conditioning, problems do still occur. It is a rare day when one or the other is not suffering from a 'niggle', be it stiffness or strain. But, as Malcolm Marshall has testified: 'Nobody goes into a Test match on behalf of the West Indies in anything less than the perfect condition for which Dennis has been responsible.' And Waight has embraced all manner of 'alternative' therapies to deal with minor strains. He tries to incorporate reflexology (Chinese foot massage to balance vital organs and alleviate muscle tension) and even acupuncture if the players are amenable. But he is also a great believer in the traditional ice methods for strains and will use ultrasound when necessary.

He pays special care to equipment, particularly footwear for the bowlers, who, he believes, need 'higher and more rigid ankle support and a flared sole to stop the rolling of the ankle. The heel should absorb shock but the material must stretch to three-quarters of an inch from the toe since bowlers exert pressure on the balls of the feet, leading to patella problems and stress fractures of the tibia. Good arch support is essential to lessen cartilage trouble and "runner's knee".'

Concern about bowlers' footwear is not exclusively West Indian of course, and there have been oft-repeated and justified complaints from the England camp, among others, about the inadequacy of boots. It seems ludicrous, bearing in mind the perilous nature in terms of injury potential of the fast bowler's trade, that the same urgent attention paid to protecting batsmen from fast bowling has not been given to safeguarding the quicks' vital assets.

Neither has the no-ball law helped the matter. Bowlers now feel that they have to anchor their back foot so that they can, with pinpoint accuracy, land the front foot in the small space between the creases as the law necessitates. This has led to a number of injuries, those to England's

Andrew Caddick and Alan Igglesden among them, although not among West Indies quicks who are seemingly more dismissive of the no-ball law. Curtly Ambrose had a problem with no-balls in the 1994 fifth Test in Antigua against England, but all Dennis Waight said was: 'His run-up is still nice and smooth.' With the best will in the world it is hard to imagine a similarly cheerful reply from another Test side's coach, although detractors will see the West Indies' attitude to the no-ball problem as some form of insolence. However, Waight's approach is 'tamper with technique at your peril', no-balls or not.

But Michael Holding, incidentally, is scornful of fast bowlers who repeatedly transgress the no-ball law. 'They just don't work hard enough on their run-ups and that's unprofessional. It certainly is no reason to revert to the old law which judged a no-ball by the placement of the back foot, not the front, as is now being suggested.

'Once you're bowling no-balls, it must enter your mind at some stage of your run-up that this one is going to be another. Once that happens, it means you're not concentrating fully on putting the ball where you want it.'

But, with the same equipment at the disposal of fast bowlers the world over, why has the rest of the world not produced quicks of the same standard? Dennis Waight says simply that he doesn't know, but that the West Indies were fortunate in having two great role models in Hall and Griffith which set the production line in motion. The truth is that other Test-playing nations have produced 'real quicks' – look at Imran Khan, Wasim Akram, Waqar Younis, David Lawrence, Devon Malcolm and Craig McDermott to name but a very few – but without the sheer numbers, quality or consistency as the West Indies. The West Indian bowlers seem to think that English bowlers are over-bowled and suffer from a coaching hierarchy which preaches technique time and again. Indeed, a former England Test player privately stated that the root cause of England's bowling problems in the early 1990s lay in the blinkered coaching and advice they were getting at Test level.

Gary Sobers, as good a judge as any, believes the West Indians are as technically correct as anyone but the difference is that they can improvise.

Imran Khan agrees: 'The great players all broke away from the classical model. Every bowler has a certain natural gift and then it is just a question of refining it.'

It is the West Indian fast bowlers' consistency of performance which is most remarkable. Other Test-playing nations have always found fast bowlers but they have not performed at the highest level with remotely the same reliability. There have been the odd outstanding performances – witness Devon Malcolm's magnificent nine for 57 against South Africa at The Oval in 1994 – but nothing to compare with the day-out, day-in feats of the West Indies' quicks.

So, what are the other sides doing wrong? The straightforward answer is:

nothing. Imran Khan believes that the West Indian pace quartet was a freak of cricket history and says his theory has been borne out since the quartet is now in decline. As Michael Holding points out: 'England tried four quicks in 1990 but it didn't work because there wasn't the quality.' But the West Indies have a natural reserve of quick bowlers which will always be available even if it cannot approach the breathtaking quality of the original foursomes. There is no more powerful incentive than emulation, so the relay of quick bowlers has appeared endless. As one fades away, so he passes the baton to a younger version. Waight points out that Hall and Griffith were the original role models, so the youngsters started coming then. And as Vanburn Holder adds: 'Hall was my idol and everyone then wanted to bowl like him. Success breeds success. Now everyone wants to bowl like Curtly Ambrose.' West Indians born since 1960 remember nothing but four fast bowlers!

And that 'chicken-and-egg' theory simply means that until another Test side gets an attack of consistent quality to equal that of the West Indies, they will not be able to tap into a similar vein.

It is worth noting here the very real fears expressed in the Caribbean a short while ago that the 'chicken-and-egg' cycle could be broken when the Americanization of sport threatened to halt the supply of world-beating bowlers. Basketball commands a great deal of television coverage in the West Indies and there was concern that the sport would attract those youngsters who in the past would have naturally turned to cricket. But Viv Richards now believes that, ironically through television, cricket is in a much more healthy state. 'Because of satellite television,' he says, 'people have been able to see the game throughout the Caribbean, every ball of this series [West Indies v. England 1993–4]. I'm not so worried about the game now: people are seeing Lara and Ambrose. Kids are picking up cricket bats and balls again. It is a healthy sign.' That's healthy from a West Indies perspective, of course, less appetizing if you are an opposing player. However, there is a growing realization that attention will have to be given to maintaining better quality pitches in the West Indies to ensure that the pace-bowling pool doesn't dry up.

But it would seem a logical progression that those 'kids picking up bats and balls again' will be even fitter than their predecessors, for not only have they seen success from their heroes which they will strive to emulate, they have also seen how hard they have worked to get there. The future recruits who will come under Waight's wing – he only works with the West Indies Test side, not any cricketers on the Caribbean domestic scene (think how much more work he could do there!) – will be at an even higher starting point than those he deals with now. That is an awesome prospect for the future.

There may be an apparent decline in the production line of the quartet, but it could well be, as some observers believe, that this is but the calm before the storm. But athleticism alone has not allowed West Indian fast bowlers to stay on top of the cricketing world for the last 20 years. They have also developed a similarly unsurpassed understanding of the technique and mentality of fast bowling.

5 | The art, craft and psychology of fast bowling

The difference between a fast bowler and a good fast bowler is not extra muscle but extra brains.

Fred Trueman

THE next vital component in the success of the West Indian fast bowlers is found in their psychological approach: the application of soul and mind, and the commitment to perfecting his skills which sets a great sportsman apart from his fellows.

One of the best examples, among hundreds, of a West Indian fast bowler making the best use of his physical and mental capabilities occurred in perhaps the most talked-about over ever played.

The third Test of England's 1981 tour of the Caribbean saw the West Indians bat first and reach a total of 265. Andy Roberts and Michael Holding then opened the bowling to Gooch and Boycott, and England's leading batsman of the 1970s has never forgotten his first over from the Jamaican.

Boycott said: 'The first delivery was short of a length and gloved me, bouncing well in front of the slips; the second was short and I played and missed as it bounced; the third nipped back and hit me on the inside of the left thigh; the fourth bounced and I played it down in front of gully; the fifth was an action replay of the fourth; the sixth plucked my off stump crazily out of the ground.'

Six balls – possibly the most testing six ever seen in a Test arena – delivered with at least five variations of body action, away or inswing, angle of attack, use of the seam and arm action, all going like a 'rifle bullet' to bowl one of the world's leading batsmen.

Holding had been warming up in the nets before the start of the innings so he was able to reach top pace from the very first delivery. The bowler himself, however, doesn't think it was the most testing over he ever bowled – although it was up there with his best. 'I knew I had him in trouble for the entire over,' he says now. 'But I bowled an over in Trinidad during a 1979 World Series game when I got Ian Chappell and Greg Chappell both out in the same over. And when you get both the Chappells out in one over, it's some achievement.

'When you are bowling, you have a plan that this ball you will bowl this way, then the next another way. But I don't think any bowler can say "I'm going to get the batsman out with this ball or that ball."

'You have a specific plan and you bowl to that and hope it will work.

'With that over to Boycott – which everybody seems to remember – I was confident that I would get him out in that over. I just didn't know which ball! It was all working for me, I was running in smoothly, I felt good and Boycott was in a lot of trouble.'

The West Indies fast bowlers are frequently referred to as a collective unit, but this view often ignores the enormous variations of style, technique and approach found within most quartets. This fact quickly becomes obvious in even the briefest conversation with anyone who knows what they are talking about.

Bob Willis, for example, as England's main, usually only, strike bowler, was in a good position to observe several different quartets and to appreciate their diverse qualities.

The greatest exponent of his craft, in Willis's opinion, was Malcolm Marshall. 'I shouldn't think many people would say him, but he was, in my mind, the most complete bowler. And he was fourth change a lot of the time! Then Joel Garner, who sometimes was completely unplayable. Then Colin Croft: all that whirling meant that the ball didn't always seem under control. That is very unnerving! He was the most difficult bowler to get out of the way of.' Willis also makes the point that the success of the West Indies fast bowlers has been achieved *in spite of* conditions in the Caribbean. 'I never had any success bowling on pitches there,' he says. 'They are very tough conditions to bowl fast in.' This is a belief endorsed by both Jeff Thomson and Imran Khan, and one which makes the Windies' achievements all the more remarkable.

Although the wickets in the West Indies do seem to be getting slower, Michael Holding makes the point that speed gets wickets because the pitches are so hard. The pitch has usually lost its shine after 25 overs and the bowlers have to put a lot of effort in to get the good players out. In England, believes Holding, fast bowlers do not need to bowl fast because the wicket gives them so much help.

Willis, as a craftsman himself, is well aware that the art of fast bowling is far from simple. But to put it crudely, if everyone could bowl fast, then most bowlers would. That obvious fact is constantly ignored by the pundits who wish to see the West Indies fast bowlers as nothing more than hired hit men: the West Indies 'mercenaries' is a term frequently bandied about by some sections of the press.

It remains an equally clear fact that the other Test-playing countries have not developed a similar attack because their quick bowlers, many as fast as those from the Caribbean, could not obtain the similar control over line or length, or master the art of swing and seam: not because the Test selectors had moral objections to fast bowling or wished to try to preserve the role of spinners in Test cricket. Bowlers such as Andy Roberts (with his two-speed bouncer), Marshall and even the supposed cricketing Neanderthal Croft (by constantly varying the angle of his run-up) took wickets as much by forward planning, as Holding says, and a command of bowling skills as by pure pace.

Critics might cite the fear and intimidation factor here, but that isn't going to hold much sway with the West Indians or most of the best Test cricketers who played against them. Imran Khan thinks that the criticism endured by the West Indies has been 'awful'. 'They weren't ever like certain Australian bowlers, with swearing for example. They never swore. They were just decent gentlemen and very skilful. And they did not get the respect they deserved.

'As for intimidation, look at any team which has had fast bowlers: would they spare the tail-enders? Which fast bowlers have spared the tail-enders? If they hung around, they would have got bouncers. That was the bottom line and the West Indies were no different. But it wasn't as if they started crying when they got bouncers. They took it. Whenever I played against them, we knew what the score was, we never had any problems.' Imran adds, 'Of course as a batsman you were frightened, everyone was. But fast bowling has to bring out a certain fear, to bring out the adrenalin and get the reflexes moving. The best players weren't hurt. The West Indies fast bowlers were some of the greatest gentlemen and anyone who says otherwise is talking nonsense.'

It follows that every West Indian fast bowler – and batsman come to that – believes that to deprive him of the bouncer, or to limit the number of bouncers he can bowl, gives the batsman an unfair advantage. Even as a former opponent, Imran Khan believes that, instead of condemning them, people should have sat back and praised the West Indies' luck to have such great bowlers to choose from. 'The bouncer law, which was initiated at the peak of the success of the pace quartet although it came into force later on, is a ridiculous law to curb their incredible fast bowling,' says Imran.

Michael Holding, known as 'Whispering Death', learned all about the fear and intimidation element from his time in Australia in 1975–6. But he doesn't think the West Indies overplayed the intimidation card. 'When Viv or Clive were at slip, you could sense what they meant by their body language or by what they said. They didn't ever say, "Knock this guy's head off" or that sort of thing. They were analysing what the batsman was doing and what he was going through.

'I am only seeing the batsman when I bowl, they are watching all the time, while I am going back to my mark.

'But intimidatory bowling is part of cricket, irrespective of what people want to see. Anybody who is bowling at 90 miles an hour is intimidating the batsman whether he is bowling short or not. When you go out and bowl three or four bouncers an over, I think that's going too far. I think umpires should take steps where that is concerned. But anybody who says that fast bowlers should not intimidate batsmen is talking rubbish. Test cricket is not for the weak, it is for the brave and the strong. If you can't deal with it, leave it.'

That view is echoed throughout the Caribbean. As Tony Cozier says: 'If a batsman backs away to a fast bowler, it is the batsman who is blamed here.'

If a Test batsman cannot avoid or hit a fast, rising ball then that is his problem, not the fault of the West Indians. Equally, most fast bowlers know not to overdo their bouncer card. The key ingredient of an effective bouncer is surprise; as a bad bouncer can be a wasted ball, so a good bouncer is rarely anticipated by the batsman.

The West Indies bowlers have of course got the bowling of effective bouncers down to a fine art: unsettling the best of batsmen and undoing their technique. Sir Gary Sobers, during a coaching engagement in Australia, said: 'Fast bowlers try to scare you with sheer pace and get you in a position where you are playing balls you shouldn't play. Once they have scared you they have got you.'

With bowling of such quality and, from a position of strength, surely the West Indies start with the psychological upper hand? Undoubtedly so, which explains why there have been comments that sides facing the West Indies expect to be beaten. But what is equally true, as we shall see in Chapter 6 when we look at the 'team machine', is that the West Indies expect to win.

As Holding has testified, the West Indian quicks will have worked out their approach to a game well before the start of play. He adds that he would have established his general strategy and thought his way through the batsmen who would be facing him. Joel Garner admits that he has taken some of the best batsmen's wickets by 'thinking them out', while Malcolm Marshall's county captain at Hampshire, Mark Nicholas, has said that the Bajan would nominate the batsmen he was going to dismiss (and how) before a match began.

Now that's confidence and even Holding doesn't believe it is possible to nominate dismissals like that! Imran Khan, on the other hand, believes that Marshall was more than capable of such a feat. 'Malcolm would be able to do that because he would try and work a batsman out and lay traps for him. At his peak he was a great bowler because he could bowl to plans. Holding, however, did not bowl to such plans, but in my mind was the most talented bowler of all time. Marshall was perhaps the more complete but Michael was sheer talent.'

In his epic *Beyond a Boundary* C.L.R. James gives the definitive account of the craft of fast bowling:

The ultimate greatness of a fast bowler is in his head. He has a series of methods of attack at his command, but where he pitches

any ball and the ball following, where he delivers one and from where he delivers another, where he quickens the pace and where he slows it down, this is the result of a psychological sensitivity and response to a particular batsman at a particular time on a particular wicket at a particular stage in the game.

To look specifically at the West Indians, from his first delivery the quick bowler knows he has to establish his rhythm so that he doesn't have to worry about his approach. It should be second nature. With Dennis Waight's training methods the West Indian quicks slot into their rhythm without too much problem. Relaxing into his run-up, the bowler will concentrate on where he wants the ball to go and what he wants it to do. Having assessed a batsman's strengths and weaknesses beforehand, as Holding says, he would endeavour not to waste one of his six precious deliveries on bowling to a batsman's strengths.

Having, he hopes, 'sussed out' the batsman, Holding provides examples of the various types of grip used. His standard grip is as follows: the first two fingers are placed along the seam, with the thumb underneath straight along the seam. For the outswinger with the new ball, he places the first two fingers along the seam, slightly slanted in the direction in which the ball is heading, the thumb underneath at an angle off the seam. For an outswinger with the old ball, the first two fingers go on top along the seam, the thumb straight along the seam. He places the shiny side opposite to the direction in which he wants the ball to go. For the inswinger with the new ball, he places the second finger closer to the seam, with the seam slanted. The thumb is almost diagonal to the seam. For an inswinger with the old ball, the shiny side is held on the inside, the dull side on the outside. The thumb goes off diagonally away from the seam.

For his run-up and delivery, he gets the desired grip on the ball, gathers momentum, eyes the target and gains maximum speed before letting the ball go.

'On your walk back to your mark,' says Holding, 'you think about the ball you bowled before, how the batsman played it and assess the batsman's reaction.'

For a case history of the art, craft and psychology of West Indian fast bowling, the best example is the devastating spell bowled by Curtly Ambrose in the Trinidad Test of England's 1993–4 tour to the Caribbean. Ambrose's 6 for 24 in England's second innings of 46 all out at Port of Spain – giving him match figures of 11 for 82 – went down as one of the greatest spells of fast bowling in history.

It is worth analysing the conditions and the fall of wickets to underline why England recorded their second-worst Test innings total (by one run) of all time and suffered deep humiliation during what Geoff Boycott described as 'the most exciting, dramatic one and a half hours of Test cricket

I've seen', and what Mike Atherton called 'the worst hour of my life'.

There was an hour or so, 15 overs, left for play on the fourth day of the third Test, the West Indies having already won the first two. The West Indies, batting first after Richie Richardson had won the toss, had scored 252. England replied with 328 – a lead of 76. They then bowled the West Indies out for 269, giving them a target of 194 for victory. A win looked possible, you might think – adding the rider, 'if they were facing any other side'.

Off the field, Richardson had been deeply hurt by another episode in the long catalogue of Caribbean insularity that followed the selection of Guyanese batsman Shivnarine Chanderpaul and the dropping of Phil Simmons from Trinidad. Irate letters had been sent to Richardson and there was a six-hour local radio show devoted to the topic. The skipper was criticized too for his decision to bat first. If the West Indies lost this Test Richardson would have faced unbridled hostility.

His fellow Antiguan Ambrose is an ally in his commitment to the unity of the West Indies team, as were Viv Richards and Lloyd before him. Ambrose was pained to see the commitment of his good friend under fire. Again we can go back to David Rudder – 'we've got to rally round the West Indies'. As Richardson was undermined so the team did rally round (although after the match Richardson admitted he had had to work hard to get the team together). After the match, Peter Roebuck wrote that the victory at Port of Spain was an important one for West Indies cricket: 'People could see that the West Indian selectors, an impressive lot, were men of honour. They could see that their splendid captain could be trusted, after all, and could rejoice in the devastating brilliance of his close friend, Ambrose. Richardson had shown the strength and the judgement to hold his team and his peoples together.'

There is little doubt that Ambrose was fired up – even more so since he later said that he had wanted to make amends for the wild stroke which caused his dismissal for 12 runs in the West Indies' second innings when it seemed they had left themselves short of a workable lead – and the rest was fast-bowling history.

Especially since Richardson took over the West Indies captaincy, Ambrose has performed outstandingly well when it has been required of him. The two trust each other implicitly, in much the same way that Lloyd enjoyed mutual faith with his fast bowlers. When Ambrose is tired, Richardson listens to him. When he isn't tired, Richardson hears him more! It is almost as if Richardson saves up his lethal weapon for momentous occasions: Ambrose took 6 South African wickets for 34 runs one morning just as it seemed that the tourists were set for victory in the 1992 Test at Bridgetown, Barbados, giving him match figures of 8 for 81; he took 7 Australian wickets for 1 run in 32 balls in Perth in January 1993. Australia had been 85 for 2 only to be all out for 119. And perhaps those narrow escapes provided the final confidence trick for what was to unfold in Ambrose's 47 balls on 29 March 1994.

At Port of Spain that evening, England, who an hour and a half earlier had thought victory could be within their grasp, were undone in 7.5 overs of an hypnotic Ambrose spell that resulted in six wickets for 22 runs.

With just an hour of play to go in cloudy, cool Trinidadian conditions, Ambrose and Courtney Walsh, who provided excellent back-up, knew they would not be required to bowl for long before a good night's rest. The pitch was tinged with green as Ambrose bowled from the pavilion end, which in itself meant that the height of his bowling hand might be lost in the dark seating behind.

His first delivery to England captain Mike Atherton was of a fullish length, fast and cut back to have the skipper indubitably leg before. England were 0 for 1. In the same over, Mark Ramprakash, with more than a hint of the chaos to come, added insult to the injury of the captain's dismissal by coming back for a non-existent second run to Courtney Walsh at long leg and suffering the ignominy of a schoolboy run-out. England 1 for 2.

Ambrose's eighth ball found the flaw in Robin Smith's defence and beat the batsman, in the middle of a disappointing series, for straightforward pace with a ball which knocked over the leg stump. England 5 for 3. Afterwards, Smith said he felt the atmosphere at the wicket was more intimidating than in any other game he had played. 'When I got out to the middle,' he said, 'I was amazed at how fired up the West Indies were. All I could hear was Richie Richardson shouting, "We want five tonight."'

Next in the firing line was Graeme Hick, never happy against West Indian quick bowling and not in a good frame of mind after dropping two simple slip catches, one of which was said to have lost the match before England even started their second innings. Ambrose must have had Hick in his sights before the Zimbabwean had even padded up. Hick, seemingly mesmerized despite surviving for five overs with Stewart, snicked an outswinger to be caught behind by Murray for six. England 21 for 4.

Then Alec Stewart, England's highest second innings scorer with 18 and the wicket that the West Indies most wanted, saw his off stump knocked cartwheeling out of the ground by a phenomenally quick ball from Ambrose. England 26 for 5.

Nightwatchman Ian Salisbury was bamboozled by Walsh, caught at first slip by Brian Lara for 0. England 27 for 6. Jack Russell was unsettled after being hit by a ball from Walsh, bowling round the wicket, and then snicked Ambrose's next ball to slip to be caught by substitute Phil Simmons for 4. England 37 for 7.

Graham Thorpe played late and saw his off stump sent flying by Ambrose for 3. England's overnight score: 40 for 8. The next morning, Walsh saw off the last two wickets of Andrew Caddick (45 for 9) and Chris Lewis (46 all out).

England second Innings, Port of Spain, Trinidad, March 1994

M.A. Atherton	lbw b Ambrose	0
A.J. Stewart	b Ambrose	18
M.R. Ramprakash	run out	1
R.A. Smith	b Ambrose	0
G.A. Hick	c Murray b Ambrose	6
G.P. Thorpe	b Ambrose	3
I.D.K. Salisbury	c Lara b Walsh	0
R.C. Russell	c sub b Ambrose	4
C.C. Lewis	c W. Benjamin b Walsh	6
A.R. Caddick	c Lara b Walsh	1
A.R.C. Fraser	not out	0
Extras (lb 6, nb 1)		7
Total (all out, 19.1 overs)		**46**

But why did England fall apart in 19 overs – or just 15 overs on that fourth day? The pitch? No, it performed quite adequately. Poor technique? Perhaps in some cases, but even the world's greatest batsmen of this or any era would have been doomed to failure in the face of Ambrose that evening. It has been said that modern fast bowlers lack aggression: try telling that to the England batsmen.

Michael Holding says: 'I don't remember seeing Curtly bowl more than a few bad balls – you could count them on the fingers of one hand. And that is what I use to assess bowling performances, not just the number of wickets taken. A lot of people take a lot of wickets but they bowl a lot of crap in between.' However, Holding believes that Ambrose, despite that performance in Trinidad, is still not a complete fast bowler, 'because he has never bowled a ball in anger around the wicket. I've never seen him do that and that is a drawback.'

Despite Holding's reservations, he still rated Ambrose's performance as one to put in fast bowling's hall of fame. And it should be pointed out that this was not hostile fast bowling, other than in the sense that fast bowling by its very nature might be termed hostile. Out of the 47 balls Ambrose sent down, only five were pitched short, while the rest were full and fast. It was controlled aggression with every ball directed at the stumps and none directed at the head.

And it was the third time Ambrose had taken at least half of the opposition's wickets in one match. More than any other bowler playing today for any side, Ambrose is the one who can turn a game in an hour. He has been variously called the cool executioner, the grim reaper, a typhoon, the towering inferno and, after Port of Spain, Hurricane Curtly.

Without doubt he is a very intelligent fast bowler. For example,

Ambrose's removal of Atherton in the second innings in Trinidad was the second time in the series that the England captain had been found wanting, on both occasions fast off-cutters trapping Atherton before he was in position.

In the heat of a Test match, Ambrose is immersed in his team, in their quest for victory. It has been said of Ambrose that he doesn't mind what people think of him, he cares only what his team-mates think.

His performance in Trinidad should perhaps serve as a microcosm of his career: fast bowling without resorting to body blows; speed with persistent accuracy. At Port of Spain it was as if he had decided on the outcome of the match as he sprinted in for his very first delivery. A year before he had complained of being worn down and tired out by Test cricket. Several commentators at the time had discounted those grumblings, saying that Ambrose's opponents should be on their guard. They were right. Ambrose has won many series for the West Indies. What will ensure that he will continue to do so, barring injury (he had a shoulder operation at the end of 1994 and missed the tour to India), is his ability to move up a gear, to 'turn it on' in a Test cauldron, just when it seems that his side are up against it. That is what marks out Ambrose as an extraordinary bowler who can be grateful to Richardson for getting the best out of him just when it seems his side might go under.

None of this could be achieved if Ambrose was not able to ally his considerable psychological depth to his physical skills, although Imran Khan believes that for a man of Ambrose's build he plays far too much cricket. 'He doesn't have the physique to be a workhorse,' says Imran, which is perhaps where Richardson's strength lies in captaining the giant Antiguan. But he still has immense stamina to call on, coupled with the art and craft to execute his psychological power.

He usually takes just 15 strides in his run-up, comparatively short by some standards (although his strides are very long). He has an upright action, with a good deal of power in the shoulder (which comes under considerable strain, hence his injury) and arm, supported by strong back muscles. As Dennis Waight points out in his comments about fast bowlers as athletes, Ambrose has an abundance of fast-twitch fibres enabling him to bowl fast without losing momentum and without straining. Because of his height – 6 ft 7 in – he can get steep bounce from the most lifeless of wickets. At the point of delivery, his arm is high – the ball is delivered from over 8 ft and this in itself causes batsmen problems – with his wrist cocked behind the ball which he delivers at a good length to deter the batsman from getting too far forward. Because of the height of delivery, the batsman's eye has to follow the ball vertically which can make the ball, travelling at such speed, a blur.

His height has obviously led to comparisons with Joel Garner but, in some ways, he is more difficult to play because of how he angles the ball.

But, like Garner, Ambrose bowls a mean yorker and can seemingly be wheeled up to order as the ace in the pack if it looks as though the opposition are getting too far ahead. And, in common with the other West Indian quicks, he can vary his pace and angle, skills for which Ambrose's Test colleague Courtney Walsh is particularly noted.

Walsh, captain of Gloucestershire, Jamaica and of the West Indies in the winter of 1994/5, is, according to his county wicketkeeper Jack Russell, the hardest bowler he has ever kept to because of his variation. (Imagine how the batsman feels, then.) Walsh made his Test début in 1984 and has been regarded as the West Indies' workhorse warrior virtually ever since. And again because of Walsh's height – 6 ft 5.5 in – his inswinging yorker is frequently unplayable.

Walsh can almost be seen 'thinking his way' through an over as he bowls it, even though the word most often used about him is 'languid'.

Each of the West Indian fast bowlers have used their craft in various ways – but all have been different and many have seemingly benefited from a lack of rigid coaching. However, with such talent on hand, all have been eager to learn from one another. Joel Garner, for instance, said of Vanburn Holder: 'He taught me how to bowl an effective outswinger when my stock-in-trade was a fast inswinger. He gave me refresher courses in gripping the ball, keeping the shine and cutting the old ball.' And of the great Wes Hall, Garner wrote in his autobiography: 'He was particularly good at explaining the difference between delivery points: where the ball is actually released, and the resulting variation in pace and length. He also also taught me the importance of direction and how to bowl accurately ... Thanks to him I came to regard fast bowling as a craft.' And Marshall wrote of Holding and Garner: 'They were always ready to help a rookie and if I now analyse what in essence they all told me it was this: never bowl exactly the same ball twice in succession – variation is the key to success.' With the overwhelming plan being to bowl fast, the West Indian quicks aim to exploit their speed, and ally to that changes in pace, flight and angle.

But while the West Indians all learnt to develop their skills from one another, neither have they been afraid to seek guidance from those outside the Caribbean. Marshall, for instance, took a lesson from Dennis Lillee: 'Dennis was bowling to me in a one-day international in Melbourne and he bowled this ball from wide of the stumps. I went to hit it through the leg-side as it pitched middle-and-leg and it cut away to miss the outside of the bat. When the ball was coming through the air, you could actually hear it whistling.'

Marshall went to Lillee after the game to find out how he did it. 'Dennis said he just rolled the wrist over the ball in delivery, something like a leg-break. He showed me how he did it and explained that the ball would either cut away once it pitched or go straight on. It is the angle of the delivery from the edge of the box along with the movement which gives the batsmen trouble.' Marshall experimented in the nets. 'I had never tried anything like that before. I had just held the ball seam-up and bowled in- and away swingers. Now I tried to bowl the leg-cutter every ball in the nets until I got it right. It took some time but eventually I found I could bowl it without any problem or reduction of pace.'

Marshall used his new-found skills to devastating effect, eventually becoming the highest Test wicket-taker in West Indian history. But does that make him the greatest of the West Indies fast men? One player is in a unique place to judge: West Indies wicketkeeper Jeffrey Dujon. He played for the Windies for 10 years and, after collecting thousands of high-velocity deliveries, had the hands to prove it.

The greatest three fast men, in his opinion, were Andy Roberts, Michael Holding and a former opponent, Dennis Lillee. Roberts, says Dujon, mastered two different bouncers: the first was delivered at just above half-pace, tempting the batsman to hook. The second would come then at full pace, often catching the batsman half-way into his stroke. The most difficult to keep to, echoing the words of batsmen when asked whom they least liked to face, was Colin Croft. 'His action always suggested that the ball was going down the leg side, so my weight was invariably on my left foot. Somehow, though, he'd move the ball away off the seam, which left me having to move quickly back to my right to collect it.' Joel Garner, on the other hand, was easier. 'Of course,' says Dujon, 'because of his height, the bounce was always higher, but he was so accurate and bowled such a good line I never really had to scamper around to him.'

But, as Dujon readily admits, the individual skills of Roberts, Holding et al. were and continue to be considerably enhanced by the team spirit within the West Indies side. Commitment to their colleagues and the continuing success of their team have meant that the sum of their skills is greater than even the West Indians themselves would have hoped.

6 | The team machine

They seem to have some inner desire inspired by a combination of God, immense pride and some collective belief in the West Indies as an entity ... This characteristic – call it heart, passion or what you will – seems to explain why they are able to suddenly raise their game to a higher level when it is needed.

Simon Hughes in *The Daily Telegraph*, March 1994

IT IS this unity, this solidarity, of the West Indies team, as well as their professionalism, that is frequently commented upon by cricketers and supporters from outside the Caribbean. It was not always so – and, of course, there will always be personality clashes in any outfit – but, as we have seen, the experience of Packer cricket, together with the inspirational leadership of Clive Lloyd, allowed the West Indies to turn a corner. The West Indies 'team machine' is vital to the operation of the pace quartet and much more besides.

Lloyd was, of course, fortunate to have a wealth of individual talents to call on, but those individuals had to be blended into a team capable of realizing their potential, not just for their own personal satisfaction but also for the good of their side. However, despite the luxury of such an abundance of expertise on hand, Lloyd cannot be presumed automatically to have had an easy job of it. It could have been quite the reverse, of course. Imagine the ego, the presumptuousness, that could develop through being possessed of genius: then compound that by the number of geniuses, both in the batting and, especially, bowling departments, that were often simultaneously present in the West Indies Test side.

In his 1926 book *The Game's the Thing*, Australian captain Monty Noble wrote that a captain becomes a 'tower of strength, a rock to lean upon in adversity. He inspires such confidence that they will work hard, keep "on their toes", and combine to give of their best no matter how long the way or how tired they are.' Noble went on: 'The great leader is the embodiment of all the hopes, virtue, courage and ability possessed by the team men under his command. If he is not, he is but the shadow and lacks the substance of captaincy.' C.L.R. James often applied Noble's words to the captaincy of Frank Worrell, but they can just as readily be used to demonstrate the manner of Lloyd's leadership. In fact, the parallels between the captaincies of Worrell and Lloyd are clear, and Lloyd himself has said that continuing Sir Frank's work was his goal.

Worrell became the first black man and the first professional to captain the West Indies on tour or for a complete series when he took the side to Australia in 1960 – *as late as 1960* – two years after the Federation of the West Indies was born. The campaign to see him installed as skipper was fierce and James, as editor of *The Nation*, the official organ of the People's National Movement of Trinidad, waged an all-out crusade, saying: 'I was determined to rub in the faces of everybody that Frank Worrell, the last of the Three Ws, was being discriminated against.' Although Worrell's West Indians lost the Australian series 2–1, the West Indies were, in Michael Manley's words, 'credited with transforming Test cricket at a moment when it seemed headed for the kind of doldrums which envelop any encounter that is dominated by the fear of defeat'. And Johnny Moyes wrote: 'Worrell alone became the leader and his word was accepted ... They learned to fight as a team. There were no divisions in the side ... The spare parts came together to form a machine which could function efficiently under the guidance of the master mechanic.' C.L.R. James noted that he was always impressed, in his many conversations with Worrell, by how the captain's judgement of an individual player was based on 'whether he was a good team-man or not. It seemed that he worked on the principle that if a man was a good team-man it brought the best out of him as an individual player.'

Worrell was determined to prove that West Indians could be as good as other Test players, but still play aggressive cricket in an atmosphere of dedication to the team. As James said at the time: 'To put it negatively, nothing was inherently wrong with us.' Worrell's work seemed to have been accomplished by the time the West Indies toured England in 1963: they won the Test series 3–1. Afterwards, he said: 'My aim was always to see the West Indies moulded from a rabble of brilliant island individualists into a real team – and I've done it.'

Worrell too, older than the rest of his side, became a father figure to his players in much the same way as Lloyd was to become. As the West Indies looked to Worrell for inspirational leadership at a time of transition, so they turned to Lloyd after the comparative lack of success of Gary Sobers's captaincy.

It was not always plain sailing for Lloyd. He received criticism from many quarters, both inside and outside of the Caribbean, about his supposed tactical naïvety. For example, the former West Indies opener Gordon Greenidge said that all Lloyd had to do as a captain was hand the ball to one of his four fast bowlers, a view echoed by former England captain Bob Willis, who said that Lloyd ran the team in the field 'as regimented as crop rotation. Lloyd would perm four fast bowlers from an impressive selection and simply wheel them up at selected stages.' (Well, who wouldn't have done?!) Imran Khan agrees, although he puts it a little more kindly, when he says, 'I never thought there was much need for captaincy there. It was just a question of holding them together, of rotating the bowlers and listening to them – after all, they were intelligent bowlers.' Lloyd's captaincy has also been denigrated as less than great because he rejected spin bowling as a positive form of attack. Tony Cozier believes: 'I don't think either Lloyd or Richards knew how to use spinners properly: they used them too defensively and more as a stop-gap.'

But Michael Holding, a champion of Lloyd's captaincy, says: 'When Clive was captain, apart from manipulating the bowlers and getting the best out of them, Clive got the best out of the entire team. We looked upon Clive more as a father figure than a captain. He was a good man-manager: he knew how to get the trust and respect and we gave it to him because he gave it to us. We would do everything he asked. If we'd bowled 25 overs on the trot and he asked us for another one, we would do it.'

Again, shades of Worrell's leadership are there in Holding's words. On the final day of the Lord's Test between England and the West Indies, led by Worrell, in 1963, Wes Hall bowled for three hours and 20 minutes, sending down 40 overs. Hall said that he did not know he was capable of bowling such a spell but the captain wanted him to so he did, not once losing pace or direction.

And Holding adds further tribute to Lloyd: 'Even if we had bowled a few overs that he perhaps wasn't quite satisfied with and he wanted to take one of us off and we said "give me one more," he would give us that one more. We had a very, very good relationship with him.

'In terms of field-placing, if he said "why do you want that field," and you'd tell him, he would give you the field-placing even if perhaps he didn't agree with it. If it didn't work, he'd say "This isn't working; let's get back to what I think." He was always willing to give us what we wanted, so we gave him everything.

'And he shared the workload as well: if you look at the end of the original four-prong pace attack – Roberts, Garner, Croft and myself – I don't think you will find that anyone will have bowled many more overs than the others. All of us bowled much the same.' To prove his point, Holding mentions the West Indies 1979–80 tour to Australia. In the three Test matches played during the series, Garner bowled 127 overs, Croft 121, Roberts 112 and Holding himself 111.

However, Lloyd was criticized for not inspiring the team when the chips were down, as in the 1975–6 series in Australia. Greenidge said that Lloyd was as 'bemused and shattered as the rest of us', and even Viv Richards – although his criticism pales into insignificance compared with his many subsequent comments about Lloyd's inspirational qualities as a captain – said then that 'the dressing room was a shambles ... no one tried to pull us together'. Lloyd was well aware that he was seen as the main cause of the dressing room disorder in Australia and admits that he felt unable to bring the chaos to an end. But, with hindsight, good came out of that awful series because it taught the young players about defeat and made them realize it was not a process to which they wanted to succumb again. The experience also made Lloyd's task of regeneration easier because the West Indies could not have fallen any lower. The only way was up.

Some 20 years on that fear or hatred of losing was noted again on England's 1994 tour to the Caribbean. After the Barbados Test, won by the tourists, England bowler Angus Fraser wrote in his tour diary: 'You should have seen the West Indies after they'd lost. Devastated. A lot more cut-up than we would be, I'm sure. Perhaps that's why they win so often.' Quite so! (And bear in mind that the 'devastated' Windies had sewn up the series by then.) A few miserly cynics would say here that, even if they don't have a chance of outright victory, the West Indies would do anything to *avoid defeat*, but those critics are categorically neglecting the 'West Indian way'. Avoiding defeat is not how they play their cricket: they are hell-bent on winning, not at all costs, but on winning with professionalism, exuberance and discipline. Nobody has put it better than Trevor McDonald when he wrote: 'The West Indian attitude is not meant to be insolent. It is rather a statement that they will not be prevented from playing the game the way they believe they must play to win.'

Lloyd introduced a more analytical approach to the game among his side, always with the emphasis on success. He was well aware that, statistically, fast bowlers were more likely to win Test matches efficiently and because of that he was able to convince the West Indies Cricket Board, cash-starved as it was, that this was the way forward. And, as the fast bowlers, together with the blazing bats, over the past two decades have consistently reaped rewards there is no danger of that approach being scrapped. Through his analytical approach to the game, Lloyd in fact encouraged freedom of expression both on and off the field, and urged thorough analysis of the opposition.

Yet while he may have had shortcomings as a tactician on the field – although in view of his phenomenal record that assumption seems small-minded – his leadership of the side in a wider sense should stand untarnished. In Trevor McDonald's biography, Lloyd stated: 'The pattern of my captaincy of the West Indies team was to a great extent dictated by the fact that the game is so terribly important for us in the Caribbean. It's much more than a game. It carries with it all sorts of aspirations and hopes of West Indian people. The key to the West Indies captaincy is realising all that.' So being captain of the West Indies does not stop at the boundary ropes as former England captain David Gower – who incidentally, as Caribbean commentators point out, would still have been playing Test cricket in 1994 if he had been West Indian – also appreciated. He said the job required 'diplomatic skill' in having to deal with players from numerous countries as well as all the political pitfalls that implies. The West

Indies captain has, in many senses, to be an ambassador in his region, and Lloyd was that and more. John Arlott said: 'Lloyd's captaincy has been marked by dignity; firm, unfussy discipline; and cool realistic strategy.' He added that Lloyd put a new and more purposeful face on his national sport, while preserving its heart.

But it is for the pursuit of professionalism among his team that perhaps the greatest debt is owed to Lloyd by West Indies cricket. He was fortunate that several of his players had the experience of playing in English county cricket and, as circumstances unfolded, fortunate too that Packer cricket came along at just the right time. That experience created a collective professional drive hitherto undreamed of among the West Indies contingent and Lloyd additionally turned it to their advantage by employing Dennis Waight post-Packer. (And that of course would not have been possible without the foresight of the board.) Waight (as we have seen in Chapter 4) has been instrumental in keeping the pace machine serviced and well-oiled but he, along with Lloyd, was equally responsible for the pre-match sessions which reinforced team spirit and togetherness, not just in the playing side but in the entire squad.

One other factor should not be overlooked in appreciating the bond between Lloyd and his team-mates: from 1983 onwards, the Test team were further united by their rejection of several huge offers to tour South Africa. In late 1982, rumours that a mass defection of West Indian cricketers to South Africa was imminent grew louder. Those rumours materialized into fact in February 1983 when a 16-strong team led by Lawrence Rowe, and including Alvin Kallicharran, Colin Croft and Sylvester Clarke, hopped on a plane to Johannesburg after finding the lure of the rand too great to resist. The authorities banned the 16 players from Test cricket for life, while individual countries, including Jamaica and Guyana, banned the players from local cricket for the same period.

Michael Manley points out in the *History of West Indies Cricket* that some people argued that the ban was an extreme action, 'to which the authorities replied, with the support of all governments and the majority of the public, that the betrayal was extreme'. Indeed the treachery was deeply felt, not least by Allan Rae, president of the West Indies Cricket Board of Control who, having heard that Rowe and Croft had categorically denied that they were headed for South Africa, told them that their 'pride was bigger than their right hands'. The very next day, the pair were on the outward-bound plane. The particular and personal grievances which may have provided the reasons for the defection of any of the 16 players are still speculated about, but for many the chance to make 'big money' for doing something at which they excelled was a prime motivator.

But those who turned down the offer from a country which pursued such an abhorrent policy as apartheid found renewed cause for solidarity, although the Test team seemed to adopt a tacit code of not publicly criticizing the 'rebel' tourists. Michael Holding refused a contract reputedly worth US$250,000 offered to him by Rowe, and both Lloyd and Richards rejected enormous sums – huge figures not just by West Indian standards but by *any* standards – dangled in front of them by South African seducers on various occasions. Lloyd as captain of the West Indian side was also invited to take the whole team to South Africa. His refusal of all offers further identified Lloyd with the West Indian team as 'one of their own' and added to the respect that he commanded throughout the Caribbean.

So, after 1983, the members of the team could look one another in the eye knowing that they stood for the same principles, that they were playing for the West Indies, with not a rebellious thought between them. The board did its bit as part of the team machine too by issuing its proposed schedule for the next seven years, which included 17 Test series, to remind their players of what they could lose by joining the trail of the 'rebels'.

From all those events behind the scenes it is fairly obvious that Lloyd's captaincy involved rather more than the 'crop rotation' of the pace quartet. But to get back to the playing field, the bowlers themselves are the first to admit that without the formidable batting line-up, plus a seemingly impenetrable slip cordon and equally effective wicketkeeper, they would not have been able to accomplish all they did. Behind the scenes, too, the West Indies board, especially under the auspices of Allan Rae, did more than keep the wheels in motion.

But the bowlers brought the ignition to start up the engine and much of the preparation for a Test series lay with them. Viv Richards says that, as captain and as Lloyd did before him, he placed great store in his bowlers before a Test. 'You never decide on the day what you're doing,' he says. 'The guys basically give you an insight into what they would like to do, which end they want to bowl from and so on. There are times when you have to pacify, it's a team effort. But you try to keep everyone happy. Short, quick spells – I've always thought that the shorter the spells, the more likely you are to have them fresh at all times, especially during the middle of the match. I've always worked on how the guy feels. And if he wants one more over – then you tend to believe him, because he's been around a while! But if a guy's tired, then you listen to him too.

'The fast bowlers are all happy for one another, they work for each other. But there is still a competitive element. If you set yourself high personal standards and you're happy with those standards, you feel that you are happy with yourself. And obviously if the guys set themselves high standards, then the team will benefit. Someone between No. 1 and No. 11 is going to have a good time but we're all vulnerable to failure in a team sport. As captain, I would try and warn people against the envious element. You have to accept that someone else is going to do well. It's hard when someone is left out and they see someone else getting the credit.

'In any other team, each individual one of the quartet would have got more Test wickets but they had to share the bowling around the West Indies side.'

Richards, in early 1985, did not have an easy time inheriting the mantle of captaincy from Lloyd with his phenomenal record as skipper. Lloyd had captained the side in 74 Tests, winning 36 and losing just 12. Of the 18 series in which he was involved as captain, just two (Australia 1975–6 and New Zealand 1979–80) ended in defeat. What an act to have to follow! Richards was given a rough ride by the West Indian press and one reporter said that a small-island player should not be made Lloyd's successor.

Richards had also been disgruntled by rumours that, despite the fact that he had been Lloyd's deputy, he was not the automatic successor. Jeff Dujon and Roger Harper had both been mentioned as Lloyd's possible replacements, and Richards felt that he was being snubbed by the board. Richards's temperament also came under the spotlight, critics saying that he was too hot-headed to be captain. Detractors, who frequently misread him as arrogant (but even Worrell had been labelled 'arrogant'!), were wrong, even though there were occasions when Richards's passionate beliefs got the better of him: he has apologized for some incidents while remaining unrepentant for others. He says now: 'I just did my job; there had to be aggression sometimes: I was aggressive when I had to be. I'm quite proud of the way I handled things. Obviously, there were a few hiccups, but over a long period you have to allow for those times.'

Those who know Richards well would not accuse him of arrogance: he is certainly a man of passion, of conviction and immense pride. In common with many of his team-mates he also relies on deeply held Christian beliefs and, in his words, has been blessed with 'God-given confidence'. And, in the manner of Lloyd, he vindicated his team to the utmost. 'I will defend my cricket till the day I die. People say that without our four quicks we wouldn't be so strong. But those are the people that just want to cripple us.'

Despite the criticism, Richards had shown himself to be tactically proficient before being appointed as captain and was able to maintain team spirit because his personality was understood by the nucleus of the team who had played under Lloyd. Richards was very 'hot' when it came to team spirit and says: 'I used to get annoyed, for example, if there was a celebration of a wicket and maybe the guy at fine leg couldn't find time to congratulate the bowler. I'd give him a ticking off for that. If we're in a huddle, no one should be left out – I say we should always be together. It doesn't look good otherwise.'

But throughout his leadership Richards, who frequently sported the Rastafarian colours of red, yellow and green on his wrist band, had to endure complaints of an anti-Asian bias, more specifically a pro-African bias, in the West Indies team. That was not new: in the early 1970s, batsman Alvin Kallicharran (who later joined the 'rebel' tour to South Africa) said: 'As soon as I got in the West Indies team, it was clear to me that the Asian guys were not going to get fair treatment. It has always been there but it has just grown and grown.' And on England's tour to the Caribbean in 1990 Richards was accused of discrimination after he stated he was proud to lead a team of African descent.

Those comments drew a statement from the opposition leader in Trinidad, saying that Richards would not be welcome on the island until he retracted those remarks. Richards in fact missed the Trinidad Test through illness. But the incident added fuel to the criticism that Richards was closely aligned with Rastafarianism, which in fact he has never completely embraced. Richards, proud to be a man of Africa, is unequivocal: 'All different races have represented the West Indies and thank God we have had an integrated team. But if one's not good enough, you cannot force one in just for the sake of having a particular player. People of all different origins will play for the West Indies again. But because of the negative vibes you get about black people sometimes, it was nice to make that statement and hope Indians and West Indians would look at the team as a collective unit. Saying that the team was of African descent – well, it is the majority and I felt there was nothing wrong with saying that.' Because of his comments, Richards was branded as racist, a ludicrous slur on such a character. But again we see there is much more to being a West Indies captain than merely rotating the bowlers.

That old chestnut of intimidation was also thrown at Richards, as it was at Lloyd, on numerous occasions, none more so than during New Zealand's tour to the Caribbean in 1984–5. During the fourth Test at Sabina Park, New Zealand's Jeremy Coney suffered a broken arm during a hostile spell from Joel Garner. Earlier that day, Richard Hadlee had bowled five bouncers in one over at Garner. Richards and the team manager Wes Hall fiercely defended the team, Hall saying after the match: 'I do not condone intimidatory bowling, but if Hadlee bowls five bouncers in an over to Garner, what do they expect the reaction to be? I say that if you do not wish to get burnt, if you cannot afford to get burnt, stay out of the kitchen … The press continues to condemn us. The umpires must determine what is fair and unfair play, not the press … The point is, why are they always getting at the West Indies? They are getting at the fast bowlers now, but they got to the spinners, Ramadhin and Valentine, in the 1950s and destroyed them with that front-foot leg-before rule.' Hall had a point: in 1950, a few batsmen complained about the relentlessness of the West Indies spin twins while broadcasters grumbled that there was no time for any comments because the overs were being bowled too quickly. It sometimes seems that the West Indies can never please anybody.

But for all the doubts, inside and outside the Caribbean, that surrounded Richards's capabilities as captain, his record as skipper is worth reiterating: in six years he led in 50 Tests, winning 27 and losing only 8. And, unlike Lloyd, he did not lose a single series. Under Lloyd and Richards, and now under Richardson, the West Indies team provided the benchmark for the opposition. How you performed against the West Indies was what really mattered.

In any circumstances, the bare facts of Richards's captaincy alone should be worthy of immeasurable praise. Unfortunately, they are not; for Richards also came under fire on innumerable occasions for his, in the words of one critic, 'menacing' approach to the game. Again that critic belittled the 'West Indian way' of playing cricket – to win. And in Richards's case that meant winning even if he himself under-performed: 'I have gained most satisfaction from what we have achieved as a unit.'

Richards maintained Lloyd's philosophy of togetherness, encouraging discussion in the dressing room, debating the strengths and weaknesses of the opposition. Each member of the team knew exactly what his job was, what was expected of him and how that job related to the other players well before the coin was tossed.

Of course, the pace bowlers were at the heart of the strategies of both Lloyd and Richards, and the latter maintained an unbeaten record even without the quality of pace that Lloyd had been able to draw on.

And as Richards had the unenviable task of succeeding Lloyd, so the latest incumbent Richie Richardson has had to assume the awesome mantle of his fellow Antiguan.

And the reaction in the West Indies? Well, from a cricketing generation accustomed to success, he was booed on his first appearance as skipper on home soil because the Windies had failed during the fifth World Cup in Australia.

But already Richardson's record is shaping up pretty admirably in comparison with that of his predecessors, in that – after only three years in charge – he still has not lost a Test series. The West Indies beat South Africa in their return to Test cricket in the one-off Test in Barbados (which was boycotted by the locals when the selectors declined to pick local fast bowler Anderson Cummins), beat the Australians in Australia and easily overcame the much-trumpeted Pakistanis in the West Indies.

Richardson was unable to take the team to India in the winter of 1994, suffering as he was from acute fatigue syndrome, and, at the time of writing, it remains to be seen how quick or complete his recovery will be. But the Antiguan clearly has the hallmarks of becoming a good Test captain with his own, equally effective, approach. Peter Roebuck wrote of him: 'His caution shows even in his tactics. Not for him the swaggering four slips of Richards or the menacing cordon of Lloyd; often he plays a waiting game, putting three men on the boundary even for Ambrose. Richards was a boxer who went in search of the knock-out, confident he had the heavier punch; his successor is less certain, more prepared to win on points.'

And Richardson has easily earned the commitment of his players, just as Lloyd and Richards did, even after enduring a similarly traumatic take-over period. He inherited merely the bare bones of a world-conquering side with Richards, Greenidge, Marshall and Dujon all boldly overlooked by the selectors with an eye to the future.

Indeed, that move by the selectors was even more courageous when you consider that the West Indies team have benefited from consistency of selection in the past. A young player in his first Test rarely feels under the same pressure as his counterpart in, say, an England side. One failure does not mean the end of the young West Indian's Test career. As Richards so succinctly puts it: 'Form is temporary, class is permanent.' If someone has demonstrated that he has enough class to be worthy of a Test place, then one poor performance will not be held against him. That approach itself engenders confidence in a side. Former opener Des Haynes believes: 'It is important you are given a decent run; it is very hard to ask a guy to deliver in one series.' Michael Holding reinforces that view, reminding us that he took only 10 wickets on his first tour to Australia. 'If I had been English, that would have been it for me.'

While Richardson does not have the firepower which was available to Lloyd or to Richards, he is unlikely to change the winning formula of employing a pace quartet or to tamper with the policy of consistent selection. And even if he does lack firepower he still has two geniuses in his side in Brian Lara and Curtly Ambrose. Tony Cozier believes that Richardson is more in the Lloyd mould of captain than Richards and hence more like Worrell, while Roebuck believes Richardson could be the best captain since Worrell. Roebuck added, in *The Sunday Times*, that: 'Richardson's team has an emotional depth. Players embrace after their daily stretches, and joyously salute each other's triumphs ... As Ambrose walks back to his mark, he often joins his captain in a clapping routine not unlike that used by England supporters during the 1966 World Cup. Few teams in sport have such fellow feeling. Richardson is lucky to have around him such men as Ambrose and Adams, Walsh and, until recently, Logie.' Not for the West Indies the little cliques which have developed in other sides where the newcomers stick together while the old-timers indulge in their coterie. Everyone is encouraged to make a contribution, in the dressing room or on the pitch, where all are seen to be geeing up the bowlers. The banter between the West Indies fielders is incessant as they all play their part. Compare this to a member of the England team playing in a Test in 1993 who later remarked: 'It was so quiet out there; nobody was talking to anyone else.'

Courtney Walsh led the Test team in India in 1994–5, of which more later, but it was hoped that Richardson, after a real break from cricket, could resume the captaincy in preparation for the Australian series in the Caribbean and the tour to England in the summer of 1995. To outsiders, Richardson does not appear as hard as Lloyd or Richards, but he has proved that he gives no quarter. He is also of the same opinion that the true strength of a side can only be measured in Test cricket. Des Haynes speaks for all West Indians when he says that Test cricket is the better game: 'It allows you to play yourselves in and show off your skills … it is the only form of cricket that still has me running to the bathroom before I go into bat.'

Indeed, it is in the Test arena that the West Indies do not believe that they can be beaten, especially in a five-Test rubber, because the pace quartet will wear the opposition down. In fact, the West Indies have only once lost the second or third match of a Test series since 1979. That fascinating statistic gives an insight into the 'team machine'. It seems that it is in the first or last Test of a series that the West Indies are most vulnerable to defeat. But if they lose the first Test – because, for example, they have underestimated the opposition (yes, it can happen) – they will come back with a vengeance to have the series sewn up by the penultimate Test.

Results of West Indies' Test series 1979–94

| Match | Played | Percentage of games | | |
		Won	Lost	Drawn
1	29	45	21	34
2	27	52	4	44
3	27	56	4	40
4	19	58	16	26
5	13	46	31	23
6	1	0	0	100
Total	116	51	13	36

Fast bowling has undoubtedly proved the critical factor for the team's success, but again it should never be overlooked that without the support of geniuses in every department the bowlers' efforts would have been in vain. Michael Holding believes that the support the quartet received from the slip fielders and wicketkeepers was vital: 'When we ran up to bowl, we only needed to hear that snick because we knew it almost certainly guaranteed a wicket! It did not cross our minds that it might be dropped. This is not to say that one didn't get away now and again but it was always a surprise when it did.' For example, in his 121 Tests for the West Indies, Viv Richards took 122 catches: now that's reliability! And in his 81 Tests for the Windies, wicketkeeper Jeffrey Dujon took 265 catches as keeper (he took two more when he was not keeper). Deryck Murray, in his 62 Tests, took 181 catches behind the stumps.

The West Indies wicketkeeper is also expected to be a mean batsman: Dujon scored 3322 Test runs at 31.94. Additionally, it was also expected that the bowlers would make runs too. As Joel Garner said in his autobiography: 'A team with four fast bowlers could easily run into trouble if it were to lose four or five quick wickets. Fast bowlers would have to make runs, not only by slogging, but through an intelligent stay at the crease. What the selection of four fast bowlers meant, if the strategy were to be successful, was that the bowlers would have to develop a different attitude to batting. We were expected to bat down to number 11.' Malcolm Marshall was not the only fast bowler who rated himself as an all-rounder: in his 81 Tests he scored 1810 runs, as well as taking 376 wickets. That's not a bad achievement for a supposedly lower-order batsman in such a successful side. Equally the other bowlers were expected to be responsible batting partners to better batsmen and to each other, as the partnership records show:

West Indies v. England:
150 for 9th wicket Baptiste and Holding, Edgbaston 1984
67 for 10th wicket Holding and Croft, Antigua 1980–1

West Indies v. Australia:
87 for 8th wicket Dujon and Ambrose, Trinidad 1990–1

West Indies v. Pakistan:
70 for 7th wicket Lloyd and Garner, Barbados 1976–7
61 for 9th wicket Dujon and W. Benjamin, Barbados 1987–8
106 for 10th wicket Hooper and Walsh, Antigua 1992–3

West Indies v. India:
130 for 7th wicket Greenidge and Marshall, Kanpur 1983–4
161 for 9th wicket Lloyd and Roberts, Calcutta 1983–4

West Indies v. New Zealand:
83 for 8th wicket Richards and Marshall, Barbados 1984–5
70 for 9th wicket Marshall and Garner, Barbados 1984–5

Put another way, the opposition cannot really consider the job done until all 11 West Indian batsmen are safely back in the pavilion!

From a crowd's point of view, seeing the West Indies bowlers giving the ball the old heave-ho is part of the spectacle of the game. The quicks always try to do their bit with the bat when the team demands it. One such example occurred, famously, in the third Test at Headingley in 1984, after Malcolm Marshall was injured during England's first innings while diving to stop a shot in the gully. With his left forearm in plaster, Marshall watched from the dressing room as Joel Garner went out to join Larry Gomes. Everybody assumed that Garner would be the West Indies' last man but someone suggested that Marshall could go out at No. 11 if required.

Garner was run out attempting to give Gomes, who was on 96, the strike and the chance to complete his century. Marshall was helped into his gear by his team-mates and ran out to join Gomes. It dawned on Marshall, as he arrived at the crease, that he could not hold the bat with two hands so his partner said he should just try to block the ball. He faced eight deliveries and even hit a one-handed four. Soon after Gomes reached his ton Marshall was out, but the psychological effect on England of having seen the West Indies No. 11 hit a boundary with one hand must have been devastating and the incident typifies the indomitable spirit of the 'West Indian way'.

His short innings also made Marshall realize that – as he was a right-arm bowler and his left arm in plaster was not hurting – he might bowl in England's second innings. The batsmen were fazed by Marshall taking the new ball at the start of their innings – the openers even asked him to cover some of the white plaster with pink tape so that it wouldn't distract them. But the Bajan just got on with the job of bowling, picking up seven wickets for 53 runs in 26 overs – all with his left arm in plaster!

Curiously, the public enemy number one of West Indies team spirit might be cricket itself, or, rather, too much cricket. Since theirs is the team everyone wants to watch, the West Indies are in demand like no other. Between mid-October 1994 and the end of August 1995, they crammed in *four* separate Test series.

The winter of 1994–5 saw the team – most of whom, remember, had been playing English county cricket in the summer of 1994 – heading first for a three-Test tour to India. While in India the team was also expected to take part in a triangular one-day tournament between themselves, the home side and New Zealand. This was due to finish in mid-December; after which the team was scheduled to travel to New Zealand for a two-Test series and three one-day matches. The team planned to arrive back in the Caribbean during mid-February; but not for any rest or recuperation. Ahead of them were four Tests and five one-day matches against a tough and talented Australian side. Once this was completed in early May, it would be straight to England for six Tests and three one-day internationals. India had pressed for five Tests but the board was well aware that they had to give the players at least some sort of break. But as well as all the cricket to be played, the travelling, packing and unpacking reaches mind-boggling proportions. More worrying is the strain on fitness and spirit that such itineraries can create, particularly in the fast-bowling department.

Overseas tours are of course vital for any board, particularly that of the West Indies, to keep their heads above water, and winning them is even more crucial. But with long absences of the Test team, domestic cricket in the West Indies has to suffer, which ultimately can only be harmful to their cricket at the highest level. Critics have stated that a few days at a regional match in the Caribbean indicate that the supremacy of the Test team is not based on a superlative domestic competition. But how can the board, when it is not in the long-term financial interests of West Indies cricket, give the players a rest?

It is left up to the individual consciences, to their mental and physical states, of the players to say 'enough is enough'. Richie Richardson's is indeed a sorry tale: he was released by Yorkshire in the 1994 season to enable him to take a complete break from cricket after he was diagnosed as suffering from acute fatigue syndrome. He said: 'I have been troubled for some months now with extreme tiredness due to the pressures of continuous cricket and haven't had a good break for many years. This has affected me mentally and physically and I have found it very difficult to concentrate during a game.' It is, to put it mildly, a sad indictment of the modern game but it is equally unfortunate that Richardson's honest influence should be lost to the West Indies in such a hectic schedule. Steve Camacho, chief executive of the West Indies Cricket Board of Control, said: 'We are worried about the situation with Richie and his return to full health is our permanent concern.'

Perhaps the only consolation lay in the fact that the West Indies were able to call on Courtney Walsh to lead them on tour. As their skipper in 1994, he was an inspiration to his county, Gloucestershire, not just on the field but off it. And, as we have seen, the off-the-field performance of a West Indies captain demands almost as much of his attention as the team does on it. The Windies 'team machine' operates in a different orbit.

The final component of that machine is easy to see from any distance and is the fortunate side-effect of their colossal achievements. It is the confidence trick. The West Indies have a confidence born out of winning. As former England skipper Mike Gatting says, 'They succeed, because they have got pride and want to keep winning.' Imran Khan agrees: 'Winning gives you that purpose and confidence. From 1976 to 1988, the West Indies were the greatest team in history. I don't care what they say about Bradman's 1948 team. They could not have been a team better than this. How could you have a *second string of bowlers* – including Clarke and Moseley – go to South Africa and destroy the likes of Pollock and Richards? Imagine the depth, imagine the belief in winning.'

The logical path of Imran's argument is, of course, that the more they keep winning, the more confident will the West Indies become, so the more unlikely they are to lose. This, of course, begs the question: how *can* they be beaten?

7 | Answering the threat

TIM CURTIS was an experienced county opener with Worcestershire, but like most successful batsmen he still usually felt nervous at the start of an innings, the adrenalin rush sharpening his reactions. But, as he watched West Indian opening bowler Malcolm Marshall mark out his run in the fourth Test at Headingley in 1988, Curtis realized that he wasn't nervous at all. Instead he was 'strangely calm'. Despite the fact that he was making his Test début, despite the fact that he was facing the world's best (and most aggressive) fast-bowling attack, the nervous energy which usually drove his batting was not there. In Curtis's own words there 'was no buzz'.

England were trying out their third opening batting partnership of the summer in that Headingley Test. The home side were two-down in the series and already Chris Broad and Martyn Moxon had been jettisoned. So, when the West Indies won the toss and put England in, it was Curtis who walked out with Graham Gooch to open England's innings. Waiting for them in the middle were Malcolm Marshall and Curtly Ambrose. As Curtis took his guard, he knew that if he survived the initial onslaught, Courtney Walsh and Winston Benjamin would pose almost as great a threat.

Although scoring only 69 runs in the four innings he played during the series, Curtis proved himself a solid enough opener and was picked for three Tests against Australia the following summer. Thinking in 1994 about his strange reaction to his Test début, Curtis (an intelligent, thoughtful man) believes that the lack of 'buzz' arose from an unconscious acknowledgement that he had little chance against the West Indian pace quartet. In hindsight, Curtis says that it was 'almost as if I had nothing to lose, I wasn't expected to do well and so my expectations were low'.

An overloaded drain, which caused water to bubble up like a spring just behind the stumps, meant that play did not begin until 2.30 p.m. Curtis had played for Worcestershire against all of the West Indian quartet before, and therefore the speed and skill of the Windies fast men came as no surprise. But, as the innings progressed, Curtis began to realize that the combination of the four fast bowlers playing together added a much greater intensity to their threat.

The first thing that Curtis noticed was that, unlike in county cricket, the bowlers never coasted through a spell. All four fast bowlers operated at top speed from their first spell of the day until their last. He could detect no particular plan of attack, with different bowlers brought on to dismiss particular batsmen, or to exploit a change in the pitch or the match situation. Instead there was an almost hypnotic sense of rotation, with pumped-up fast bowlers rushing to the wicket every ball like the 'monsters' in some particularly intense computer game.

But, as the game progressed, he realized he was up against a simple and ruthlessly operated game-plan. In the late 1970s the West Indian batsmen had eradicated some of the flashy stroke play which had seen them lose ground to more disciplined sides in the past. Now Curtis had direct experience that the fast bowlers had forgone the extravagance of trying to smash the stumps out of the ground (or remove the batsman's head from his shoulders) every ball and had instead opted for a disciplined style of bowling that produced fewer of the bad balls which batsmen needed to begin building an innings. With four fast bowlers the West Indies had left themselves with very little margin for error. If two of the fast bowlers bowled poorly enough to loosen the stranglehold on the batsman, the Windies had no alternative means of dismissing the opposition. It was an all or nothing policy which, if the pace quartet was to operate effectively match after match, required total commitment to maintaining a predetermined and very demanding length, line and pace. The plan was simple, but its execution was not.

Curtis's second shock was to see Gooch caught behind off Marshall after just 37 minutes' play. 'I wasn't used to seeing Graham get out,' remembers the Worcestershire opening batsman.

The next surprise for Curtis was just how hard it was to score runs. He knew he would have to be patient against the pace quartet, but the stranglehold they were able to place around the English batting was something he had never experienced before. The stock ball was banged in just short of a length with relentless accuracy. Most members of the pace quartet are well over 6 ft in height, which means they can bowl this length 'naturally' and not risk the loss of accuracy which striving for extra effort can produce.

Curtis found that most deliveries were pitched too short to drive, too full to cut or pull and directed so 'straight' it was almost impossible to nudge singles down to long leg or through the slips. To score any runs off this sort of bowling required the batsman to play 'a high-risk shot'. Curtis was fast learning that the West Indies pace bowlers' biggest weapon is not fear, but frustration. The difficulty of scoring runs quickly enough to develop the rhythm needed to play a long innings is nearly always the first factor that Test batsmen mention when asked why the Windies pace quartet poses such a challenge.

Curtis's experience is typical. When Gooch was dismissed for 9, little more than half an hour had passed and England's score was still only 14. Almost an hour later when Curtis finally fell lbw to Winston Benjamin, the team's score had crept up by only 29 more runs. Curtis had batted for just over an hour and a half, received 71 balls, hit one four and scored 12 runs.

Curtis saw it as his job to see off the new ball, to 'absorb' the energy of the West Indies attack. He demonstrated the bravery for which he is renowned on the county circuit, by taking Brian Close as his role model, recognizing that what energy he couldn't absorb with his bat or pads he would soak up with his body. Curtis adopted his normal approach to batting, setting targets to survive 10, 20, 30 overs. But, as the game continued, he soon discovered that the energy of the West Indian pace attack (because at least one fast bowler was always relatively fresh) was almost impossible to 'absorb'. In the four Test innings he played that summer, Curtis batted for six hours and 48 minutes. His shortest innings was 69 minutes and his longest 151. He received 305 balls during that period, but managed to score just 69 runs and hit 8 fours.

Curtis can now see that he fell for the West Indies' three-card trick in his first three innings against the pace quartet. In each case he had batted for more than an hour and a half. But in each innings the lack of scoring opportunities meant that he struggled to develop 'a sense of fluency'. If, at this point, one of the fast bowlers delivers a 'hittable ball', the surprise factor, combined with the over-eagerness (even desperation in some cases) of the batsman and the speed of the delivery, can often produce the dismissal other more threatening balls failed to. In his first three innings, Curtis was consecutively lbw to Benjamin for 12 (playing across a straight ball), bowled by Ambrose again for 12 (driving too late at an over-pitched delivery) and caught behind off Benjamin for 30 (driving at a slower ball). It was only in the fourth innings when a Marshall inswinger had him lbw for 15 that frustration played no part in his dismissal.

It was in this last innings that Curtis recognized another factor behind the success of the West Indian fast men. The pace quartet's ability to bowl so straight ball after ball, over after over, makes it vital for a batsman to get into line behind each delivery. To move too far over to the leg or off-side immediately raises the possibility of being bowled. But Curtis discovered that once a batsman does this, he will find himself in a catch-22 situation. He will immediately find himself playing balls, the majority of which would pass safely over the stumps (Marshall's stock ball for instance would pass a batsman of normal height at about hip level). A short leg will be brought in to exploit the situation and the batsman will have to make yet another split-second decision. If he plays a defensive shot, he runs the risk of edging a catch off a ball that wouldn't have hit the stumps; if he lets it go the delivery might be slightly less short than usual and bowl him or trap him lbw. It is, of course, simply a matter of judging the length, but at 90 m.p.h. that is easier said than done.

Curtis found that the accuracy of the West Indian bowling was just one of the ways in which the pace quartet would exercise control over a batsman. He says: 'You always felt you were being dictated to, you could never turn the tables because they never bowled enough bad balls and when they did hit the odd bad patch there were still few deliveries which you could hit. When the poor delivery did come it was likely to be a bouncer that looped high over your head or a fast leg-side full toss.'

The fact that the West Indies pace quartet had gained the psychological upper hand over Curtis before he had even faced them underlines just how many hurdles a batsman has to overcome when trying to combat the Windies pace attack. The fact is, not a single batsman has managed to average above 50 against the West Indies since the pace quartet became established as the Windies' main weapon during the 1979 World Cup in England.

Leading batsmen against the West Indies 1979–94*

	Tests	I	NO	H S	Runs	Av	100s	50s
M.E. Waugh (A)	10	17	2	139	707	**47.13**	2	4
Salim Malik (P)	7	13	3	102	456	45.60	1	3
M.D. Crowe (NZ)	7	13	1	188	544	45.33	3	1
B.M. Laird (A)	6	12	0	92	540	45.00	0	6
G.A. Gooch (E)	26	51	2	154	**2197**	44.84	5	13
K.C. Wessels (A/SA)	8	15	0	173	670	44.67	1	6
R.A. Smith (E)	15	27	4	175	1024	44.52	3	6
D.B. Vengsarkar (I)	17	28	2	159	1119	43.04	4	6
D.C. Boon (A)	18	34	4	149	1285	42.83	3	7
A.J. Stewart (E)	10	19	2	143	716	42.12	2	2
G. Boycott (E)	9	18	2	104	663	41.44	1	4
S.M. Gavaskar (I)	11	20	2	**236**	745	41.39	3	1
A.R. Border (A)	**31**	**59**	7	126	2052	39.46	3	**14**
S. Mohammad (P)	6	12	2	86	378	37.80	0	3
D.M. Jones (A)	10	19	2	216	631	37.12	1	1

* We have chosen to measure batsmen's performances against the West Indies since the 1979–80 Test series against Australia. Although pace quartets were often picked for the West Indies in the six years before that rubber, they often contained fast-medium bowlers such as Holder and Julien or were weakened by the absence of leading players contracted to the Packer 'Circus'. The most recent series to be taken into consideration is England's 1994 tour of the Caribbean. The figures in bold are the world records against the pace quartet. Batsmen who played fewer than five Tests against the pace quartet have not been included.

But the real dominance of West Indian fast bowlers over their Test opponents is demonstrated by the number of leading batsmen who have failed to come to terms with the pace quartet.

Batting record for each Test country v. West Indies 1979–94 (ranked by average – qualification five matches)

New Zealand

	M	I	NO	H S	Runs	Av	Difference between average against West Indies and overall average Diff
M.D. Crowe	7	13	1	**188**	**544**	**45.33**	−1.75
J.J. Crowe	7	13	1	112	395	32.92	+6.68
G.P. Howarth	7	12	0	147	394	32.83	+0.39
J.V. Coney	10	17	3	83	458	32.71	−4.86
R.J. Hadlee	10	15	3	103	389	32.42	+5.26
J.G. Wright	10	18	0	138	535	29.72	−8.10
K. Rutherford	6	11	0	12	41	3.73	−23.42
Total						30.29	−3.69

Record for New Zealand against the pace quartet in bold

England

	M	I	NO	H S	Runs	Av	Diff
G.A. Gooch	**26**	**51**	2	154	**2197**	**44.84**	+0.97
R.A. Smith	15	27	4	**175**	1024	44.52	−0.51
A.J. Stewart	10	19	2	143	716	42.12	+2.74
G. Boycott	9	18	2	104	663	41.44	−6.28
A.J. Lamb	22	42	3	132	1342	34.41	−1.68
D.I. Gower	19	38	3	154	1149	32.83	−11.42
M.A. Atherton	10	18	0	144	589	32.72	−5.69
P. Willey	13	25	5	102	642	32.10	+5.20
G.P. Thorpe	5	9	0	86	239	26.56	−6.94
G. Fowler	5	10	0	106	260	26.00	−9.32
G.A. Hick	9	16	0	96	391	24.44	−7.76
B.C. Broad	6	12	0	55	266	22.17	−17.37
I.T. Botham	20	38	1	81	792	21.41	−12.13
W. Larkins	7	14	1	54	266	20.46	−0.08
M.R. Ramprakash	9	16	0	29	283	17.69	+0.99
M.W. Gatting	9	17	0	56	258	15.18	−21.57
Total						31.92	−5.68

Records for England against the pace quartet in bold

Australia

	M	I	NO	H S	Runs	Av	Diff
M.E. Waugh	10	17	2	139	707	**47.13**	+6.05
B.M. Laird	6	12	0	92	540	45.00	+9.72
K.C. Wessels*	8	15	0	173	670	44.67	+3.54

	M	I	NO	HS	Runs	Av	Diff
D.C. Boon	18	34	4	149	1285	42.83	−3.40
A.R. Border	**31**	**59**	7	126	**2052**	39.46	−11.10
D.M. Jones	10	19	2	**216**	631	37.12	−9.43
M.A. Taylor	11	21	1	144	678	33.90	−13.08
S.R. Waugh	12	21	2	100	591	31.11	−11.59
G.S. Chappell	6	12	0	124	356	29.67	−24.19
W.B. Phillips	7	14	0	120	394	28.14	−4.14
K.J. Hughes	15	30	2	130	774	27.64	−9.77
G.M. Wood	12	23	1	111	603	27.41	−4.97
D.W. Hookes	6	12	0	51	328	27.33	−7.03
J. Dyson	5	10	1	127	243	27.00	+0.06
G.R. Marsh	10	19	0	94	453	23.84	−9.35
G.M. Ritchie	6	11	0	78	244	22.18	−13.02
Total						**34.36**	**−6.36**

*Including one Test for South Africa

Records for Australia against the pace quartet in bold

India

	M	I	NO	HS	Runs	Av	Diff
D.B. Vengsarkar	17	28	2	159	**1119**	**43.04**	**+0.91**
S.M. Gavaskar	11	20	2	**236**	749	41.39	−9.73
M. Azharuddin	6	9	0	61	298	33.11	−13.99
M. Amarnath	11	20	0	117	655	32.75	−9.75
S.V. Manjrekar	5	8	1	108	215	30.71	−9.26
R.J. Shastri	**19**	**33**	5	107	847	30.25	−5.54
Yashpal Sharma	6	11	2	63	249	27.67	−5.78
Kapil Dev	**19**	32	2	109	750	25.00	−6.13
Arun Lal	8	14	0	93	340	24.29	−1.74
B.S. Sandhu	5	8	3	68	99	19.80	−10.77
A.D. Gaekwad	11	20	0	72	374	18.70	−11.37
Total						**30.62**	**−7.56**

Record for India against the pace quartet in bold

Pakistan

	M	I	NO	HS	Runs	Av	Diff
Salim Malik	7	13	3	102	456	**45.60**	**+1.53**
Shoaib Mohammad	6	12	2	86	378	37.80	−9.02
Javed Miandad	**15**	**26**	0	114	**831**	31.96	−20.61
Imran Khan	13	23	5	**123**	560	31.11	−6.58
Asif Mujtaba	5	9	0	59	175	19.44	−6.08
Ramiz Raja	11	21	1	62	382	19.10	−11.62
Mudassar Nazar	5	10	0	41	184	18.40	−19.69
Total						**28.80**	**−10.30**

Record for Pakistan against the pace quartet in bold

Of the 57 batsmen who have played five or more Tests against the pace quartet since 1979, only 13 have averaged over 35. This compares with 15 whose average was below 25. And remember these were players who were persevered with for at least five games. There are many less 'successful' batsmen who were dropped before they played their fifth game.

Australia's batsmen have the best record against the West Indian bowling attack over the last 14 years, but it is perhaps New Zealand who have reason to be proudest of their performance. Although the seven New Zealand batsmen averaged just 30.29 during their 10 games against the West Indies, they did much better than could have been expected of them. Their comparative performance against the West Indies is better than that of any of the other Test-playing sides. And if the somewhat rogue figures of Ken Rutherford are removed, New Zealand's batsmen were almost as successful as Australia's and achieved a level of performance against the world's best bowlers that matched their overall record.

The relative success of New Zealand's batsmen against the West Indies fast bowlers appears to stem from the troubled 1980 tour. As already explained in Chapter 3, concerns over the quality of the umpiring and some immature behaviour on the part of the West Indians led to many of the pace bowlers effectively 'giving up' for the majority of the series. When New Zealand toured the Caribbean five years later, the West Indian fast bowlers spent most of their energy trying to remove the heads of the visiting batsmen. This loss of temper, combined with bad weather, meant that the first two Tests were drawn. It was not until the two teams arrived in Barbados that the West Indies got their revenge for their only series defeat in the last 15 years. In Barbados, on a lightning-fast wicket, Marshall was virtually unplayable, taking 4 for 40 and 7 for 80 as New Zealand were bowled out for 94 and 248.

The bad-tempered relations between the two teams did not appear to have improved by the time the West Indies returned to New Zealand two years later. During the first Test the West Indies gained a first innings lead of 117, but then an attack of Marshall, Garner, Walsh and Holding could not prevent the home side running up 385 for 5. The second Test was won easily by the West Indies, but in the third Test the wheels came off again. The West Indies were bowled out on a difficult wicket for 100 (Richard Hadlee 6 for 50). In reply New Zealand totalled 332 for 9, with Marshall taking 1 for 75 from 27 overs and Walsh 1 for 78 from 24, being particularly guilty of overdoing the short-pitched delivery and therefore wasting the helpful conditions. The result was a win for New Zealand by 5 wickets.

New Zealand (along with Sri Lanka arguably the weakest side in world cricket) played three series against the West Indies (unquestionably the strongest) during the 1980s. The West Indies won one series, but lost the first and drew the last. Compare this with the West Indies' performances against England in the 1980s of five straight series victories and it is clear that New Zealand did far better than anybody could have expected. There is no doubt that the challenge of playing the West Indies brought the best out of the notoriously stubborn New Zealand batsmen. But it was the ill-disciplined approach of the fast bowlers that was the main cause of the West Indies' under-achievement against New Zealand. As such it is the only major black spot on the psychological approach shown by the Windies pace quartet in 15 years of Test cricket. To date, the West Indies have not played New Zealand in a Test match (largely for economic reasons) since March 1987, although they were due to take part in a two-Test series against the Kiwis during February 1995.

If Australia are the West Indies' sternest foes and New Zealand the surprise package, it is the two sides from the Indian sub-continent that have had most problems with West Indian pace. Only two of the 18 Indian and Pakistan batsmen to have played in five or more Test matches against the West Indies really came to terms with the pace attack.

It is hard to pin down a single reason why batsmen from the Indian sub-continent should have under-achieved to such a degree against the West Indian fast bowlers. The lack of familiarity with truly fast bowling is obviously one factor, especially in India, but there appear to be others.

In Pakistan, pitches were often prepared to suit the home side's bowling strength – that of fast bowlers Sarfraz Nawaz, Imran Khan, Wasim Akram and Waqar Younis. Of course, fast bowling was the Windies' strength too and games between the two sides in Pakistan were often very low scoring. For example in the 1986–7 series Pakistan recorded innings totals of 159, 328, 131, 77, 239 and 125 for 7 in the three Tests. The West Indies fared only a little better, making 248, 53, 218, 240 and 211. Imran Khan took 18 wickets in the series at 11.05, while Tony Gray captured 14 at 16.21, Marshall 16 at 16.62 and Walsh 11 at 17.72.

In India, the batsmen did not have to cope with difficult pitches, but they were faced with an inferiority complex just as debilitating. With the exception of Kapil Dev and India's first ever Test opening partnership of Amar Singh and Muhammad Nissar, India had not produced a Test-class pace bowler. In a game increasingly dominated by pace, the Indians became used to being on the receiving end from nearly all the other Test-playing nations. Despite the success of India's spin-bowling greats, there is a strong belief that India will only be able to hold its head up in the cricketing world once it has produced at least two consecutive generations of fast bowlers. In India, despite all the evidence to the contrary, fast bowlers are seen as the real match-winners and the Indian batsmen walking out to do battle with Curtly Ambrose or Courtney Walsh find it hard to forget this.

However, two batsmen from the Indian sub-continent did manage to overcome most of these disadvantages. Salim Malik did well enough given the poor batting around him, but it was Dilip Vengsarkar whose performance really shines through.

Vengsarkar was always singled out for special treatment by the West Indian fast bowlers because they believed that the willowy Indian could not play fast bowling. This was patently untrue, but it did not stop the Windies pace men, especially Malcolm Marshall, peppering Vengsarkar with short-pitched deliveries on regular occasions. The Windies bowlers were further irritated by the fact that for much of the mid-1980s Vengsarkar was the world's best batsman according to the then newfangled Coopers Deloittes ratings. The Windies thought this was patently rubbish (in their minds Viv Richards was still number one) and the point was sharply made by Malcolm Marshall when he found himself on the opposing side to Vengsarkar in the game organized to celebrate the bicentenary of the MCC in 1987.

The players chosen for the MCC and Rest of the World sides were meant (injuries permitting) to represent the best 22 players on the planet. The game was played in the best of spirits, but when Vengsarkar came to the wicket after Marshall had dismissed his West Indian team-mate Desmond Haynes, a note of aggression entered the match. Marshall went round the wicket and fired a torrent of short-pitched balls past Vengsarkar's chest, until he eventually fended one to Graham Gooch at slip. Marshall won that particular duel, but it was Vengsarkar who won his own personal battle with the Windies fast bowlers.

Incidentally, in the MCC game, Marshall showed himself a class above even the great bowlers assembled for the match. On the flattest of Lord's pitches the best pace bowlers in the world returned the following figures:

	Overs	Maidens	Runs	Wickets
Imran Khan	38	10	130	2
Courtney Walsh	40.1	18	156	2
Kapil Dev	31	8	75	1
Richard Hadlee	23	4	73	0

Marshall's figures were:

	Overs	Maidens	Runs	Wickets
	22.3	3	63	4

Marshall was given the match award for the most successful bowler on the basis (as one observer commented at the time) of 'sheer, sharp reality'.

The winner of the batting award in that match was Sunil Gavaskar who made 188, although Marshall reckoned he had the great Indian batsman lbw without scoring first ball and did bowl him for a duck in the second innings. Gavaskar had great success against the West Indian bowlers during the 1970s, scoring 774 runs at the outrageous average of 154.80 in his first series against the Caribbean side. But the 1980s saw Gavaskar struggle to get anywhere near those performances against the higher pace and skill of the pace quartet. In the first 10 matches that Gavaskar played against the West Indies in the 1980s he scored just 513 runs at the paltry average for a great player of 28.50. Because of this the Indian captain Kapil Dev took the unprecedented step of dropping India's batting master down to No. 4 during the sixth and last Test of the 1983 series in India. However, the replacement opener Navjot Singh was a complete failure, being caught in the slips for a duck during Marshall's first over. A few balls later Vengsarkar suffered the same fate and Gavaskar walked to the wicket with the score at 0 for 2.

Wickets continued to tumble around Gavaskar until Ravi Shastri arrived at No. 7 with the score on 92. The young all-rounder got resolutely in line and Gavaskar proceeded to play one of the great innings against the Windies pace quartet. He batted for 10 hours and 44 minutes and faced 425 balls. His undefeated score of 236 contained 23 fours, and remains to this day the highest individual score by an Indian batsman and the largest score made against the West Indian pace quartet. It was also Gavaskar's 30th Test century, which took him past the previous record set by Sir Donald Bradman.

Apart from his innings during the sixth Test, Gavaskar appeared to have significant problems in combating the pace quartet. During the 1970s, Gavaskar was considered one of the four greatest players of fast bowling. However, it seems the 1980s pace quartet presented a challenge which went beyond anything he had experienced in the previous decade. The two other masters of fast bowling, Barry and Viv Richards, for different reasons never had the chance to test themselves against the West Indian pace quartet in a Test match, but the remaining member of the foursome did and had as difficult a time as Gavaskar.

Greg Chappell's Test scores against the West Indies during the 1970s were: 42, 14 not out, 106, 56, 1, 51, 41, 31, 123, 109 not out, 13, 43, 52, 182 not out, 6 not out, 4, 48 not out, 68, 54 not out. This gave him a record of 19 innings, 1044 runs, average 80.31. He scored four centuries and five 50s. But from the arrival of the fully fledged pace quartet in the 1979–80 series, his performance was seen to slump sharply, a decline all too clear from his Test scores during the 1980s: 74, 124, 19, 22, 0, 31, 0, 6, 12, 0, 61, 7. Chappell played 12 innings during his last two series against the West Indies and made only 356 runs at an average of 29.67. He scored just one century, two 50s and recorded three ducks.

The Chappell of the late 1970s had just emerged from three years with the Packer 'Circus'. There he had to combat a more or less unrelenting diet of fast bowling from the West Indian and Rest of the World sides. It is not unreasonable to suggest that he was shell-shocked.

But the fact that the two best players of fast bowling who had a chance to test themselves against the pace quartet in Test cricket failed to rise to that challenge has not stopped their less talented colleagues trying to find a way to gain the upper hand over the West Indian quicks. As there are many people in Britain today who have little memory of a Labour government, so there are those in the cricket world who now struggle to remember a time when the West Indies (and particularly their fast bowlers) have not ruled the roost. As with each lost election post-mortems would start on how the Labour party could make itself electable in Britain, so with every crushing series victory for the West Indies, various theories have been floated as to how to hold up this seemingly unstoppable juggernaut.

Many of the theories devoted to how the West Indies might be defeated have centred around the right 'type' of batsmen to combat the West Indian pace bowlers. When tour parties are assembled to go to the Caribbean, along with the established members of the side, at least one player will usually be picked because he is deemed a 'good player of fast bowling'. England did it in three consecutive tours of the West Indies with Peter Willey, David Smith and Wayne Larkins. Likewise, batsmen who have done reasonably well against other opposition have found themselves dropped before the start of a series against the West Indies because the selectors believed they lacked the 'guts' or the technique to deal with the pace quartet. These players were usually identified by their performance against the West Indies when compared to that against other Test sides.

The faster you bowl, the harder I'll hit it: batsmen who met the challenge of the West Indian pace quartet

	Difference between average against West Indies and overall average
B.M. Laird (A)	9.72
J.J. Crowe (NZ)	6.68
M.E. Waugh (A)	6.05
R.J. Hadlee (NZ)	5.26
P. Willey (E)	5.20
K. Wessels (A/SA)	3.54
A.J. Stewart (E)	2.74
Salim Malik (P)	1.53
M. Ramprakash (E)	0.99
G.A. Gooch (E)	0.97
D.B. Vengsarkar (I)	0.91
G.P. Howarth (NZ)	0.39
J. Dyson (A)	0.06

The Windies bunnies: batsmen who failed the challenge

	Difference between average against West Indies and overall average
G.S. Chappell (A)	−24.19
K.R. Rutherford (NZ)	−23.42
M.W. Gatting (E)	−21.57
Javed Miandad (P)	−20.61
Mudassar Nazar (P)	−19.69
B.C. Broad (E)	−17.37
M. Azharuddin (I)	−13.99
M.A. Taylor (A)	−13.08
G. Ritchie (A)	−13.02
I.T. Botham (E)	−12.13
Ramiz Raja (P)	−11.62
S. Waugh (A)	−11.59
D.I. Gower (E)	−11.42
A.D. Gaekwad (I)	−11.37
A.R. Border (A)	−11.10
B.S. Sandhu (I)	−10.77

So, exactly what type of player does best against the West Indies? Well, for a start, there does seem to be some truth that a mental and physical toughness does give batsmen some advantage against the West Indies pace quartet. In professional cricket they do not come any tougher than Peter Willey, Kepler Wessels, Alec Stewart and Graham Gooch. All four were not only born fearless, but also had the toughness to soak up the physical punishment which a long innings against the Windies pace quartet is bound to produce. Sheer stubbornness plays its part too: Bruce Laird, Jeff Crowe, Mark Ramprakash, Geoff Howarth and John Dyson did not have the steel-hard constitutions that Wessels et al. had, but they all had the strength of will to play long, defensive innings against the four fast men.

The proof of the need for physical and mental toughness when playing against fast bowling is provided by Graeme Hick. The Zimbabwe-born batsman was expected to take to Test cricket as a duck takes to water. However, his first series, against the West Indies in England during 1991, produced just 75 runs from seven innings. Ambrose dismissed him six times out of seven as the West Indies singled Hick out for special treatment, realizing the damage he could do to their cause if he became comfortable at the crease. The Windies bowlers were also inspired by the memory of an innings played by Hick against the 1988 West Indian tourists. Hick's century in that match gave him a thousand runs in the month of May, but few of the opposition players applauded him when he reached the milestone,

An ideal made flesh: Wes Hall was the archetypal West Indian fast bowler with a beautiful side-on action, which ran seamlessly into a sweeping follow-through
(Hulton Deutsch).

The last time the wheels came off: Michael Holding kicks the stumps out of the ground in frustration as an appeal to have New Zealand's John Parker caught behind is turned down. The West Indies lost the 1980 rubber 1–0; the last time, to date, that they lost a series.
(Allsport).

The daddy of them all: shouldering his way to the wicket, Andy Roberts was the trail-blazer for the pace quartet and became the second West Indian after Gary Sobers to pass 200 Test wickets *(Adrian Murrell/Allsport)*.

The supposed cricketing Neanderthal: Colin Croft was the member of the pace quartet most likely to deliver the ultimate unplayable ball and the one that batsmen least liked facing (Allsport).

Poetry in motion: a real athlete, Michael Holding had the action that fast bowlers around the world tried to emulate, and many regarded him as the quickest in cricket history (Allsport).

Raw recruit: Wayne Daniel played as a 19-year-old on the West Indies tour to England in 1976 alongside Roberts, Holding, Holder and Julien but fell out of favour with the West Indian selectors *(Adrian Murrell/Allsport)*.

A giant among fast bowlers: at 6 ft 8 ins, 'Big Bird' Joel Garner's trademark was a toe-crunching yorker and his good length deliveries leapt up at batsmen's ribs, making run-scoring nigh impossible *(Adrian Murrell/Allsport)*.

The eyes have it: Sylvester Clarke was similar to Malcolm Marshall in technique but closer to Colin Croft in temperament, which kept him on the fringes of the Test side *(Adrian Murrell/Allsport)*

WORLD SERIES CRICKET
WORLD

WORLD SERIES CRICKET
WEST INDIES

WORLD SERIES CRIC
AUSTRALIANS

Another world: Clive Lloyd led his West Indian team into the Packer 'Circus' to face Ian Chappell's Australians and a Rest of the World side, captained by Tony Greig *(Allsport)*.

Sharing the load: as captain, Clive Lloyd knew how to get the best out of his bowlers, including Michael Holding who says, 'We would do everything he asked' *(Allsport)*.

Bowling to order: Malcolm Marshall took hundreds of
wickets by forward planning and capitalized on an intelligent
approach to his craft with an explosive open-chested delivery
(Adrian Murrell/Allsport).

Rally Round the West Indies: fans in Guyana rejoice in their victorious team
(Ben Radford/Allsport).

One of cricket's most macabre dismissals: England's Mike Gatting was out
hit-wicket after a ball from Marshall removed part of his nose. Despite his gruesome injury, Gatting places no blame on the bowler *(Adrian Murrell/Allsport).*

Victim of the game-plan: England's Tim Curtis, an experienced county opener with Worcestershire, discovered that the West Indian fast bowlers' biggest weapon was not fear, but frustration. Here he is clean bowled by Curtly Ambrose at the fourth Test at Headingley in 1988 *(Adrian Murrell/ Allsport).*

The team machine: the strategy of the pace quartet meant that the West Indies fast bowlers were expected to contribute with the bat as well as the ball. At Headingley in 1984, Malcolm Marshall famously did his bit for the cause, batting one-handed after suffering a broken arm in the field to enable Larry Gomes to reach his century *(Adrian Murrell/Allsport).*

Athletes of the highest calibre: physiotherapist Dennis Waight has trained the West Indians, particularly the pace quartet, to adopt a fitness ethic that has reaped many dividends, not least in the fostering of team spirit in his pre-match work-outs on the outfield *(Adrian Murrell/Allsport)*.

Looking good, feeling good: Patrick Patterson shows the obvious advantages of Dennis Waight's approach *(Adrian Murrell/Allsport)*

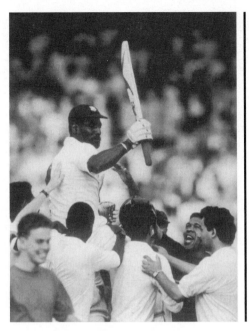

All for one, one for all (Take One): Viv Richards did not have an easy time inheriting the captaincy from Clive Lloyd but he quickly earned the respect of his team. In his last series, in England in 1991, his team-mates chaired him off the field at Edgbaston after another memorable victory *(Adrian Murrell/Allsport)*.

All for one, one for all (Take Two): joy at taking a wicket is not confined to the bowler, jubilation spreads throughout the team machine *(Adrian Murrell/Allsport)*.

The workhorse warrior: Courtney Walsh pushes himself to the limit for the sake of his side and varies his pace greatly, making it difficult for the batsman to pick up the length of each ball *(Ben Radford/Allsport)*.

Very, very, *very* fast: Patrick Patterson was a fearsome sight for a batsman. He possessed an aggressive streak and was frequently unplayable *(Ben Radford/Allsport)*.

The grim reaper: at 6 ft 7 in, Curtly Ambrose is the one bowler in international cricket today who can turn a match in a trice and destroy everything in his way *(Simon Bruty/Allsport)*.

'Real quick': Ian Bishop, with his superb action and good temperament, formed a formidable new ball partnership with Ambrose but his injury problems have been unusually difficult to cure for a West Indian fast bowler *(Adrian Murrell/Allsport)*.

Under pressure: Richie Richardson has the hallmarks of becoming a great Test captain after surviving, with credit, a traumatic take-over from Viv Richards. He was diagnosed as suffering from acute fatigue syndrome in the summer of 1994, a worrying blow for the West Indies *(Ben Radford/Allsport)*.

believing that he had been caught behind early in his innings. But despite all this a man who had scored 10,000 first-class runs by the age of 24 should have been able to cope. The reason he couldn't was simply that facing a four-pronged pace attack made him almost uncontrollably nervous. The proof of this came during research carried out by Mike Morgan as part of his BSc in Sports Science at Liverpool University. Hick was wired up to a heart monitor and subjected to a bowling machine delivering balls at 90 m.p.h. ('real quick' in other words). His heart rate rose from 55 beats per minute to 137. Against 'slow' bowling his heart rate was 130 b.p.m. Hick's nervousness against fast bowling was highlighted by the fact that his team-mate, Tim Curtis, recorded a b.p.m. 10 slower against fast bowling than against spin bowling.

Hick's failure against the West Indies during his first Test series was also, in all likelihood, due to another factor which has made more than one batsman struggle against the pace quartet – his side-on stance. And that technical deficiency in turn increased his unease because he knew the West Indies would exploit it.

Now the side-on stance is the foundation of traditional batsmanship. Much of its appeal to the older commentators is that it provides a link with past heroes (which of course the quartet does not – their very modernity jarring), but many good judges also believe it has technical advantages against the short-pitched ball. Ted Dexter, perhaps second only to Viv Richards in post-war cricket as a dismisser of fast bowling, certainly believes this. A side-on stance, he says, gives a smaller target for a bowler and makes it easier for the batsman to sway out of the way of a short ball.

But much has changed since Dexter's time and many more balls are bowled at stomach or chest (as opposed to head) height (especially by the Windies quartet), making swaying out of the way a riskier and more difficult proposition. Batsmen have to play many more defensive shots on the back foot and, against the extreme pace of the West Indian fast bowlers, it is often difficult to move back behind the line quick enough. Very often the result is a catch to short leg.

Both Hick and Steve Waugh have suffered from this problem, and both have taken the same step to remedy it. They have adopted a stance which is now more 'open', with more of the chest facing the bowler. Now they are in a better position to play a defensive stroke, or an attacking shot for that matter, to a short-pitched ball angled in at their body. Hick adopted the tactic in time for the 1994 tour of the Caribbean and significantly improved on his performance during 1991. Waugh changed his style following the 1993–4 series against the Windies and has recently enjoyed great success against South Africa's four-strong pace attack.

Significantly many batsmen with open stances have done well against the West Indies, Kepler Wessels for example. Another, Englishman Peter Willey, was described by Michael Holding as the 'hardest man to bowl at' in Test cricket. Of the West Indian batsman, Desmond Haynes has given his career a new lease of life by adopting a more open stance.

Looking at the list of champions and under-achievers, there doesn't seem much evidence to support the claim that short men do better against the pace quartet. This widely held belief is based on the assumption that many short-pitched balls will pass harmlessly over the head of smaller men. In fact what happens is that the stock West Indian delivery which passes a batsman of 'normal' height at about hip height tends to zero in on the chest of shorter batsmen, making it even more difficult to play. Mind you, the 6 ft 6 in Australian batsman Tom Moody is firmly of the opinion that being tall encourages the bowlers to bounce you and Sunil Gavaskar is adamant that his lack of inches made it easier to avoid short-pitched balls, so maybe it's a case of swings and roundabouts.

The side-on stance apart, few batsmen have succeeded in using anything but conventional methods to subdue the pace quartet. The most notable exception has been Australian batsman Mark Waugh. He has been the most successful batsman against the West Indies in recent years largely because he has adopted the high-risk strategy of stepping away to the leg side and lifting short-pitched deliveries from the pace bowlers over the top of the slip cordon. It is similar to the tactic adopted by Sir Donald Bradman to counter the short-pitched bowling of the English bowlers during the 1932–3 series in Australia. For a player of such abundant ability it seems a short-sighted move and the tactic was noticeably less successful during the second series in which he employed it. The all-out attack method adopted by Waugh was an echo (albeit from a less accomplished batsman) of that used by Richard Hadlee. The New Zealand all-rounder disliked facing fast bowling and did not intend to hang around while the West Indian pace bowlers softened him up (a prospect always likely for opposition fast bowlers).

It would be inaccurate to accuse any of the batsmen in the 'failures' list of cowardice in the face of West Indian fast bowling. Indeed, players such as Mike Gatting, Ian Botham and Greg Ritchie are renowned as tough cookies. It is perhaps Greg Chappell's 'shellshock' which comes closest to feelings of fear affecting the performance of a batsman. Poor technique against fast bowling seems to account for the majority of the players in this list. Ken Rutherford, Gatting, Mudassar Nazar, Chris Broad, Ritchie, Ramiz Raja, A.D. Gaekwad and B.S. Sandhu all scored runs against other sides but had their shortcomings exposed against the West Indies. Many would also put Gower in this category, although others would ascribe his relatively poor performance to failure of temperament when facing the highest pace.

The remaining batsmen on the 'bunnies' list are harder to pigeon-hole. Javed Miandad and Botham are perhaps the easiest to deal with. Both are batsmen who have to dominate their opposition mentally and tactically if they are to score runs. This is almost impossible to do against the Windies pace quartet, such is their skill and, particularly, because of the small number of deliveries from which it is possible to score. This soon frustrates players like Botham and Miandad, for whom an inability to keep their score moving is almost an affront to their manhood. This was most famously demonstrated during the second Test of England's 1980–1 tour of the West Indies. The story is recounted by Botham's England team-mate John Emburey.

'It was during the second Test at Barbados. Holding was bowling very well and Botham just couldn't get his bat anywhere near the ball. Eventually he just threw the bat on the floor as if to say "I can't play this stuff." Eventually he was out, caught behind off Holding for 26 and he comes storming into the dressing room shouting "What can you do? You can't do this, you can't do that." And there's all us tail-enders sitting there thinking, "We haven't got half the talent of this man and he's making a song and dance about not being able to play the bowling. What chance do we have?"'

For the record, after Botham was out, Bairstow, Emburey and Dilley all went for a duck, while Robin Jackman managed just 7 runs. England slumped from 94 for 6 to 122 all out, with Peter Willey left high and dry on 19.

On returning from the West Indies tour, Botham travelled with Somerset for a county championship game against Lancashire. When he went out to bat, who should be waiting for him but Lancashire's then overseas player Michael Holding. Botham told his partner, opening batsman Peter Roebuck, that he wouldn't survive the over. He didn't: he was out first ball, his confidence shot to pieces.

Botham and Miandad are so used to establishing dominance over their opponents that on the few occasions (usually against the West Indies) they find themselves outclassed they (at least temporarily) give up.

Sometimes, of course, their very urge (indeed, their need) to assert themselves speeds their downfall. During the first Test on England's 1986 tour of the Caribbean, Botham was doing a good job of repairing England's first innings with Allan Lamb. After 4 wickets had fallen for 83, Lamb and Botham had played sensibly to take the score to 120. But Botham then decided to take Marshall on, provoking the bowler to go around the wicket and feed Botham with a number of bouncers. The bait was too tempting for Botham and he soon hooked Marshall down long leg's throat. His dismissal exposed the tail to the Windies bowlers and England were dismissed for only 39 more runs.

The presence of three remaining players on the 'bunnies' list is something of a mystery. Two are Australian, and Mark Taylor and Allan Border would seem to be exactly the type of players to score runs against the West Indies, both possessing guts and talent aplenty. Yet they both average around 10 runs lower against the West Indies than they do against other opponents. Their under-achievement might have much to do with the identification by the West Indies of Australia (particularly in the late 1980s and early 1990s) as the major threat to their world crown. The West Indies, of course, also had the memory of 1975–6 to drive them on.

These two batsmen, along with David Boon, were the backbone of the Australian batting and the West Indies pace men knew that their dismissal would provide the major step towards beating them. So, like many times before in many different circumstances, they raised their game. It took the super-hard approach of Boon to withstand the onslaught and even then the nuggety No. 3 averaged three and a half runs less against the Windies than he did against other opponents.

Border could also cite another factor which might account for his relative lack of success against the West Indies. The Australian captain played 31 Tests against the pace quartet, which is five more than the next man (Graham Gooch). On his retirement during the Australian close season of 1993, he was the only batsman from England or Australia to play in every series his team contested against the West Indies pace quartet. Other long servers from these countries such as Gooch, Gower, Lamb and Boon missed at least one series, in the case of the last two because their Test careers did not begin until the mid-1980s. Players from other countries such as Miandad have also been unlucky enough to have careers which coincided with the dominance of the West Indies fast bowlers, but Australia and England played twice as many games during the 1980s and 1990s against the Caribbean side as against other Test teams.

In series during the early and mid-1980s Border was called on time and again to save his side. Often he appeared the only Australian batsman prepared to summon up the intense concentration and physical courage needed to counter the hostile West Indian pace attack. The heroics began in the third Test of the 1981–2 series in Australia. Coming in at 17 for 4 in the first innings he top scored with 78 out of 238. In the second innings, with Australia trailing by 151 runs, Border was promoted to No. 4 and after beginning his innings at 35 for 2 scored 126 out of 386. Despite Border's efforts, Australia still lost the match by 5 wickets.

But it was during the 1983–4 series in the Caribbean that Border staged perhaps the greatest one-man stand against the pace quartet on their home soil.

Allan Border v. the West Indies 1984

	Team score at start of innings	Individual score	% of team total	Result of match
1st Test – 1st innings	55 for 3	5	2	
2nd innings	42 for 3	54	20	Drawn
2nd Test – 1st innings	16 for 3	98*	38	
2nd innings	114 for 4	100*	33	Drawn

3rd Test – 1st innings	158 for 3	38	9	
2nd innings	65 for 4	8	8	WI won
4th Test – 1st innings	14 for 1	98	37	
2nd innings	50 for 1	19	10	WI won
5th Test – 1st innings	22 for 1	41	21	
2nd innings	7 for 1	60*	38	WI won

The West Indies, inspired by Marshall, Garner and Holding, were at the beginning of a winning stretch lasting 11 consecutive games. They were arguably the strongest side in world cricket, since the 1968 South Africans and the Australian batsmen were simply overwhelmed: all except Border. In six of Australia's 10 innings he scored more than 20 per cent of his team's total. In three, he made well over a third, remaining not out at the end of the innings. Border sold his wicket dearly and the fact that his team-mates did not sickened him. It is no wonder that Border found it hard to summon up the same level of performance in subsequent equally hard-fought series against the West Indies.

Significantly Border and Taylor were respectively captain and vice-captain of the Australian side during most of the recent games with the Windies. Before he became captain, Border played 13 Tests against the West Indies and scored 1037 runs at 46.14 with two centuries and eight 50s. After he was made skipper, he played a further 18 Tests, scored 1015 runs at 33.83, hit just one century and only six 50s.

Rival teams have long suspected that the West Indian fast bowlers single out opposing captains for special treatment. David Gower, for instance, was roughed up by Michael Holding in a match against Jamaica just before the first Test of the 1986 series. These suspicions seem to be confirmed by the fact that eight of the 16 players (including the last 'bunny', Mohammad Azharuddin) on the list of those who have struggled against the West Indies were either captains or vice-captains of their national sides at the time. By contrast, only three of 13 players on the list of those who achieved particular success against the West Indies were captaining their sides at the time.

Batsmen who do struggle against the pace quartet often find it very hard to escape from the firing line. Australian batsman Tom Moody is just one of the many who has suffered this intense examination of a batsman's skills. 'Unlike many Test bowlers, the Windies fast bowlers are nearly always guaranteed to bowl six good balls at you every over,' says Moody. 'It is often impossible to get the single needed to rotate the strike and this means that a batsman can be pinned down and worked over for six balls. If you are in trouble against one of their bowlers, there is no escape. Batsmen are also prevented from running singles and exchanging the strike, which means they can't build up the rhythm needed for a long innings, and the bowler's concentration is not disturbed by having to bowl at a different batsman in the course of one over.'

This 'working over' of batsmen usually takes one of two forms. If the batsman is relatively unknown to the West Indians he will be tested out for any weakness. Once weaknesses are found, however small, they will be ruthlessly exploited. The most famous example, of course, of this battering away at a perceived weakness came in the first over of the second Test during England's 1981 tour of the Caribbean. Opening the bowling to Geoffrey Boycott, Michael Holding forced the England opener on to the back foot with five consecutive short-pitched balls (none of them bouncers) and then produced a lightning fast delivery to bowl him off stump with Boycott's normally immaculate forward defensive shot suddenly riddled with uncertainty.

The various members of the West Indian pace quartet never tire of working out how to dismiss batsmen. A good example is the dissection they carried out on Mike Gatting's technique in the mid-1980s. Gatting was second only to Graham Gooch as a run scorer in English cricket during the 1980s, but his nine Tests against the West Indies brought him less than 300 runs at an average of 15. As Gatting readily admits, the pace quartet worked him out pretty quickly. They knew he was a good back foot player, so they pitched the ball up and swung it into his pads. Gatting was bowled or caught behind so many times that he began thrusting his pad far down the wicket with his bat held high over his head, as far away from the ball as possible. The result was him being given out lbw without playing a shot to deliveries that he could have defended with his bat. Gatting made the misjudgement because the pace quartet (particularly Malcolm Marshall in this case) had picked apart his technique, and left him unsure of even the basics of when he should play at a ball and when he should leave it.

But, as Gatting points out, he is not the only strong back foot player to get this treatment. Robin Smith's first three series against the West Indies had produced 704 runs and left him as the only batsman in world cricket averaging over 50 against the pace quartet. But by the start of England's 1994 tour of the Caribbean, the Windies had had plenty of time to do their homework. They refused to give Smith the short balls outside the off stump (which they used to dismiss David Gower) and this prevented him from playing his favourite square cut, dramatically reducing his run rate. When he was thoroughly frustrated and out of sorts, a few sharp short balls directed in at the body would force him back on to the stumps and then the *coup de grâce* would be administered by a fast, well pitched-up ball. The result of this tactic was that in his nine Test innings on the tour Smith was bowled twice, lbw three times and caught in the slips four times. Until he made 175 on a featherbed wicket in Antigua during the drawn fifth Test, Smith had scored just 145 runs in eight innings at an average of 18.

The talents of the West Indian bowlers rarely cause just one set of problems for a rival team's batsmen. For example, while one batsman can find himself pinned down by the pace bowlers' relentless accuracy, others can be starved of the strike using the same methods.

Imagine a situation in which two batsmen are facing the West Indian fast bowlers. One is a relatively inexperienced player who has just come to the wicket, the other is an established Test player with 30 runs already under his belt. The rookie batsman takes strike at the start of an over and is worked over by one of the quartet. Next over the experienced batsman might nudge the first ball for a single but would then have to watch helplessly as the young player is grilled by the fast bowler. This could go on for six overs with the experienced batsman getting a single early in the over and then standing at the other end with no means of escape as his young team-mate gets the treatment. Finally the young player is out and the batting side now has two problems, a new batsman coming to the wicket and an established player who has played perhaps less than 10 deliveries in the last half an hour. The batsman must get used to the extreme speed of the bowling all over again; that is, if the pace quartet give him the chance.

Even if he survives, he will be relatively powerless as he watches the pace quartet deal with his team-mates one by one. He may try to shield incoming batsmen against the pace attack. This is sometimes possible against one particularly threatening bowler, but not two – especially not two as accurate as most of the members of the Windies pace quartet. Countless middle order batsmen have looked on in horror as the pace quartet disposes of the last half of the batting order for a handful of runs, leaving them startled and stranded on 20 not out. This, of course, brings us on to another difficulty faced by batsmen combating the West Indian Test attack: the fact that the pace quartet are rabbit hunters par excellence.

The proportion of runs scored by tail-enders against the West Indies is lower than against any other Test team. Today, lower order batsmen are often well equipped to deal with medium-fast bowling and all but the best spinners, but the great majority can only afford to concentrate on defence against the West Indian pace quartet. John Emburey, for example, had a Test batting average of nearly 23, but he will readily admit that he lacked the technique to combat the pace quartet. He and the other tail-enders in the England side were reduced to 'blocking out maidens'. Useful if an established batsman is at the crease, but next to useless if the tail has been left to its own devices. Emburey started the 1986 tour of the Caribbean batting at No. 7, which he now admits was 'a bit frightening'. He finished the tour at No. 10 and his eight innings in the series had brought him just 64 runs.

The England off-spinner saw his job as supporting any front line batsman who had survived. He and his team-mates regarded it as a considerable bonus if the last five wickets could add even only 60 or 70 runs, but such was the quality of the West Indian bowling that this was rarely possible.

Only three times in 10 innings did the last five wickets add more than 50 runs.

Emburey noticed that the West Indies always seemed to be able to pace their game-plan so that the second new ball greeted the arrival of the first tail-enders. Apart from that he noticed no change in the Windies tactics when tail-enders came to the wicket. The same method of bowling just short of a length and then pitching one up which was usually so successful against the front line batsmen was also adopted against the lower order players.

Although tail-enders were usually given the instruction to 'stick around for as long as you can' when they went out to bat, most front line batsmen have been left to work out their approach to playing the pace quartet for themselves. Tim Curtis, for example, remembers being given no particular instruction by the experienced Test batsmen in the side on how to play the pace quartet. Instead the only message (repeated like a mantra throughout the dressing room) was that if two batsmen managed to build a partnership they should squeeze every last possible run from it. Gooch, Gower and Lamb made it clear that the Windies would often appear to be going off the boil only for a wicket suddenly to fall (perhaps through the frustration factor) and the pace quartet to pour through the breach, carrying all before them. The period following the end of a long stand against the West Indies is always a dangerous one for their opponents. New batsmen must adjust quickly to the speed of the bowling and the fast bowlers step up a gear to make the most of the situation.

The knowledge that against the West Indies the fall of one wicket is usually followed by the loss of two or three more is shared by all their Test opponents. Curtis says that this knowledge produced a dressing room atmosphere at Headingley in 1988 in which all were expecting a wicket to fall at any moment and for that to spark some sort of collapse. This attitude was no doubt encouraged by the Windies' 2–0 lead in the series, but there was also a danger of the batsmen's fears becoming a self-fulfilling prophecy.

Curtis did not have to wait long for a powerful demonstration of the pace quartet's ability to transform a match. After England had slumped to 80 for 4 in the first innings, Lamb and débutant Robin Smith took the attack to the pace quartet, adding 103 in just over two hours: 183 for 4 on a helpful Headingley wicket was no bad position, and England had just begun to think in terms of winning the match and levelling the series at The Oval when Lamb tore a calf muscle and had to retire. The West Indies saw their chance and took it. Ambrose produced an 'evil lifter' to have Smith caught behind (183 for 5), while new captain Chris Cowdrey lasted 12 balls before falling lbw to Marshall for a duck (183 for 6). Marshall then produced a leaping ball which the cumbersome Pringle could only edge to Dujon (185 for 7) and Ambrose spread-eagled Jack Richards's stumps with a super-fast delivery (185 for 8). Four wickets had fallen for 2 runs in the space of 26 balls and only some long-handle from fast bowlers Dilley and Foster allowed England to reach 201 before Ambrose struck again. It was a scenario that has been repeated time and again wherever the West Indies have played Test cricket during the last 15 years.

The pace quartet's widely known ability to turn even the most secure match position into a rout gives their team a massive psychological advantage. This is particularly useful for the West Indian captain on the odd occasions when he needs to bring on his part-time spinners in order to give the fast bowlers a brief rest. Curtis describes how the batsman facing Gomes, Richards, Hooper or Adams is often haunted by indecision. After being pinned down by the pace men for so long, the inoccuous deliveries of the slow bowlers (calling them spinners is usually a misnomer) appear almost unbearably tempting and logically they do offer the chance of increasing the run-rate beyond the miserly limit allowed by the fast bowlers. But the batsmen also know that, if they lose their wicket to a rash stroke against the slow bowlers, the fast bowlers will be immediately reintroduced and that a batting collapse becomes a real possibility. In any case the batsmen also know that the reintroduction of the fast bowlers is never more than half a dozen overs away and that wickets need to be preserved for that moment.

Examine the records of the West Indies' most used 'fill-in' bowlers over the last 15 years and the caution with which they have been treated becomes clear. The number of wickets they have taken and their bowling averages make it clear that these were not match-winning spinners, yet their economy rate is equal to if not better than that of their fast-bowling colleagues, many of whom were themselves masters of tight bowling. It is also interesting to compare their figures to those of John Emburey, England's front line spinner for most of the 1980s and the acknowledged master of 'defensive' or 'negative' slow bowling.

Light relief? The pace quartet's support bowlers

	M	Balls	Runs	Wkts	Av	Runs/ 100 balls	Overs/ test
V. Richards	121	5170	1964	32	61.37	37.99	7
H.A. Gomes	60	2401	930	15	62.00	38.73	7
C.L. Hooper	40	4559	1966	35	56.17	43.12	19
Compared with:							
J.E. Emburey	63	15211	5564	147	37.85	36.58	40

Hooper has averaged nearly 20 overs a Test because, until recently, he alone had to shoulder the fill-in bowler's role, whereas in the early and mid-1980s the load was shared by Gomes and Richards.

Just as the batsmen can feel under pressure when facing the Windies' relatively unthreatening slow bowlers, they can also find themselves at a loss when trying to maximize any advantage they have over the Windies' fast bowlers. After 15 years of West Indian dominance, sides that find themselves with the upper hand know how rare it is and how, if they squander the chance, they are unlikely to get another during the series. They also know that the West Indian team, particularly the pace quartet, tend to react to the situation by raising their game. The combination of these two factors tends to result in the sort of pressure few batsmen can handle. South Africa's first Test against the West Indies was one such case (see Chapter 3) and so was Curtis's second.

The fifth Test of 1988, held at the Kennington Oval, saw England gain a first innings lead of 22 over the West Indies. When the home side had extended their lead to 72 without losing a wicket on the evening of the second day they looked well placed to snatch a consolation victory in the last game of the series. In the 19th over of England's reply Curtis was lbw for 15 to Marshall, then Robert Bailey was bowled by Benjamin with the first delivery of the 20th over and Smith trapped lbw with the last for a duck. In the space of two overs England had slumped to 55 for 3 and effectively surrendered the initiative. England totalled 202 in their second innings and lost by 8 wickets.

Incidentally England were to beat South Africa in almost exactly the same fashion on the same ground six years later.

So, what is the recipe for success against the West Indian pace quartet? Well, not being the captain or playing in a side which can threaten the West Indies seems to help. A good technique is also a major advantage, but (as Miandad and Azharuddin found out) it is often not enough. No, facing the West Indian fast bowlers is a physical and psychological test of nerves, and it is the players who rise to this challenge who are the best bets against the pace quartet. This is not to say that every batting line-up pitted against the West Indies should be filled with macho lunkheads who walk to the wicket muttering about all the awful things they are going to do to these over-rated West Indian fast bowlers and once on strike take a few bouncers on the chest just to show they are not scared.

The West Indies fast bowlers are too talented and operate a strategy that is too well thought-out to be fazed by such a simple-minded approach. The batsmen, such as Botham, who have tried to out-muscle the West Indies fast bowlers have nearly always failed. During even the most productive innings against the West Indies, the fast bowlers will have countless moral victories and the number of balls off which it is highly risky to attempt a scoring shot means that the batsman is never going to have his score racing along. It is next to impossible totally to dominate the West Indian fast bowlers and that

removes an important component of most successful Test innings. It effectively means that a batsman must adopt a different mental approach to an
innings against the West Indies, as well as deciding whether he will change
his batting style. He must search for a way to gain the holy grail of modern
Test batsmanship: a career average of above 50 against the West Indies.

Malcolm Marshall, asked in 1992 which current player he most admired,
named Graham Gooch 'for his dedication and hard work'. This is not surprising given that the Essex opener has come closest to discovering the
secret of combating the West Indian fast bowlers. Gooch has played six
series against the West Indies and 'failed' in only one of them.

G.A. Gooch v. the West Indies 1980–91

Series	M	I	NO	H S	Runs	Av	100s	50s	Position in England averages
1980	5	10	0	123	394	39.40	1	2	3
1980–1	4	8	0	153	460	57.50	2	1	1
1985–6	5	10	0	53	276	27.60	0	4	2
1988	5	10	0	146	459	50.00	1	3	1
1989–90	2	4	1	84	128	42.66	0	1	2
1991	5	9	1	154*	480	60.00	1	2	3

Gooch managed a number of notable achievements against the West Indies.
For a start he scored centuries against them in four series, an unparalleled
feat during the era of the pace quartet. He also withstood the extra burden
of captaincy, averaging 53.92 during the eight games he was in charge.

Gooch's one 'bad series' was the 1985–6 tour of the Caribbean. Gooch
had recently completed his three-year ban for touring South Africa with a
'rebel' team. He knew what sort of reception he was likely to get in the West
Indies and was not keen on making the trip. After he was finally persuaded
to join the tour, Gooch found all his worst fears justified with protests cul-
minating in a stinging attack by the Antiguan deputy prime minister Lester
Bird. Gooch was enraged as, after earlier comments by Bird, there had been
an agreement that neither side would raise the issue again. Gooch demanded a right of reply, which he claimed was denied by the Test and County
Cricket Board, and then decided to ask for permission to pull out of the
fifth Test in Antigua. He changed his mind when faced with the reality of
letting down his team-mates and breaking his contract with the TCCB. On
the tour Gooch became a lonely figure, his gloom deepened by England's
5–0 defeat in the Test series, criticism over the level of commitment displayed by the English players, and constant 'sex and drugs' allegations levelled at Ian Botham by the tabloid press.

But even in the midst of this turmoil, Gooch played one innings which set him apart from his team-mates. The second one-day international in Trinidad was rain-hit and the game reduced to 37 overs a side. The West Indies were put into bat and England captain David Gower watched helplessly as the home side reached 229, with Viv Richards making 82 off 39 balls.

England were faced with the prospect of scoring at more than six an over against an attack of Garner, Patterson, Walsh and Marshall. Botham was promoted to open the innings with Gooch, but was soon out. Gooch then decided that enough was enough and, taking advantage of the playing rules which allowed only two men outside the fielding circle for the first 15 overs, started to hit out. He hooked Garner three times during his opening spell and, when Garner was replaced by Walsh, the Essex opener smashed a good length delivery over mid-on for six. Gooch reached his 100 off 100 balls and England were faced with the task of making 9 runs off the last over. The opener made 6 of them and England won by 5 wickets, G.A. Gooch 129 not out. The real power of Gooch's stroke play is perhaps best reflected in Joel Garner's bowling figures. The giant Bajan was undoubtedly the greatest limited-overs bowler ever, yet during this game his 9 overs cost 62 runs.

Gooch is typically modest when asked about his success against the West Indies. He claims, with good reason, that his game is best suited to combating the extremes of sharply turning spin or all-out pace. He is bold and definite in attack or defence and this can, as he admits, cause him problems when a medium-pacer is moving the ball around.

His upright stance with his bat raised was developed before he had faced the pace quartet. It was originally devised to 'stop myself moving about at the crease' and to 'keep my head still', but it does also give Gooch specific advantages when facing fast bowlers. The hundredths of a second saved by not having to raise the bat off the ground to the horizontal before swinging it up into the back lift are often valuable against the pace of the West Indian fast bowlers. Essentially Gooch also combines his raised bat stance with a head which stays rock steady as the bowler runs up and delivers the ball. This is the mistake often made by players who try to copy Gooch. As they wait for the ball, their bats and heads wave from side to side. Gooch, by contrast, apart from a couple of brief tenses as the bowler nears the wicket, appears carved from marble.

Gooch also cites his physical fitness as another factor underlying his success. Often criticized for placing over-reliance on fitness, Gooch can always point to himself as the prime example of the benefits of circuit training and five-mile jogs. At the age of 40 Gooch was considered the best batsman in the world, which would be unthinkable in the days of limited-overs cricket without a commitment to physical fitness training. And once he lost the England captaincy, Gooch began racing round the outfield like someone who does his winter training with West Ham Football Club, which of course he does.

Gooch describes a long innings against the West Indies as 'a war of attrition' and claims that his physical condition helps him maintain the concentration he needs. He argues that once your energy level falls below a certain point you cannot give full attention to your game. A moment's thought, as Marshall brings his arm over, about how good that end-of-play bath is going to feel can be fatal.

Just how much of a battle playing the Windies often is can be underlined by comparing two of Gooch's innings played less than a year apart at the height of the Essex opener's powers.

At Lord's in July 1990 Gooch scored 333 against India; in June the following year he took 154 off the West Indies. Despite the fact that he scored over twice as many runs in the first of these innings, Gooch received only 30 per cent more balls. Against India Gooch scored at a run every two minutes, against the West Indies it was a run every three minutes. Incidentally, considering the criticism the West Indian fast bowlers often receive about the time it takes to bowl their overs, it is interesting to note that the Indian attack (which contained two front line spinners) delivered their overs no quicker than Ambrose, Patterson, Walsh and Marshall.

Despite his generally high level of fitness, Gooch takes little for granted. Before a series against the West Indies, he goes through a series of exercises designed to get him quickly into the rhythm of playing high pace and the short-pitched ball. He points out that he has always been strong off the back foot and that this makes preparing for a West Indian series, in terms of technique, simply a matter of practising to increase the quality of his already high-class pull, cut and hook shots. It is the foundation of strong back foot strokes (such as those possessed by Allan Lamb, Robin Smith and David Boon) that is necessary before you can attempt to take on the pace quartet. Gooch has also worked hard on how to play the genuine bouncer safely. Like Robin Smith, when not playing a defensive or attacking shot to a short ball he usually weaves out of the way while dropping his hands. He prefers this to ducking, as he can keep his eye on the ball and there is no danger that a sharply swinging delivery might glance off an upraised bat and be caught by the wicketkeeper or slips. Psychologically, too, the former England captain does not like the idea of bowing his head to any fast bowler.

Many batsmen in the past have seen no need to prepare their game for a confrontation with the West Indies. They believe that if their technique in domestic cricket or against other Test sides is good enough to get them into their national team, it will be good enough to work against the West Indies. But this is simply not the case. None of the batsmen with experience against the pace quartet would advise any young player dramatically to alter his game when playing the West Indies, but they would warn him to prepare. The pace quartet very rarely bowl half volleys, so it is no good relying on the drive to bring you a good proportion of your runs. The batsman must decide which strokes will bring him runs – the cut, pull and leg glance for example – and practise them intensively. The terms of an innings against the pace quartet are always dictated by the bowlers. They create a challenge which is peculiar to batsmen facing the West Indian Test team. To ignore the nature of that challenge, however unnatural it may feel, is to fail it.

Gooch's motto while England captain was 'If you fail to prepare then prepare to fail.' He put this belief into practice most memorably before England's 1990 tour of the Caribbean. A fierce training schedule was developed and put into place at the pre-series training camp at Lilleshall. Unlike in previous tour warm-ups, there was an emphasis on testing and improving physical stamina for both batsmen and bowlers. In the past, England batsmen had prepared for a Caribbean tour by knocking up against English medium-pacers. This time, coaches were instructed to throw balls from 18 yards and bowling machines were cranked up to 90 m.p.h.

But perhaps Gooch's boldest move was in the selection of his batsmen. England had just lost a six-match home series against Australia 4–0 and the team's batting line-up was in some disarray after no fewer than 13 batsmen had been tried in order to counter Terry Alderman's subtle swing. The situation was made worse when four of the batsmen (Mike Gatting, Kim Barnett, Tim Robinson and Chris Broad) in contention for the West Indies squad joined the last 'rebel' tour of South Africa. Ian Botham had already declared himself unavailable for England's tour and Gooch was facing a real shortfall in experience. Given this background, Gooch's decision to omit David Gower, his immediate predecessor as England captain, from the tour party seems amazing. But the new England captain knew that Gower's record against the West Indies was none too impressive, a fact overlooked by many critics of the decision, and reasoned that his apparently laid-back attitude would sit uneasily with the new 'up and at 'em' approach that he and manager Mickey Stewart were to instigate.

Gooch examined the ranks of county batsmen to discover those who would have the guts and mental strength to withstand the West Indies pace quartet. In a re-run of Tony Greig's decision to counter Lillee and Thomson with the grey-haired David Steele, Gooch chose Wayne Larkins as his opening partner. Larkins had had a good season in county cricket, but he was 36 years old (the same age as Gooch) and had not played Test cricket for eight years. However, Gooch believed that Larkins's positive approach to playing fast bowling was what was needed. For the same reason, the uncapped Alec Stewart and Nasser Hussain, as well as the relatively inexperienced Rob Bailey and David Capel, were all selected. Robin Smith, the one batting success of the Ashes summer, and Allan Lamb, who had twice averaged over 40 in a series against the West Indies, completed the line-up. The more solid, but less enterprising, talents of Curtis, Martyn Moxon and Chris Tavare were all passed over, as was Mike Atherton.

Gooch adopted a very clear policy of picking the 'type' of batsmen who stood the best chance of doing well in the Caribbean and then building on those talents by employing a carefully structured training programme. On the 1986 tour the English batsmen were pitched straight from what was effectively a cricketing holiday into the life-threatening situation that was presented by the combination of the West Indian bowlers and an under-prepared Kingston pitch. Four years later, England's batsmen were already well on their way to being battle-hardened by the first Test. The West Indies were caught off guard and England won that first game by eight wickets and would have won the second but for a brief rain storm. Graham Gooch was injured in the second Test run-chase and after that the carefully constructed tactics of the English team slowly began to unravel. But despite the eventual 2–1 series victory for the West Indies, Gooch's tactics had been vindicated. In the context of a highly competitive series against the world's strongest side, Larkins, Stewart and Hussain were all a success.

When the West Indies came to England in 1991, Gooch stuck to similar tactics, giving the stubborn Ramprakash an extended run in the side and bringing back Stewart for the fifth Test which England won to halve the series. Again Gower, who had been second to Gooch in the averages during the 1990–1 Ashes series, was not picked. In the three series before the 1990 trip to the Caribbean, England had lost 14 Tests and drawn 1. With Gooch in command the record was played 9, lost 4, won 3, drawn 3.

During the two series against the West Indies, players such as Ramprakash and Larkins both played a number of long innings against the pace quartet. Lacking the technique of Gooch or Smith, they found that they had to cut out a number of their normal scoring strokes. Despite the fact that this dramatically slowed down their run-scoring speed, both remained positive at the wicket and alive to any scoring chance that might come along.

Remaining positive is the factor which Gooch believes is most important during an innings against the West Indian pace quartet. It was a message he says he impressed on all the English batsmen during the 1990 and 1991 series, although 'some listened and some didn't'. He explains that 'being positive' does not mean hooking every bouncer or trying to drive good length balls over mid-on's head. It is much more about a mind set which allows the batsman instantly to forget about the previous ball which nearly took his head off or screamed past his outside edge and to treat the next delivery primarily as a scoring opportunity.

One of those who did listen to Gooch's advice was Alec Stewart, the only player to score two centuries in one match against the pace quartet. 'As a batsman, I just try and be the boss,' he claims. 'In a way it's arrogance, but in a positive way. You're proving you are better than who you are playing against.' Gooch's main disciple uses the same approach to deal with the physical threat of short-pitched bowling. 'You've got to believe you're good enough to get out of the way of the ball,' he says.

In Gooch's game, positivity manifests itself in a number of ways. For example, he used positive thinking to loosen the hold Malcolm Marshall was beginning to get on him after a series of lbw dismissals. Instead of worrying about Marshall's late swing as he went out to bat, Gooch recalled the centuries he had scored against the fast bowler in county and Test cricket. With Geoff Boycott in the early 1980s, Gooch made sure he and his partner kept up a running dialogue during any partnership to counter the siege mentality the pace quartet's relentless attack can produce. Batsmen can also have real trouble maintaining concentration when there is a gap of 45 seconds between one delivery and the next. A partner's exhortation ('Come on, only half an hour to lunch') can work wonders.

The idea of taking a positive approach to scoring runs in Test cricket is hardly a novel one; indeed the majority of batsmen would say that they operated in this way. Mike Gatting, for example, describes the secret of playing a long Test innings as simply 'hanging around, setting yourself the target of surviving the first half an hour, the first hour, the next session – confident in the belief that if you remain positive and are a good enough player the runs will start to come'.

What is different against the West Indies is that it is much more difficult to maintain a positive attitude because of the quality of the bowling, as Gatting found out to his cost. Because of the speed of the West Indian bowling, batsmen are always operating at the very limit of their reactions and this means that the hundredth ball of a batsman's innings can cause him as much trouble as the first. The realization that things are not likely to get significantly easier as an innings progresses is perhaps the biggest barrier to remaining positive when facing down the pace quartet. There is no plateau to be reached after scaling the mountainside.

On the 1986 tour of the Caribbean there was much talk by the English batsmen of the 'death ball' which one of the pace quartet would eventually produce to snare a batsman's wicket. The result was England's talented stroke-makers throwing the bat with wild abandon in the hope of making a few runs before they were cut down. Alternatively, many other Test series against the West Indies over the last 15 years have seen opposition batsmen frozen into inactivity as the fear that the fall of one wicket will most likely herald a dramatic collapse weighed heavily on the batsmen's minds. Both these scenarios, of course, fuel the Windies' towering self-belief and eat away at their opposition's already shallow confidence. Being positive in a dressing room full of graveyard humour or nervous wrecks is a lot more difficult than being positive when surrounded by players all keen to tuck into New Zealand's or India's pop-gun attack.

A simplistic approach, such as the all-out attack methods favoured by

England's batsmen during the 1986 tour, is very rarely likely to be success-ful. According to Gooch, the correct approach to combating the West Indian quartet is a question of achieving the right balance between follow-ing a disciplined game-plan (after all, as any Test batsmen will tell you, the Windies fast bowlers are the most disciplined participants in international cricket) and refusing to let the constant pressure they are able to exert result in an overly negative mind set. For example, Gooch explains that this kind of balanced approach is important when deciding whether or not to play the hook shot against the quartet. A positive player will always try to score as quickly as possible (and with so many short-pitched balls, the hook shot is one of the best ways to do this). The game-plan, however, may dic-tate that the bounce is too uneven, the field setting too restrictive or the bowling simply too quick. What is important is to start with the positive attitude of wanting to play strokes and then apply caution where necessary, not the other way round.

Gooch became aware of the importance of taking the attack to the West Indian bowlers (whenever possible) during the 1980 and 1981 series. During these two series Geoffrey Boycott would respond to the challenge of the West Indian fast bowlers by retreating behind his immaculate defence. Boycott would reach the end of the session knowing that he had played well against the world's best bowlers, only to glance at the score-board to find, to his horror, that his score had advanced by only 20 or so runs. Boycott's resulting worries about his ability to counter the pace quar-tet affected not only him, but (as he was widely regarded as the world's best opening batsman) the confidence of the whole team. Gooch noted the effect on Boycott and reasoned that, if this was how negative thought could affect a man talented enough still to average over 40 in the nine Tests he played against the pace quartet, what would it do to a less experienced or skilful player?

It was a positive attitude that enabled Gooch to play what was arguably the greatest ever innings against the pace quartet. The first Test of the Windies' 1991 tour of England was played on a helpful pitch at Headingley. The situation a few overs into England's second innings was remarkably similar to that of the fifth Test of 1988. After gaining a first innings lead of 25, England reached 38 and then lost three wickets to Ambrose while another 20 runs were added. But this time Gooch was in no mood to give in. He found a willing partner in the débutant Mark Ramprakash who helped him add 78 for the fourth wicket. Then Ambrose struck again and dismissed Ramprakash, Robin Smith and Jack Russell as England struggled to 124 for 6. Surely the pressure would be too great now, England's nerve would break and the Windies would romp home again? But, no, Gooch went on, refusing to be fazed by the wickets tumbling around him. He found another stubborn partner in Derek Pringle and England ended the third day on 143 for 6, 168 runs ahead, with Gooch, playing a captain's innings, on 82. It was the first period of play during a rain-hit fourth day that transformed Gooch's innings from the very good to the great. He took his stand with Pringle to 98 and soon after reached his century. He had faced 240 balls and batted for over 5½ hours. With Pringle's dismissal, Gooch opened his shoulders and moved on to 154 off 331 balls as the tail was swept away by Marshall and Walsh. Gooch's innings had been performed on a bowler's wicket against the best bowling attack in the world and his undefeated 154 out of England's 252 represented the sixth most dominant individual innings in Test history. Gooch was able to score off only a quarter of the balls he received, but still managed to remain fluent. A glance at the run chart shows that he mixed thumping off-side drives to well pitched-up deliveries with powerful hooks, cuts and pulls to the inevitable short-pitched deliveries that followed to record most of his 18 fours.

Gooch believes the innings to be the greatest he has ever played because he managed to rescue England twice after the West Indies had, as usual, clawed themselves back into a winning position through a burst of apparently irresistible fast bowling. But there are plenty of other reasons for Gooch to be proud. His 154 brought England's first home victory over the West Indies for 22 years. It was made against the world's strongest bowling attack – Ambrose, Patterson, Walsh and Marshall – on a helpful wicket. It was only the sixth example of a batsman carrying his bat for England and only the third time somebody had done it against the West Indies. And all through the power of positive thought!

Gooch might have been forgiven for muttering some unkind words about the Headingley groundsman as he walked out to face the world's best fast bowlers on a helpful track. But not a bit of it. Gooch rejects the idea that English groundsmen should prepare flat pitches whenever the West Indies arrive in the hope of drawing the fangs of their fast bowlers. All this does, says Gooch, is to make the English seam bowlers totally ineffective, while the Windies fast bowlers can still rely on speed through the air and extra bounce. Better to prepare a seaming wicket which the English bowlers can exploit. Headingley was such a pitch and Phillip DeFreitas (8 wickets for 93), Steve Watkin (5 for 93) and Derek Pringle (4 for 52) out-bowled the pace quartet and, along with Gooch, won the game for England.

Gooch claims to have a bruise for each of the 154 runs he scored at Headingley and there is no doubt that courage takes a major part in playing successfully as a Test batsman against the West Indies. The issue of intimidation and short-pitched bowling is discussed at length in Chapter 8, but on a technical point it is worth recording that Gooch, Gatting et al. recognize that on certain pitches they are likely to get more than their share of 'throat balls'.

Geoff Boycott believes that being hit by a ball can sometimes be a good thing, because it 'wakes you up' and provides a sharp reminder that your concentration is slipping. Gooch doesn't go quite this far, but he does appear largely unconcerned about the physical danger of facing the Windies pace quartet (except on dangerous wickets). He says that he has never worried about being hit during an innings against the West Indies and that to do so would fatally undermine the most complete of techniques. He acknowledges that other batsmen do become physically scared when facing the pace quartet, but can offer them no words of advice. 'I don't really understand why I can go out and bat against Marshall and Ambrose without being scared,' he says. 'It's just something I was born with.'

8 | Nasty, brutish and short(-pitched)

THE West Indies appeared to be living on borrowed time in early 1991. They had enjoyed 10 years on top of the cricket world, a period of dominance unprecedented since World War 2, but now age was catching up with their senior players. Gordon Greenidge was 40, Viv Richards 39, Jeff Dujon and Desmond Haynes 35, and Malcolm Marshall 31.

The Australian team which arrived in the Caribbean during February, on the other hand, was on the crest of a wave. They had lost only one Test during the previous two years, and had beaten England conclusively both at home and abroad, as well as overcoming a strong Pakistan side in Pakistan. During the same period, the West Indies had lost three games, drawn a series against Pakistan, narrowly defeated England in the Caribbean and only shown anything like their old form during a 3–0 demolition of a weak India side.

The Australian team of 1991 was a tough and talented unit. Their batting line-up drawn from Geoff Marsh, Mark Taylor, David Boon, Allan Border, Dean Jones, and Steve and Mark Waugh was the strongest in the world. But, perhaps more importantly, in Craig McDermott, Merv Hughes, Bruce Reid and Terry Alderman they had a fast-bowling line-up which appeared on paper as good as the current Windies quartet, especially as that lacked the injured Ian Bishop.

To begin with, the two sides seemed to be following the script, with Australia winning the one-day series 4–1. But then, after a rain-ruined first match, the West Indies annihilated Australia in the second Test, winning by 10 wickets. The third game was also spoilt by the weather, but in the fourth match the West Indies clinched the series, thanks to an overwhelming victory by 343 runs. At the end of the series, the 'past-it' Marshall headed the bowling averages with 21 wickets at 20.81. Patrick Patterson had 18 at 22.72, Courtney Walsh 17 at 25.06 and Curtly Ambrose 18 at 27.39. Of the Australian batsmen only Mark Waugh and Taylor averaged above 35.

The Windies had done it again. They were back on top and the envy of the world's cricketing powers – one of the greatest teams in any sport in history. Most in the West Indies team believed their achievements had justly earned them the respect of cricket followers across the globe. But they were wrong. Next stop for the Windies team after the Australian series was a trip to England for a five-match series. Soon after their arrival the June edition of *Wisden Cricket Monthly* hit the streets. Its editorial, by David Frith, was entitled 'An unappetising tour'. It read:

Another invasion is upon us by a West Indian team which is the most fearsome, the most successful and the most unpopular in the world. Their game is founded on vengeance and violence and is fringed by arrogance.

How incredible it was to learn that when the series against Australia had ended, the West Indies captain, Viv Richards, 'demanded' that the world's cricket authorities clamp down on intimidation and abuse. Thus spoke a man who was supposed to be in charge, and yet who is invariably at the very centre of the war-dances. 'People should be made to realise', he says, 'that no individual is bigger than the game.' How true. How very true.

Richards even claimed that this sort of thing was happening everywhere in cricket. From where he stands it might appear thus, but in fact such ugliness does not perpetually soil England's matches with Australia, New Zealand, India or Sri Lanka, or many another contest. West Indies, for their part however, have become embroiled in one sour series after another.

Their supporters will insist that bitterness arises from the fact that West Indies have been so steadily victorious. This may be close to the truth, but there is a vital additional factor to be identified, and that is that these matches have long since become manifestations of the racial tensions that exist in the world outside the cricket-ground gates. Just when cricketers of both sides should be teaching ordinary folk how to co-exist and enjoy honourable sports combat, a damaging counter-image emerges.

It has not been uncommon of late to hear cricket-lovers talk of ignoring this summer's one-day internationals and Test matches in favour of county cricket. The visitors' over-rate will be poor (and the Test and County Cricket Board are letting them get away with it). This, tactically, will almost certainly be matched by the home side. There will be no variety in the West Indies attack, with no slow bowler of Test class in the squad. And we have seen it all oh so many times before. What on earth persuaded the TCCB to invite them back a year early?

At least play will cease at 7pm, even if West Indies, in seven hours' play, have bowled only 75 or 80 overs. By capitulating on that point too the TCCB at least have curtailed everybody's inconvenience. West Indies cricket needs this tour urgently, having suffered another financially disastrous home series. And yet they have out-bluffed the TCCB completely by refusing to accept controls over bouncers and fast, high full tosses. So it is left to the umpires:

> and we know well enough how lacking in the right stuff they usual-
> ly turn out to be.

In the same issue, Frith answered a letter complaining about his view of the Windies' use of the bouncer by writing:

> There is more to bowling than the ugly bouncer flying straight at the teeth, and West Indies' bowling success, upon which their 15-year dominance has been based, has been heavily reliant on the short, fast ball. This has seriously depleted cricket as a spectacle: though not, of course, in the Caribbean, where, as Australian opener Mark Taylor recently observed, a square-cut for four by a visiting batsman will bring but a murmur of appreciation while a bouncer – much less three in a row – raises a frenzy of delight from the bleachers.

In the subsequent issue of his magazine, Frith followed up his editorial with one entitled 'Just to clarify . . .'. Frith believed his comments had been misinterpreted, particularly since extracts from the June editorial had been sensationalized by the *Daily Mirror*. So, in July 1991, Frith wrote: 'The statement that the West Indies' success has been based on "vengeance and violence" seems almost deliberately to have been misunderstood in certain quarters. In refuting the "vengeance" comment ("retribution" might equal-ly well have been used), some West Indian cricket supporters have firmly rejected the notion while, in the same breath, pointing to the living hell served on the 1975–76 West Indians in Australia . . . This was precisely the point.'

But if the West Indies needed confirmation that they were going to be greeted in England more like rampaging barbarians than conquering heroes, they only needed to look as far as the UK's other major cricketing magazine, *The Cricketer*. Former England Test all-rounder (and son of Sir Len) Richard Hutton had just taken over as editor. He was feeling his way, but it was clear that his sympathies did not lie a million miles away from those of Frith. His June editorial read:

> The key question is how those who pay the admission money will react to another one-sided series, in which the tactics of one of the protagonists are likely to have ugly tendencies. There is a depriva-tion about much of West Indian cricket, both of opponent and spectator.
>
> Almost 300 (i.e. 12 per cent) of Australia's total runs (during the 1990–91 series) came in extras, which is far from the bonus it might appear to be. Overall the West Indies bowled 141 no-balls and con-ceded 85 leg-byes. Leg-byes are symptomatic of ill-directed bowl-ing, which when delivered at West Indian pace virtually denies the batsmen an opportunity of scoring from the bat. Of even greater

deprivation is the no-ball, the late calling of which under current regulations makes it unlikely that the batsman can change his stroke. Unpunished no-balls are an evil. They disrupt the flow of the game, waste time and kill cricket. No-balls bowled by the West Indies amounted to 23.5 overs of dead cricket and, at their unacceptable over-rate of 12 an hour, equated to a total time wasted of two hours. This wastage is duplicated if opposition bowlers are as prolific. When no-balls were called on the back foot a batsman would be disappointed with less than a boundary. Crude arithmetic, therefore, would point to Australia, admittedly ignoring their own transgressions, having been deprived of around 400 runs, which over the course of a series is the difference between losing and being prevented from winning.

Cricket lovers should be equally enraged by the consistent objections of the West Indian Board to host countries' proposals to make cricket more appealing to the spectator. For an organisation whose domestic cricket is insolvent and which depends for survival on shared funds generated from its overseas tours such a stance is unlikely to be well received.

There is much to admire about the athleticism of the West Indian fast bowling, but little aestheticism. Classical principles no longer apply. Their bowlers look inside the arm rather than over the left shoulder. The open-chested approach from an angle wide of the crease puts the ball on a nasty line and closes down the off-side. The extinction of the out-swinger, with the inexplicable exception of Marshall, reduces the game to one side of the wicket.

The over-rates during the 1991 series were slow, by both sides, and the Windies still bowled as many no-balls as they had in the Caribbean. However, the two sides got along famously, the bouncer barrage never appeared except at The Oval in the fifth Test (more of this later) and all five games were well attended. The crowds in fact flocked to one of the most exciting and evenly fought series in years, with England winning the first and fifth Tests, the West Indies the third and the fourth. But the Windies' critics remained convinced that this series was an aberration and stuck to their guns. The result of the mounting pressure against the Windies' 'style' of play was the imposition of the 'one-bouncer-an-over' ruling.

So, what exactly are the West Indies accused of? The case for the prosecution seems to divide into three allied, but distinct, accusations. The first is that they rely on violence rather than skill to win Test matches. Endless short-pitched balls mean that those batsmen who aren't carried off injured start to fear for their lives and then become a softer target for the pace quartet.

The second charge is that the Windies bowlers attempt to gain an unfair advantage over opposing batsmen by maintaining a pathetic over-rate. This has the twin effect of reducing the scoring opportunities of opposing teams and of keeping the fast bowlers fresh. The Windies are also accused of 'depriving' both opposing batsmen (and the paying public) by failing to control the number of no-balls and virtually unreachable leg-side deliveries they bowl.

The third charge is less specific than the others. It is that by always relying on four fast bowlers, the West Indies have made the game less interesting to watch. They are accused of killing off variety and encouraging the neglect of swing, seam and spin bowling.

These are the 'bare bones' of a case that is often dressed up in the kind of emotive language that David Frith used in his 1991 editorial. Just as West Indian commentators such as Michael Manley would claim that the success of the pace quartet has given the socially and economically deprived areas of the Caribbean a rallying point, so its critics accuse it of helping destroy a once beautiful game and of encouraging a Black v. White split in world cricket.

Of the three charges levelled against them it is the allegations of intimidation that provoke the fiercest response from the Windies' critics. England's arrival in the Caribbean for the 1994 tour of the West Indies was greeted by the *News of the World* with a sports page splash headlined 'Bloody Windies! England tour of terror'. The article, by David Norrie, detailed the list of injuries inflicted on batsmen by the pace quartet and began: 'Mike Atherton's troops landed last night in the bloodiest battlefield in the sporting world.' And, for once, many in the conservatively inclined British cricket establishment would have found themselves agreeing with the views of a tabloid newspaper.

In the middle of the 1991 series between England and the West Indies, the English delegation to the International Cricket Council succeeded, at the second attempt, in restricting the number of bouncers in an over to one per batsman. A bouncer was defined as a delivery passing over the shoulder of the batsman 'standing upright in his crease'. Before this change in the law, it was simply left to the umpires to decide if a bowler was trying to intimidate a batsman.

The introduction of the new bouncer rule was accompanied by a ruling linking the failure to average 15 overs an hour to a system of stiff fines. Many in the Caribbean believed that, after over a decade of West Indian dominance, the other Test-playing nations had finally decided enough was enough and made a conscious decision to shift the balance of world cricket. In other words, they believed that the two decisions had little to do with improving the quality of cricket played at Test level, but were instead directly aimed at reducing the effectiveness of the pace quartet. Some outside the Caribbean (including Imran Khan) openly agreed with this conspiracy theory, but there was much greater agreement that the West Indies' unbeaten record might now come to an end.

The one-bouncer-an-over rule was introduced on 1 October 1991 and lasted three years before it was repealed. During that period the results of the three Test series and two one-off games the West Indies contested were:

v. South Africa 1992 (at home)

M	W	L	D
1	1	0	0

v. Australia 1992–3 (away)

M	W	L	D
5	2	1	2

v. Pakistan 1993 (at home)

M	W	L	D
3	2	0	1

v. Sri Lanka 1993 (away)

M	W	L	D
1	0	0	1

v. England 1994 (at home)

M	W	L	D
5	3	1	1

In total the West Indies played 15 Test matches, winning 8 of them, drawing 5 and losing only 2. More significantly, they maintained their record of not having lost a series since 1980. The win over Australia had been set up by a controversial one-run victory in Adelaide, but they destroyed the home side in the final Test to secure the rubber and in every other series they were in commanding form from beginning to end.

The Windies appeared to take the new regulations in their stride and were marching on to new successes. But they had failed in one area and that was to successfully adapt their game to the new over-rate regulations. The increased use of Carl Hooper still did not prevent the Windies incurring heavy fines in most games for breaching the new regulations.

Some greeted the West Indies' continuing success by claiming that the bouncer ruling was not that restrictive. In theory, it still allowed hundreds of bouncers in a day's play. Of course, the actual number bowled was much less, and more importantly the ruling removed much of the 'surprise' factor from the short-pitched ball. Once the batsman had received his 'one for the over', he could 'relax' for the remainder of the six balls. As a tactical weapon the bouncer's effectiveness was much reduced, but the Windies' results during this five-year period seem to suggest that the pace quartet could maintain their dominance over batsmen without relying on it. The individual records of the pace quartet tell a slightly different story.

West Indies fast bowlers (1 October 1991–1 October 1994)

	M	Ov	Mdns	Runs	Wkts	Av	Difference between average prior to 1/10/91
C.E.L. Ambrose	15	648.5	202	1377	79	17.43	−5.7
I.R. Bishop	7	247.5	53	607	30	20.23	−0.35
W.K. Benjamin	8	272.2	77	687	25	27.48	+5.79
K.G. Benjamin	7	233.5	45	728	26	28.00	*
A.C. Cummins	3	45	8	144	5	28.80	*
C.A. Walsh	15	561.4	132	1482	48	30.88	+5.93
B.P. Patterson	2	66	5	232	2	116.00	+89.96

*Kenny Benjamin and Anderson Cummins both made their débuts after 1 October 1991

Ambrose and Bishop have had no trouble at all dealing with the new playing restrictions; indeed, during the last four years Ambrose has become more a force of nature than a mere bowler. Patterson's two games during the early 1990s make a sensible comparison impossible, although with speed as his main (some would say only) weapon the bouncer rule would perhaps have affected him the most. Of the two bowlers whose performance did noticeably decline during this period, other factors appear to have had a greater influence. Winston Benjamin had an impressive start to his Test career and gained a bowling average which flattered his talent. He was never one of the Windies' front line fast men until Marshall's retirement and Bishop's injury problems created new opportunities for him. His average during the three years from October 1991 perhaps gives a better indication of his ability. In any case, of all the West Indies quicks, Benjamin uses the bouncer least and would therefore be less affected by the new restrictions.

The decline in Walsh's performance is potentially the one to which critics could most reasonably point to support their claim that, without the indiscriminate use of the bouncer, West Indies fast bowlers become significantly less effective. But in Walsh's case it is possible to plead mitigating circumstances. The tall Jamaican had operated as the stock bowler in the Windies side for the majority of his career. He had also been carrying a weak Gloucestershire attack almost without a break since 1984. The introduction of the one-bouncer rule coincided with the retirement of Marshall, the recurrence of Bishop's injury troubles and the failure of Patterson to establish himself as a first choice member of the pace quartet. By default Walsh found himself moved up from second change to sharing the new ball with Ambrose. At the age of 29, Walsh had to forget seven years of bowling to contain and switch to all-out attack. It was not his natural game; Gloucestershire captain David Graveney had after all called him the best old ball bowler in the game and it showed.

Walsh's performance is therefore a red herring and it remains a fact that the top flight West Indian pace bowlers were able to operate within the new restrictions without it affecting the quality of their performance.

It did not take long for most Test-playing countries to realize that they had made a mistake by introducing the ruling. Former Pakistan captain and ex-ICC member Imran Khan, for example, had always been against it, arguing that a similar rule in county cricket had helped undermine the ability of English batsmen to play fast bowling. Many thought that it actually encouraged the use of the bouncer, with every bowler of over medium-pace thinking that, as he was now restricted to only one bouncer an over, he was damned well going to use it. It also put the umpires in a difficult position. If a bowler was managing to intimidate a batsman while only bowling him one bouncer an over, umpires knew that they were on shaky ground if they intervened. They still had the power to step in if they thought intimidation was going on, but how would they justify the action, in the media glare which accompanies most international games, if the bowler had appeared to follow the letter of the law on short-pitched bowling? The one-bouncer-an-over rule also did not make any allowance for the ability of the batsman ... and it had not stopped the West Indies.

Australia, as well as the West Indies, had always been unhappy with the one-bouncer rule, former Australian captain Ian Chappell fearing that it would be a 'formula for tedium' as medium-paced trundlers replaced unfairly penalized fast bowlers. In July 1994, following a proposal by the Australian delegation, the ICC replaced the one-bouncer-an-over law with a new ruling. Under the new law, short-pitched bowling is deemed 'unfair' if by its 'length, height and direction' and its 'repetition', it is likely to inflict 'physical injury on the striker'. This definition of unfair bowling will be applied 'irrespective of protective equipment and taking into account the relative skill of the striker'. Under the new regulations a bowler can deliver a bouncer at the same batsman twice an over, with any subsequent delivery passing over the shoulder of the batsman being called as a no-ball.

The new rule puts the ball firmly back in the umpire's court. It will require him to exercise his judgement as to when the batsman is in danger. Critics of short-pitched bowling, such as David Frith, claim that this is very unlikely to happen. Instead Frith says: 'The reality will almost certainly be that the bully boys, their whining pleas having been met, will ping away to their hearts' content.'

Whatever the outcome of the new ruling, the move must be applauded for removing the question of intent from the umpires' deliberations. Under the old ruling an umpire had to decide whether the bowler intended to 'intimidate' the batsman. In other words the umpire had to decide whether a bowler was thinking as he ran into bowl: 'If I give him one up the hooter, will he be scared of my bowling?' It is after all impossible to intimidate somebody who is not scared of you. Today the umpire only has to read his own mind: 'Is the bowling of *this* bowler at *this* time likely to injure *this* batsman?'

But the linking of the intimidation/injury and bouncer rules is a relatively irrelevant one when it comes to the West Indian pace quartet. Although the Windies fast bowlers do use over-shoulder-height bouncers to unsettle batsmen, they are perfectly capable of unsettling them without getting the ball above chest height.

Most non-West Indian fast bowlers tend to bowl the majority of their deliveries to two very different lengths. Their stock ball will be pitched on or just outside off stump, passing the batsman about half-way between knee and hip. If the batsman was looking too comfortable on the front foot, the bowler will deliver a bouncer designed to bounce at head height over the stumps. This will occasionally be followed by a yorker if the batsman stayed rooted on the back foot.

The stock ball for the West Indian pace quartet, if left untouched by the batsman, will pass over the off or middle stump at a height level with the batsman's stomach or chest. This is what is known as a 'West Indian length'. The Windies stock ball would not necessarily be pitched that much shorter than the stock ball of, say, an Australian or English fast bowler, but the extra pace combined with the height of the bowler means that it is likely to bounce higher. For the West Indian fast bowler to produce a wicket-taking ball which would be sure to hit the stumps, he must bowl a yorker. But this is a high risk strategy: if he pitches the ball a little too full, he will deliver a full toss; if a little too short he serves up a nice juicy half volley. No bowler wants to do this, a Windies fast bowler least of all.

There is a real fear among West Indian fast bowlers such as Marshall that 'people won't think much of you' if a batsman is able to drive them freely. There is no doubt that many West Indian fast bowlers react to emphatic front of the wicket shots as if they were a direct slur on their manhood. Hooks, pulls and cuts are all right because they are the counter-punch to blows of the bowler. But in the West Indies, a clinical front foot shot is often seen as a sign that a quick bowler has not proved himself fast enough and that the batsman is now comfortable enough to commit himself to front foot shots early enough to make them effective. Speed, of course, is rightly worshipped in the West Indies and to have your ability to bowl 'fast enough' questioned by repeatedly being driven off the front foot can be highly damaging to your reputation.

There have been non-West Indian fast bowlers who have bowled a West Indian length, such as John Snow and Jeff Thomson, and they have usually been singled out some time during their careers as 'headhunters'. However, former Australian captain Ian Chappell is not alone when he describes these deliveries as 'just a damned good ball', whose outlawing would be difficult and unfair.

The critics of the West Indies pace quartet have been motivated by all sorts of reasons – a belief that the game was being devalued, a concern for the safety of batsmen, jealousy and racism being among them – but the debate has been fuelled not by the bouncer, but by the Windies stock ball. The stock ball from a West Indian fast bowler, if the batsman fails to either hit it or get out of the way, will probably hit him somewhere between the thigh and the chest rather than crashing safely into his pads. The 'likelihood of injury' when facing this type of bowling is therefore sharply increased and if you have four West Indian fast bowlers playing in one team then the 'danger' moves up another notch.

This is why the bouncer rule as far as the West Indian fast bowlers go is a red herring. The most consistently dangerous ball they bowl is *not* the bouncer, which most accomplished Test batsmen will see early enough to duck, but the ball that explodes from a length to strike a player in the chest or throat. To cut down on the number of injuries suffered by batsmen facing West Indian fast bowlers, the ICC would have to pass a rule insisting that the majority of deliveries should pass the batsman below waist height.

Many would claim that there is a historical precedent for taking steps to curb the threat of physical injury to players from fast bowling, citing the aftermath of England's notorious Bodyline tour of Australia in 1932–3.

Pelham Warner, ironically the manager of the English team which introduced Bodyline, was later to condemn the tactic, declaring, 'One of the strongest arguments against this bowling is that it has bred, and will continue to breed, anger, hatred and malice.' Many would argue that the Windies pace quartet were guilty of engendering similar feelings in their opponents. Cries of 'Bodyline!' can still be heard from crowds at Test matches the world over in which the West Indies are taking part. For these ill-informed loudmouths, any bouncer or short-pitched delivery which causes a batsman some discomfort is a product of Bodyline bowling. But Bodyline involved much more and in its impact was a world away from the tactics employed by the West Indian fast bowlers.

A batsman facing a Bodyline attack would find every ball pitching on the leg stump and bouncing from short of a length to pass him shoulder high. All but one of the fielders were placed behind square on the leg-side in what was known as the leg trap. The inner ring of fielders running from short square leg to leg slip were there to catch deflections from defensive shots, while the outer ring from deep square leg to deep fine leg were positioned to snaffle attacking shots. The length and direction of the bowling meant that it was highly risky to play any shot in front of the wicket and almost suicidal to play any off-side shots at all. For the bowlers, the peculiar nature of the field meant that it was impossible to vary the length and the direction of the attack. The only possible variety was the odd pitched-up delivery on the leg stump in an attempt to bowl a batsman behind his legs.

Bodyline was also a completely defensive method of bowling: it was primarily devised to stop Don Bradman scoring, not to get him out. With two notable and famous exceptions, any batsman who tried to attack the bowling was soon dismissed. This meant that the batsman had little choice but to wait until three Bodyline bowlers (Larwood, Voce and Bowes) tired or the English captain Jardine, seeing that the batsmen were not prepared to take any risks, switched his plan of attack.

This kind of stalemate does not happen when the West Indian pace quartet are operating. Batsmen are restricted in the choice of shots they can safely play, but they do have a choice. And, unlike the Bodyline attack, the great majority of deliveries are not directed at the leg stump, but on an off or middle stump line in an attempt to secure a snick to the wicketkeeper or slips. Look at any batting chart of a lengthy Test innings against the West Indies and you will see that, although the majority of scoring shots are square of the wicket and perhaps 60 per cent are on the leg-side, there are plenty of signs of strokes in front of the wicket and through the off-side.

The rule changes which followed the Bodyline tour were directed at restricting the number of fielders behind square on the leg-side, not with curbing short-pitched bowling. The legislators of the 1930s realized that it was the restrictive field placing that posed the greatest threat to the game's standing 'as a fair contest', not the short-pitched bowling, and amended the rules accordingly. They could have quite easily destroyed Bodyline by banning short-pitched bowling (regardless of whether it was directed at the leg stump or not). But they did not, recognizing it as a legitimate part of the game. As Mike Gatting said, when we asked him whether the injuries he had suffered against West Indian fast bowlers preyed on his mind when he went in to bat: 'If you're worried about getting hit by the ball, you shouldn't be playing Test cricket.'

But what about the argument that the restriction of short-pitched bowling is justified on the grounds that it reduces the physical danger faced by the batsman? We are not about to follow the macho line that physical danger is 'an essential part of the game', but the possibility of injury has always been present in cricket. Would the people who argue against short-pitched bowling in the 1990s have protested at the legalization of overarm bowling in 1864? This was the moment in the game's development when the *real* danger of a batsman being struck on the upper body was first introduced. And why is the banning of short-pitched bowling any more legitimate than replacing the traditional cricket ball with something made of a softer material? After all, cricket is virtually alone in sport in asking the striker to risk injury by placing his body in the direct flight of such a hard object. In baseball, for example, the striker has to stand away from the ball in order to get enough room to swing his bat.

Not for one moment would we suggest that no West Indian fast bowler has ever gone too far and deliberately tried to hit a batsman. These are men who need plentiful reserves of aggression to do their job properly and even the mildest of off-the-field characters, such as Michael Holding or Courtney Walsh, suppress that side of their character while play is in progress. This has always been the way with fast bowlers from the days of the 'Demon' Spofforth onwards. Former West Indies captain Viv Richards readily agrees that some West Indies fast men had a mean streak which sometimes got out of hand, although he claims he never encouraged it.

Holding's view of the intimidation debate is typical of most members of the West Indian pace quartets: 'It would be naïve and misleading of me to claim that I never bowl bouncers without trying to intimidate the batsman. On the contrary, I want him to be aware that if he gets on to the front foot against me he might find himself in trouble – in other words he might get hurt. But that is quite a different thing from actually *wanting* or *intending* to hurt him. I have no desire to hurt anyone. But I do want to get batsmen out as quickly as possible, and if that means pitching a few in my half of the wicket in order to keep him on the back foot, I – like any other fast bowler – will do what the law and the umpires allow. The flatter and slower the wicket, the more important it is for the fast bowler to let the batsman know that he mustn't feel safe on the front foot'.

Holding does admit that there have been times when the West Indian pace quartet have 'overdone the short-pitched bowling' (although he was only ever once warned by an umpire for intimidation). However, even if the Windies pace men are deliberately trying to injure or intimidate the batsmen, which 99 per cent of the time they are not, rather than simply using the short-pitched ball as a tactical weapon, attempting to reduce the physical threat posed by the West Indian pace quartet by dramatically restricting short-pitched bowling would be both an inconsistent and a counter-productive move.

There is no doubt that such a ruling would cut down on the number of injuries and it would probably force the West Indies to abandon their pace quartet strategy and start to pick spinners. But to many it would set an uncomfortable precedent for the future governance of the game by radically altering the way in which the players from one of cricket's spiritual homes play the game. The bouncer and the short-pitched ball in general are part of any West Indian's cricketing life from the moment he can pick up a bat or a ball. This is a result of a cocktail of sporting tradition, natural exuberance, culture and physique.

Former England fast bowler Bob Willis tells the tale of sitting with Michael Holding watching England all-rounder Chris Lewis limbering up before resuming his innings during the 1994 series in the Caribbean: 'Chris

Lewis was practising on the edge of the field and getting one of the England guys to throw the ball slowly at his head so that he could practice ducking. Michael just fell about laughing! He could not believe that someone was practising ducking! If you go and watch Red Stripe or club cricket in the West Indies they bowl two or three bouncers an over and the batsman is just trying to hit them out of the ground. That is why the West Indies will say, when they see a batsman in trouble against the short ball, "Why doesn't he try and hit the ball?" '

The combative West Indian attitude towards fast bowling is best expressed by the 'Master Blaster', Viv Richards: 'A fast bowler thinks that because he has got a ball, he is the most aggressive person on earth. I always thought that I had a bat, and that's my form of defending myself. You get the stare and the glare from fast bowlers. Lillee used to do it a lot. But if you stayed there long enough, there was only going to be one winner. The bowler has to turn around and walk back to his mark. He has to be the one to break eye contact and walk away. You can just stand in your crease and let your eyes bore into his back.'

In other words, Richards thought he could turn the tables on any fast bowler who was trying to 'intimidate' him. That is the West Indian way of playing cricket and has been since the start of the century. It is no wonder that Richards has little time for players who complain about short-pitched bowling from the Windies quartet.

'I was never intimidated by any fast bowler. I always thought that, even if I was hurt, it would be while I was doing something I thoroughly enjoyed. You do care about getting hurt, but you tend not to worry too much about it. You must think to yourself, "I am tough enough to stick this out." I think that is what is wrong with some Test cricketers who fail against the Windies. They are just not tough enough, they are not willing to grit it out.'

Viv Richards himself had only limited exposure to the bowlers who made up the pace quartet, but he experienced enough to understand the challenge facing Test batsmen from other countries. He faced most of the great West Indian fast bowlers in English county cricket, but there they were operating on their own. A sterner test was provided by domestic cricket in the West Indies, where teams such as Barbados (whose bowling line-up in the late 1970s was Garner, Clarke, Daniel and Marshall) and Jamaica were often able to field a Test-class fast-bowling attack. These games were often played at the end of long overseas tours to Australia, New Zealand or the Indian sub-continent and Richards was conscious that he was 'not always able to give of his best'. His record against Barbados at the end of the 1991 season was 22 innings, 601 runs, average 27.32. Against Jamaica it was only a little better, his 653 runs against the island being scored at an average of 34.36.

He scored just four centuries and three 50s in a combined total of 41 knocks against the twin homes of West Indian fast bowling, so had a strong incentive to moan (while not on Test duty) about the methods of Garner, Marshall et al. But he never has, nor has he moaned about the tactics employed by any fast bowler.

In fact, on some occasions he has actively encouraged them. During the third Test of the West Indies' 1979–80 series against Australia, Aussie fast bowler Len Pascoe decided to sort Richards out. Now, Pascoe was a genuinely aggressive character whose eagerness to get rid of the batsman 'one way or the other' often boiled over into something approaching madness. Early in his spell during the West Indies' first innings, Pascoe unleashed three consecutive bouncers at Richards. 'That'll be enough, Lennie,' said umpire Max O'Connell, only for Richards to shout from the other end of the pitch, 'Don't stop him, Max.' Pascoe, naturally enough, went ballistic and in the process completely lost control. Richards scored 76 and Pascoe disappeared at the rate of six an over.

Ban the short ball and in all likelihood the game's popularity within the Caribbean would begin to crumble, not because the Test team started losing, but because the West Indian way of playing the game had been changed 'unnaturally' from outside. If that happened, cricket would lose its last stronghold on the American continent and the rolling tide of Coca-Cola culture would sweep on.

Insisting (for example) that the majority of deliveries must pass the batsman below chest height would directly interfere with a way of playing the game that has developed organically in the West Indies as a product of the climate and culture. The same approach might see the banning of Pakistan's swing bowlers, Indian and Sri Lankan spinners, and English seamers. All have skills which are products of their physique, climate, culture, and their country's cricketing 'style' and 'knowledge' and which give them an advantage over their opponents. But are they 'unfair' advantages? Obviously not. But why then were there calls to ban the googly as South Africa's quartet of leg spinners won game after game against England in the run-up to World War 1? The googly was unplayable, said its critics, it would destroy off-side play (a charge also levelled at the swing bowling of George Hirst and Fred Root), and leave uncertain batsmen dithering and strokeless as they wondered which way the ball was going to turn. Of course the googly had no such effect, but the debate it provoked of unfair versus fair is always much easier to decide in retrospect.

Any game which is strong enough to cope with changes as dramatic as having the bowler switch from underarm to round-arm to overarm deliveries is strong enough to cope with one country's unusually deep pool of fast-bowling talent. The game may change because of the fast bowlers' influence and it might not be as attractive as the game it replaced (although we would disagree), but any sport which does not evolve will soon be deserted by the two sets of people who sparked and encouraged that evolution: the game's innovators and its most ardent fans.

There is one final factor that underlines how inconsistent and illogical a decision to ban short-pitched bowling would be. No one has yet satisfactorily explained the difference between Holding's desire to make sure that the batsman doesn't feel 'safe' on the front foot and the pull, sweep or cut shot which a batsman uses to scatter a ring of close fielders. Both are replying to the tactics of their opponent (be it a batsman playing repeatedly off the front foot or a bowler attempting to dismiss a batsman by bowling to a close-set field) by making it clear that unless there is a change of plan somebody will get hurt. The batsman or bowler concerned does not want to hurt his opponent, but he is being thwarted in his ambition to score runs or take wickets and is well within his rights to respond within the laws of the game.

If the tactics of the Windies pace quartet are 'unfair' then, after over a decade of dominating international cricket, it would not be surprising to find that their Test opponents would have little respect for them. But that is simply not the case. You will struggle to find an experienced Test batsman of the 1980s or 1990s who thinks that players such as Malcolm Marshall, Michael Holding and Curtly Ambrose were anything other than great bowlers. Indeed, as Tim Curtis readily admits, most players have 'total respect' for the members of the pace quartet

That is not to say that the arrival of the pace quartet did not shake up the ranks of the world's best batsmen. From his position at square leg for the West Indies, Vanburn Holder could see that the batsmen were 'a bit unhappy, a bit uncomfortable' when they first encountered the twin attack of Michael Holding and Andy Roberts. At times during the 1976 series against India and the following tour of England, Holder for the very first time 'felt sorry' for the batsmen of the opposing team as they struggled to cope with the short-pitched assault of the pace quartet. His summary of the situation is pithy and to the point: 'It was so quick, they couldn't play it.'

But, nearly 20 years later, that surprise element has gone and the batsmen of the world have a pretty good idea what they are in for. Batsmen don't exactly rub their hands together in glee when faced with the prospect of combating the pace quartet, but they do recognize it as the ultimate test of their technique and temperament.

Most of these batsmen dismiss without a second thought any allegation that the Windies bowlers were trying to intimidate them. They admit to being apprehensive when faced with the likelihood of attempting to combat the quartet on an uneven wicket, but in most circumstances they recognize that, for the West Indies, the throat ball is a tactical weapon they will use sparingly in order to retain the surprise element.

Graham Gooch, public enemy number one as far as the pace quartet is concerned, is well aware that on anything other than a featherbed, the pace quartet is unlikely to waste many deliveries by bouncing them over the batsman's head, but that on flat wickets the short-pitched ball is used as a major part of the game plan. To prove the point he refers to the fifth Test during the 1991 West Indian tour of England.

The game was played on a typically flat Oval wicket, and the Windies quartet of Ambrose, Marshall, Walsh and Patterson recognized that they would have to rely on the short ball to unsettle the batsmen. The best example came in England's second innings with the home side attempting to score 146 to win the match and draw the series. Even on the fifth day the pitch was perfect, but with England's score on three, Patterson produced a ball which leapt from just short of a length at Hugh Morris's throat before jamming his fingers against the bat handle and flying through to Dujon.

Gooch, who scored 60 and 29 in England's five-wicket victory, remembers that there were 'probably more bouncers bowled during the first session of that match than during the rest of the series put together'. He instantly dismisses the idea that the Windies are bouncer-happy, claiming that only 'very flat wickets' are likely to produce a torrent of short-pitched bowling. In the Windies' view, the groundsman has chosen to shift the balance in the favour of the batsmen and this makes it legitimate for them to use every method at their disposal to even out that balance. There are unlikely to be many experienced Test bowlers from any country who would disagree.

Tim Curtis agrees with Gooch's analysis. He describes the members of the Windies quartet as 'shrewd cricketers, who only use bouncers when it suits them'. In his four Test innings against the quartet, Curtis says that he received few bouncers because players such as Marshall and Walsh, who had played against him in county cricket, knew he was a courageous and technically correct player of short-pitched bowling. They realized they had a better chance if they pitched the ball up and, as Curtis remembers, 'they were right'.

In fact, Curtis goes so far as to say that many English Test batsmen tend to worry about being hit by a West Indian fast bowler more when they meet them individually during county games. In a Test match the threat is so ever-present that most experienced players will become accustomed to the possibility of being hit and therefore learn successfully to block it from their minds. In a county game, a batsman will constantly be thinking, 'I wonder if Sylvester Clarke is playing today' or 'I'll stay down at this end for two more overs; they'll have to give Holding a rest soon'. In a Test match, most batsmen will steel themselves to facing down the pace quartet. In county cricket, all but the toughest players will be hoping to avoid the opposition's West Indian quick and therefore are unlikely to be as mentally well prepared when they see Wayne Daniel or Joel Garner rushing to the wicket. The very contrast between the speed of the West Indian bowlers and their English county team-mates is also likely to provide a sharp reminder of the potential physical danger the batsman is in as the first throat ball explodes from the pitch.

If any batsman has reason to resent the use of the bouncer by the West

Indian fast bowlers it is Mike Gatting. The Middlesex and former England captain was the victim of one of the most macabre dismissals in international cricket, out hit wicket after a ball from Malcolm Marshall had removed part of his nose. Marshall's bouncer during the first one-day international of England's 1986 tour of the Caribbean had hit Gatting square between the eyes on the bridge of his nose. When Marshall went to retrieve the ball, he found it covered in blood and with a piece of Gatting's nasal bone wedged into the leather. The fast bowler, sickened by the sight, reeled away and left the fielding to one of his colleagues. Gatting was forced to return to England for surgery and ended up missing all but the fifth and final Test of the tour. However, despite the gruesome injury the bouncer inflicted, Gatting places no blame at all on Marshall and appears remarkably unaffected by the whole episode.

'It wasn't a very good wicket and it probably wasn't a very good shot. Miscalculations happen and unfortunately this one had an unpleasant result. But I didn't change my game after I got hit. Maybe I'm a bit more watchful, but you can't play any differently or alter your whole attitude to the game just because you got pinned.'

Another who, it might be thought, would bear a grudge against the West Indian pace quartet is England and Warwickshire opening bat Andy Lloyd. Lloyd made his début on the international scene during the West Indies' 1984 tour of England. Picked for the three one-day games which preceded the Test series, he did well and was an automatic selection for the first Test. His Test career lasted around 30 minutes. A Marshall bouncer, skidding through low as usual, cracked Lloyd just above the right temple. Lloyd soon discovered that he could not see properly out of his right eye and was forced to leave the field. He suffered from blurred vision for about six weeks and was forced to miss the entire 1984 English season. Lloyd never again rediscovered the form that had won him his England place.

But Lloyd, like Gatting, does not blame Marshall: 'The only time batsmen have trouble with short-pitched bowling is when the bounce of the ball is not "true". It may seem that the West Indies appeared to bowl excessively short at times during the series, but the England batsmen only found themselves in trouble when the bounce was uneven. Surely it's the pitches that must be watched and regulated, so that they produce an even bounce, rather than an over-strict regulation of short-pitched bowling.'

It is a point also strongly made by Michael Holding: 'On good cricket wickets with an even bounce – no matter how fast they may be – people generally do not get injured. Barbados, Perth, Brisbane and Madras all come to mind as good Test wickets in recent times. You can bowl flat out on these pitches and feel that you are unlikely to hurt anyone. Nor is the bouncer likely to be much use except as a surprise ball. If you want fewer injuries in cricket – and of course we all do – look neither to the laws, nor to the bowlers – look instead to the groundsmen.'

Gatting also dismisses the notion that the Windies use the bouncer in an indiscriminate manner, but neither does he think they bowl it as 'a last resort'. The former England captain has seen many of his team-mates come under fire from the pace quartet, but in each case he had the feeling that the bowlers (and their captain) were operating to a 'plan' which was instigated following careful thought. The plan might be triggered by a number of factors such as the state of the wicket, the state of the game, or the reaction of the batsman to an exploratory bouncer or two. And it is not only nervous defensive play that might get a batsman a working-over. Gatting has seen players such as Robin Smith and Ian Botham look to attack early bouncers, not seem totally in control of their hook shot and then be fed short-pitched balls until one proves fatal. As Gatting says, 'They'll take any batsman on.'

One factor that can spark a bouncer assault from the pace quartet is when a tail-ender sticks around for a couple of overs and it is the use of bouncers against tail-enders that has brought some of the heaviest criticism down on the heads of the pace quartet. The West Indian fast bowlers tend to have little patience against tail-enders since they are used to knocking over a side's last four wickets very quickly. England's John Emburey confirms that it doesn't take too long for a lower order batsman 'to get one up the nose'.

Bob Willis admits that he was 'terrified' when he faced a West Indian fast bowler. Particularly unnerving was Wayne Daniel: 'I thought that, with all the effort and strain that "Diamond" [the nickname given to Daniel by his Middlesex team-mates because of his value to the side] put into his delivery might mean that he would let slip an unintentional head high full-toss.'

The commonest complaint levelled at the tactics adopted by the Windies fast bowlers against the tail-enders is that they bowl few yorkers, the traditional way of dismissing batsmen with poor technique. However, this ignores the fact that the defensive technique of lower order batsmen has improved markedly over the last 20 years. The arrival of one-day cricket, in which all 11 players are expected to be able to score at least 20 runs if called upon, has meant that players such as Devon Malcolm, who are complete mugs with the bat, are few and far between. Even supposed rabbits like Peter Such have shown the ability to bat defensively against Test-match bowling for over an hour on more than one occasion. The West Indian fast bowlers realize this and know that, if they don't force tail-enders on to the back foot, they are likely to suffer the same frustration as other Test sides.

The only exceptions to the West Indies fast bowlers' dislike of the yorker have been Joel Garner and Curtly Ambrose. However, they often used the block hole ball because their great height made it especially difficult to pick up the ball's flight. Both the pacemen used the yorker consistently against all types and qualities of batsman. In fact Ambrose is more likely to bowl a yorker at front line batsmen with a high back lift (such as Graeme

Hick or Graham Gooch) than he is against Angus Fraser or Phillip DeFreitas.

John Emburey says that the Windies fast bowlers will often reserve a first ball bouncer for tail-enders who are known either to be particularly timid against short-pitched bowling or for their stubborn rearguard actions. Sometimes, especially with experienced Test opponents, the West Indian fast bowlers will perform a double bluff and keep the batsman guessing by saving the bouncer for the second, third or even fourth ball. For many lower order players the nervous tension created waiting for this first 'surprise' bouncer is enough on its own to force them into making a mistake. The members of the pace quartet appear to have an encyclopedic knowledge of how most tail-end batsmen play the bouncer. This 'forearming' is particularly a problem for English players who come up against individual members of the West Indies' Test attack week in, week out on the county cricket circuit.

Research by Dr Michael Biddulph at the University of Nottingham suggests that a short-pitched delivery from a front line West Indian fast bowler will take roughly half a second (490 milliseconds (ms)) to reach the batsman. Top class batsmen, through a combination of talent and experience, often need as little as 120 ms to react against this kind of delivery. This gives them a safe margin for error even if they wait until the ball has pitched (after roughly 240 ms). However, tail-enders on average take around 320 ms to react and their inability to gauge correctly how high a short-pitched delivery will bounce can have them fending desperately at a head-high ball or ducking into another which they could have safely defended.

However, although Emburey admits to being 'intimidated' by the West Indian fast bowlers, it is *not* by their use of the bouncer: 'They bowl just short of a length and you know you are not going to get any half-volleys because of the fields that they set. You are prepared to hit everything off the back foot, but gradually they start to pitch the odd ball up and very quickly get you lbw or caught behind. They are very intelligent bowlers and you know they are not going to give you too many balls to hit. In particular they gave you nothing to drive. You couldn't score, which meant you couldn't get away from the strike. That was intimidating.'

One thumping drive off the front foot by a tail-ender is usually all it takes for the pace quartet to decide to teach the batsman a lesson. But they do not always use the bouncer to make their point. Devon Malcolm struggled to cope with Courtney Walsh during the closing stages of the first Test on England's 1994 tour of the Caribbean after unleashing a few forceful front foot shots. Walsh went round the wicket and fired delivery after delivery into Malcolm's body, the ball rarely bouncing above waist height, but it nearly always avoided the batsman's tentative defensive prods and struck him repeatedly on the body. Tim Curtis, watching the game on television, thought it 'wasn't too clever' and a rare example of the Windies fast bowlers going over the top (David Frith thought it was 'obscene'). But Walsh was indignant, declaring, 'How is it possible to intimidate somebody below the waist?', adding that he had 'never aimed a ball at anyone in my life'. In this case it was the angle of the delivery, and the fact that Malcolm kept turning his back after the ball was bowled, which was causing the batsman problems. It is the pace quartet's stock ball which causes tail-enders most difficulties and this again underlines that the majority of intimidation allegations arise from the pace quartet bowling a standard 'West Indian length'.

The pace quartet's attitude towards tail-end batsmen is also coloured by their own batting pretensions. With the exception of Patrick Patterson, almost all the West Indian fast bowlers believed they were placed a couple of places lower in the batting order than they should have been. There was much competition between members of the various quartets as to who would bat at No. 8 behind one of the two Murrays or Dujon. Once that spot had been filled then the remaining three players would battle it out for No. 9 and so on. Because the members of the pace quartet take their batting so seriously, they do not expect any special treatment from opposing bowlers. They do not seek revenge for bouncers bowled at them (though that normally comes in the natural flow of events), but just accept it as part of the game. This is one of the reasons why Walsh reacted in what appeared to be such an off-hand manner to the battering he gave Devon Malcolm. Comments such as 'The man had a bat to protect him' may seem callous given Malcolm's batting prowess, but all Walsh was doing was expressing the widely held West Indian belief that, if a player wants to play Test cricket, he must expect no quarter. In their eyes, the fact that Malcolm constantly turned his back on the deliveries directed at him from around the wicket by Walsh was stupid and undignified.

None of the West Indian pace quartet (even Patterson) would have played Walsh's bowling that way and Malcolm's actions (especially as they came from a West Indian fast bowler, albeit one playing for England) caused them some embarrassment and even anger. They would stand up and try to play those deliveries, so why didn't he? Even a first ball snick to the wicketkeeper was better than this show of incompetence and apparent lack of nerve.

The West Indies bowlers have also had to contend with the improvement in protective clothing which has emboldened many tail-enders faced with a rampant fast bowler. However, there are many in the West Indies who believe that the widespread use of helmets and protective clothing has actually reduced the ability of batsmen to face down the pace quartet.

Viv Richards never wore a helmet, even when batting against his West Indian team-mates, and he believes that many of the batsmen who were 'not willing to grit it out' attempted to gain some grit by wearing one. In his eyes this was and is 'the wrong reason' for wearing a helmet because, as he explains, the Windies pace men soon realized that many of the batsmen who came to the wicket encased 'in a suit of armour' were not wearing all the protective gear simply to stop themselves being injured, but to give them the courage they naturally lacked. This realization immediately gave the West Indian bowlers a psychological advantage over the batsman – something Richards was determined never to do – regardless of the speed of the bowling.

In Richards's view the amount of protective clothing worn by modern batsmen against even the extreme pace of the Windies quartet has got 'totally out of proportion'. He traces the root of the problem back to the Packer 'Circus' when the established (mainly Australian) Test batsmen contracted to take part suddenly found themselves facing half a dozen very quick fast bowlers from the West Indies, South Africa and Pakistan, and panicked. For many of those players, wearing a helmet was 'totally out of character' and, according to Richards, has led to today's situation in which batsmen walk to the wicket expecting to be hit and having covered themselves in protective clothing for that eventuality. They are resigned to 'soaking up the punishment', rather than attempting to avoid it as good players from Bradman to Richards have always done. Many other commentators, including former Australian captain and brilliant hooker Ian Chappell, have claimed that many of the injuries inflicted by the West Indian fast bowlers are the result of the slow reactions of a player whose sight line is obscured by a grille and who is mentally hiding behind what he hopes is an impenetrable forcefield.

But there is a counter-argument which claims that improving protective gear has dramatically cut down on the number of injuries inflicted by fast bowlers, particularly those from the West Indies. And the statistical evidence would seem to support this.

Injuries caused during Test matches by fast bowlers*

	Bowlers from		
	The West Indies	The rest of the world	Total
1979–81	5	9	14
1982–4	10	9	19
1985–7	6	8	14
1988–90	5	3	8
1991–93	1	4	5
Total	27	33	60

*Only injuries which prevent players from batting (sometimes only temporarily) during a match are counted

This table seems to suggest that Test cricket has become much safer over the last 10 years. Injuries to players were four times higher in the years

1982–4 than they were during 1991–3 and the number of injuries caused by West Indian fast bowlers has shrunk by 90 per cent. The one-bouncer-an-over rule might have something to do with the decline in injuries during the early 1990s, but the trend appeared to have been well established by then, despite the ever-increasing number of Test matches.

There might be other factors associated with the fall in injuries, such as the number and quality of fast bowlers playing during each period. *But what is plain is that intimidation rapidly appears to be becoming a non-issue.*

The number of injuries inflicted by fast bowlers from outside the Caribbean is a reminder that it is not always the West Indian bowlers who have taken the initiative in adopting hostile bowling tactics.

This has been especially true in the case of the Australians. Before the West Indies' 1984–5 tour of Australia, former Test wicketkeeper Rod Marsh issued the war cry which has been repeated endlessly during the Caribbean side's period of dominance. It was time to 'fight fire with fire', he said, time to 'crack a few skulls'. Marsh claimed that since the Australians knew they were going to get their fair share of bouncers, they should get their retaliation in first and be prepared to take the punishment the West Indian quartet would allegedly dish out in return (especially to the Aussie quick men).

Marsh's comments were quickly rubbished by Richie Benaud and Ian Chappell. West Indian captain Clive Lloyd was simply puzzled, saying: 'It's amazing when they finish playing what they end up saying. He [Marsh] never said that when he was playing. All of a sudden brutality comes into it. We just want to play good cricket. I think it is rather silly, really. We are going out to play cricket in the right manner. We are not setting out to injure people.'

Despite Chappell's warning that in a head-to-head confrontation between the two countries' fast bowlers, the West Indians would come out on top, the Australians went into the first Test with four pace bowlers – and they lost the match by an innings and 112 runs. At the end of the series (which the West Indies won 3–1), three Australian batsmen had been forced to retire hurt, against one West Indian, and Benaud said the home side had no one to blame but itself since it had set the terms for the series.

Perhaps the last word on the contentious subject of intimidation should come from a 'neutral' observer, doyen of Test umpires Dickie Bird. Bird claims that he is happy with the onus placed on the umpire by the rules attempting to curb potentially dangerous bowling. In over 20 years as a Test umpire, Bird has only had to warn a handful of fast bowlers for intimidation and in the majority of cases the 'unfair' play has stopped right there. He describes the one-bouncer-an-over rule as 'farcical', believing the umpire already had sufficient power to curb intimidation.'

Bird also believes that short-pitched bowling, within reason, can add to the game's spectacle. 'The short-pitched delivery is a legitimate part of the fast bowler's armoury and it would be wrong to deprive him of it as long as it does not get out of control. It would take away *the most exciting spectacle in the game* [our italics], and that, at a time when desperate attempts are being made to lure spectators to cricket grounds, would be entirely counter-productive.'

If supporters of the West Indian pace quartet can be relatively sure of rebutting most criticism about their alleged over-use of the bouncer, they are on considerably less secure ground when it comes to defending their over-rate. The West Indies do (in general) bowl their overs more slowly than any of their opponents. The calculations used to show this usually ignore the facts that the West Indies bowl more no-balls (of which more later) and take more wickets than their opponents which tends to (naturally) slow down their over-rate. Nevertheless there does seem to be a case to answer.

There is little problem in justifying the tactical use of slow over-rates. If the Windies bowl at 13 overs an hour, their opponents can cancel out any advantage by doing the same (as England did during their 2–2 series against the Windies in 1991). And, of course, the Windies did not invent the slowing down of over-rates for tactical reasons; that is normally attributed to Len Hutton during the 1954–5 tour of Australia when he relied on the three-pronged pace attack of Tyson, Statham and Bailey. But what about the poor paying spectator? In the Caribbean there is little concern over the issue. The Windies keep winning after all, but the over-rate also suits the 'soon come' attitude prevalent on most of the islands, and many supporters are so busy discussing the finer points of the last delivery that they don't complain if the next doesn't come along for a minute or so. It is not too much of an over-statement to say that most West Indian cricket supporters consider the issue of over-rates an irrelevance. But that is not the view of most of the game's professional observers in the rest of the world, particularly in England.

Significantly, over-rates and the West Indies' slow progress first became an issue during their 1980 tour of England. During this series a combination of bad weather and slow pitches meant that four of the five Tests were left unfinished. However, it was the rate at which the West Indian fast bowlers got through their overs that received most of the blame, at least from English commentators.

Many overseas players believe that the English are obsessed with over-rates for no good reason, pointing out that English county cricket has the highest over-rate targets in the world and one of the poorest attendance records.

Former Pakistan captain Imran Khan, for example, is convinced there is little connection between falling crowds and slow over-rates. 'The two best series that I have played in were against the West Indies in Pakistan during 1986 and the Caribbean two years later (both of which finished 1–1 with one game drawn). During both those series there were times when the over-rate fell to about 12 an hour. This was partly due to the long run-ups of fast bowlers and partly due to the hot conditions, especially in the West Indies. Yet at the end of the series there was not a single complaint about slow over-rates from the crowd or the media. The quality of cricket provided was of such a high standard that no one even noticed the over-rates.'

Imran attempts to support his case by pointing out that a year after Pakistan's ding-dong battle with the West Indies in the Caribbean, his team took on Australia at home. Over-rates during this series (between two high-class sides) reached 19 per hour. But the cricket was, surprisingly, of a poor quality and the series was scheduled outside the normal Pakistan cricket season. The result? Empty stands. Imran points out that in India, where over-rates often climb above 20 an hour with sides fielding three or even four front line spin bowlers, Test match crowds have declined since peaks reached in the 1970s. He also notes that on the few occasions that atten-dances have been poor during series featuring the West Indies, the reason might have rather more to do with familiarity breeding apathy than any-thing else. For example, the Windies' 1988–9 series in Australia attracted disappointing crowds. But whereas the West Indies had only toured Australia three times between 1961 and 1975, they made a further seven trips during the next 14 years. Of course, the West Indies had won all the series during this period and Australia, of all cricket-watching nations, does not care to watch losers, unless it is Australia inflicting the defeats.

West Indian commentator Tony Cozier agrees with Imran's conclusions and points out that when India boasted its great spinning quartet of the 1970s (racing through the day at more than 20 overs an hour), they rarely drew large crowds outside their own country.

Former West Indies captain Clive Lloyd is adamant that the various attempts over the last 10 years to insist on a compulsory number of overs in a day is nothing more than 'an attempt to reduce the effectiveness of our pace attack'. From a physical fitness point of view, Dennis Waight believes that, if the authorities persist with their over-rate clampdown, the Windies, out of sheer necessity, will be forced to develop spin bowling. Certainly the issue began to assume a high profile during the period from 1982 to 1984, when the West Indies (and some would say their pace quartet) was at its strongest. The first crunch point came at the ICC's 1982 meeting when a proposal to limit the length of a bowler's run-up was outvoted. The next crisis point came just before the West Indies' 1984 series against England, when the English Test and County Cricket Board asked the West Indies Cricket Board of Control to agree to a minimum number of 96 overs in a day's play. The West Indies (who were in the middle of a run of 11 straight Test match victories) refused and won the series 5–0. Four years later they did agree to a minimum of 90 overs a day and still won the series 4–0.

Lloyd argues that insisting on a set number of overs a day means that batsmen will know they only have to bide their time against the fast bowlers before they are taken off and replaced by a spinner to improve the over-rate. Lloyd and Imran Khan both agree that, if over-rate quotas are rigidly enforced, fast bowlers will be restricted to short spells and/or shorter run-ups, hindering their effectiveness and preventing them from developing their game. Interestingly, Lloyd claims that fast bowlers who learn their game in the West Indies Red Stripe competition, where there are no over-rate targets, develop more stamina than those brought up in English county cricket, where there are, because their spells are not artificially terminated by concerns about the over-rate.

But over-rate targets do not only hinder the development of fast bowlers, according to Lloyd. He claims that 'spinners are also unable to take their time in returning to their mark and thinking about where they will be pitching the next delivery. We hardly see anyone in the modern game flighting the ball; experimentation is almost extinct.'

Lloyd's argument is essentially that over-rate targets do not encourage good bowling or good bowlers. He contends that, instead of trying to attract bigger crowds by promising a set number of overs, administrators should instead create interest in the game by concentrating on ways of improving the quality of the players involved.

Lloyd's call for 'quality', not 'quantity' is echoed by the leading bowler of his period as West Indian captain, Michael Holding. The graceful fast bowler argues that an over-rate target 'encourages robotic rather than enthusiastic participation by the fielding team'. And as far as attracting crowds go, Holding has a simple answer: 'If the paying public are so upset with the quantity of cricket in a day during any Test series played by the West Indies, they certainly don't show it by keeping their money in their pockets and staying away. However one-sided the Test series may have been, the stands have still been sold out in advance. It is the anticipated quality of cricket that brings people piling through the turnstiles, not just the prospect of seeing a lot of overs bowled in a day.'

Many of the West Indies players also claim that they would be happy to bowl their overs at a faster rate if some way could be found of cutting down on the fiercely packed programme of matches they are expected to play. The West Indies are always in demand as world champions and are rarely idle. If they are not involved in fully fledged Test series, they are likely to be taking part in one-day tournaments such as Australia's annual World Series or the growing number of one-off mini world cups organized in and around the Asian sub-continent. The West Indian bowlers might be expected to get their rest between May and July, when most nations do not play cricket. But of course most members of the pace quartet will be taking part in English county cricket, expected to turn out for 17 four-day county championship matches, 17 Sunday league games, and as many Benson & Hedges and NatWest trophy games as their team qualifies for. Fred

Trueman may have bowled over 1000 first-class overs in an English season, but with one-day cricket included, the workload of a West Indian fast bowler taking part in county cricket as an overseas recruit would not be far short of that. And Fred was able to enjoy the odd winter off, and long, relaxing cruises at the beginning and the end of overseas tours.

Of course the West Indies fast bowlers are unlikely to want their income reduced to the same degree as the number of games they are expected to play. This means that they will want to be paid more per game and this adds another dimension to the problem.

The Windies appear to believe that asking them to bowl at anything more than their 'natural' rate (i.e. between 12 and 15 an hour) would reduce the 'quality' of their cricket. They also claim that quality has made them world champions and this is what draws the crowds. And it is true that it is highly unusual to hear crowds complaining about the over-rate, if the cricket is good. Of course, some would argue that, after 15 years of West Indian fast bowlers taking 45 seconds for each delivery, they don't know any better. And the Windies would also claim that if they did speed up their over-rate the only result would be that they would defeat most sides inside four days and some inside three, therefore depriving spectators of up to two days' full cricket and the administrators of up to two-fifths of their potential takings.

But are quality and quantity as mutually exclusive as the West Indies claim? Obviously not, as they believe they could speed up their over-rate if they did not have such a heavy workload. And it does seem that the Windies are picking up bad habits. In the early 1980s the quartet of Roberts, Holding, Garner and Croft were able to maintain an over-rate of between 14 and 15 an hour. By the early 1990s, the quartet of Marshall, Ambrose, Walsh and Patterson had slipped to between 12 and 13. In the final analysis it will be up to the spectators to decide on the merits of the West Indies' argument. If they feel they are being short-changed they can stay away. West Indian cricket relies almost exclusively on the money earned from both Tests and one-day internationals. If takings from these games started to decline dramatically, and the invitations to visit the 'big-money' countries of England and Australia started to come less frequently, then change would come pretty quickly.

The Windies believe that they are simply playing their natural game, which unfolds at under 15 overs an hour. Although their argument about too-demanding targets affecting the quality of the game holds some weight, it does seem that they have become a touch lazy over the years: 15 overs an hour is close to the natural rhythm of West Indian cricket; 12 is not. But perhaps any team which remained champions of the world for over 15 years and did not become that little bit arrogant would hardly be human. If spectators believe that 'laziness' has got out of hand then it is up to them to show their displeasure by not coming to the games. In this context the administrators' constant pressure to improve over-rates by the use of fines is almost irrelevant. The International Cricket Council appears to have set a reasonable benchmark of 90 overs a day. It is now time for them to devote their energies to other, more pressing issues (such as encouraging the game in Africa, and combating the increasing popularity of American sports in the Caribbean and Asia) and let the 'paying public' pass judgement.

The Windies use much the same argument over the bowling of no-balls that they do over the question of over-rates. In Clive Lloyd's words, no-balls are 'almost inherent in the repertoire of fast bowlers'. And, given the fact that the West Indian quartets are composed of out-and-out fast bowlers, their no-ball record does not seem that bad. Compare their record to that of South Africa in their 1970 series against Australia, for example. In that series South Africa's three leading wicket-takers (Peter Pollock, Mike Procter and Eddie Barlow) were all fast bowlers. In the two games in which Barlow played the largest part, South Africa conceded 32 and 23 no-balls respectively. Prior to the 1960s, fast bowlers bowled fewer no-balls because the back foot no-ball rule was easier to comply with.

However, the West Indies *do* bowl more no-balls than their opponents and because of the speed of their bowling, the no-ball call often comes too late for the batsman to take advantage of it. This situation does favour the Windies, but to penalize them just because their bowlers have learnt to bowl fast hardly seems fair. The correct solution to the problem would be to revert to the back foot rule. This is a rule change supported by Sir Donald Bradman, among many others, for a number of reasons. But one of the main attractions of a change would be that umpires would be able to call no-balls quickly enough for the batsman to react, even when facing the West Indian quartet.

The third main charge against the pace quartet – that the West Indies by relying solely on four fast bowlers have impoverished the game both tactically and aesthetically – is perhaps the most damning and the least explored.

It is claimed that the success of the West Indian pace quartet has encouraged other Test nations to try to pack their sides with fast bowlers, and to ignore the claims of spin bowlers. Certainly the sight of a Test team taking the field with four pace bowlers and no front line spinners is much more common than it used to be. However, the current South African team – which incidentally was greeted in England by the mainstream cricket press with almost unalloyed joy despite the fact that their game-plan is based on utilitarian batting and unrelieved fast-medium bowling – is the only side consistently to play a pace quartet. All the other Test nations have remained relatively loyal to the preconception of a 'balanced' side.

True, when faced with the competing claims of a spinner and pace bowler of apparently equal ability and experience, the modern Test selector is more likely to opt for the fast man. Picking a fast bowler instead of a spinner is often seen as the 'safe option' and the best way to avoid press criticism should anything go wrong. But this scenario has more to do with the insecurity of selectors from other Test nations – and the Windies pace quartet can hardly be blamed for that. After all, their own selectors displayed the courage of their convictions by rejecting convention and playing four fast bowlers. When selectors from other countries have stuck to their guns and picked their best bowlers regardless of their type (e.g. the pairing of May and Warne during the 1993 Ashes series) they have usually benefited.

We live in a safety-first age and the pace bowler is seen as the safest bet, but again the Windies are hardly to blame for this. The real culprits are likely to be a mixture of one-day cricket, heavy bats and seamer-friendly wickets. It is these factors that have meant that the last 25 years, while being a golden age for fast bowlers, have produced very few high-class spinners.

There is only one clear-cut case of the success of the West Indies pace quartet influencing another Test side in an unhealthy fashion. After India's success in the 1983 World Cup (in which they defeated the West Indies, Roberts, Holding, Garner and Marshall included, in the final), India went pace mad. In the cup-winning skipper, Kapil Dev, India already had their first Test-class fast bowler since Mahmood Nissar and Amar Singh in the mid-1930s. India had always craved a strong fast-bowling attack and, even though the cup-winning quintet of Dev, Sandhu, Madan Lal, Binny and Amarnath was hardly fearsome, they believed that the future for the country's Test team lay in copying the West Indies. For most of the rest of the decade, India picked a series of pace bowlers (who were really nothing more than medium-paced trundlers) in the hope that they would turn out to be a second Kapil Dev. None of them did, but in the mean time talented spinners such as Maninder Singh had their careers constantly disrupted.

English cricket has also been prone to this belief that the discovery of a set of high-quality fast bowlers would be the Test team's salvation. But rather than arising from a desire to imitate the West Indies, this belief is based on some vague notion of wanting to return to a golden age when England had fast bowlers popping out of coal mines all over the country. In truth, English cricket has produced perhaps two dozen world-class fast bowlers in the last 120 years and there have been great stretches (1905 to 1925 and 1945 to 1954 for example) when England had no Test-class fast bowler, and plenty of others when it has had only one.

Despite this, the search for a set of bowlers to match Trueman, Statham and Tyson remains as strong as ever, and it has been given a new edge by the growing into maturity of the children of the Caribbean immigrants of the 1950s. England now had its own chance to have its own West Indian pace quartet if it chose. However, the selectors have largely resisted this temptation and, for example, Lawrence and Malcolm never played in the same Test team. The English selectors have wisely decided not to try to copy the West Indians and the most successful Caribbean immigrant to play for England has turned out to be Phillip DeFreitas, a classic English fast-medium swing and seam bowler.

Another area in which the West Indies pace quartet is alleged to have had a malign influence is in the amount of short-pitched bowling Test batsmen have to face. There is no doubt that some sides have attempted to engage the West Indies in a bumper war. But as they have nearly always come off second best, the more intelligent (such as Craig McDermott) have studied the Windies' tactical use of the bouncer and taken a more level-headed approach.

There are also more out-and-out fast bowlers playing Test cricket now than at any time – during 1994, for example, the West Indies regularly fielded four, Pakistan and Australia three, and England two – so this will increase the amount of short-pitched bowling in Test cricket as a matter of course. True, the success of the Windies quartet (and other fast bowlers in the 1970s, 1980s and 1990s) may persuade medium-pace bowlers (such as Brian McMillan) to try out a short-pitched delivery. But, in most cases, if a bowler can deliver a good bouncer he will bowl it regardless. If he doesn't, but still insists on pitching short, he will be hit out of the attack and eventually dropped from the side. If your average county seamer is bowling more bouncers now than he has done in the past, this is again more likely to be the fault of poor-quality wickets which make this kind of delivery hard to play. How many times have we seen an English fast-medium bowler brought up on under-prepared county pitches repeatedly banging the ball half-way down a Test pitch, cancelling any chance of swing or seam and getting caned into the bargain?

The only reason that these sorts of bowlers might try to kid themselves that they can emulate the Windies fast bowlers is that the wickets they normally bowl on deceive them into thinking that they are the next Holding, Marshall or Croft. Their Australian counterparts, for example, brought up on wickets of even bounce, soon realize that they had better leave the bouncers to the fast men and concentrate on perfecting the arts of swing and seam. A perfect example of this came in 1993's England v. Australia clash at Headingley. The pitch, for once, was a batsman's paradise and Australia scored 653 for 4 declared in their first innings. England went into the game with one fast bowler and three medium-fast seamers. When Allan Border declared after reaching his double century, the figures of the three medium pacers read: Ilott 51 overs, 11 maidens, 3 wickets for 161 runs; Caddick 42 overs, 5 maidens, no wicket for 138 runs; Bicknell 50 overs, 8 maidens, 1 wicket for 155 runs. When England batted they were dismissed for 200 and 395, losing by an innings and 148 runs. Their chief destroyer was Paul Reiffel, a typical English-type seam bowler. Keeping the ball up to the bat he took 8 wickets, 2 bowled, 2 lbw and 3 caught behind or in the slips.

But what about matches actually involving the West Indies? Are they poorer spectacles and less 'good' as games of cricket because of the Windies' reliance on four fast bowlers? The Windies' supporters would argue for a start that, since their team are the most dominant world champions cricket has ever known, any game they are involved in is going to be highly charged. The sight of the world's best annihilating even weak opposition is usually worth watching, even if it is a case of simply marvelling at the ruthless application of the skills which produce their dominance. It was precisely this sort of fascination that packed stadiums wherever the Harlem Globetrotters played. The result was not in doubt, the attraction was in seeing how it was achieved.

'Aha', say the critics. 'Our point exactly. The West Indies win in a way that is ugly, vicious and boring. All you get is four fast bowlers pounding in over after over, banging down bouncer after bouncer. Their bowlers display little skill (and no variety), just brute strength *and* they take five minutes to bowl six balls. And you can't even enjoy yourself by watching the batsman, because those few balls he can hit will nearly all be short and on the leg-side, severely restricting his range of strokes.'

The issues of over-rates and intimidation have been dealt with earlier in this chapter, but what about the accusations of a lack of variety and skill, and an essentially defensive bowling strategy?

The skills of the West Indian pace men are examined in depth elsewhere in this book, and here it is only necessary to say that bowlers such as Roberts, Walsh and Marshall could bowl almost any delivery to order, while even such a relatively uncomplicated bowler as Croft had a command over a leg-cutter that few of his contemporaries in Test cricket could match. The idea that the number of leg byes conceded by the West Indies is the result of bad bowling is also ridiculous. The large number of leg byes results from the sheer speed of the Windies quartet which means that the ball will cannon off the batsman's pads at great speed. Some of the West Indian fast bowlers might occasionally concentrate on the leg stump, but they do this for tactical reasons. As any Test batsman will tell you, the Windies front line fast bowlers combine great speed with unerring accuracy.

Variety is another matter and, although most quartets contain four fast bowlers of a quite different type, they are still all fast bowlers. But here again the West Indies would put forward the quality argument. Who would you rather watch: the rather ordinary spin or medium-pace bowlers who make it into some Test teams, or four bowlers, all admittedly of the same type, but in near total command of their craft? Variety is an attractive feature of any bowling attack, such as those possessed by Australia or Pakistan, but while the Windies struggle to find a world-class spin or medium-pace bowler then they would argue that their four-fast-bowler strategy still provides the better entertainment. It is also worth making the point that the sight of Holding or Ambrose rushing to the wicket is still one of the greatest visceral thrills in cricket and one which is not dulled by repetition.

The West Indies' strategy for dismissing opposing batsmen is based on frustrating those players who can cope with the initial onslaught of pace and movement. This is a very disciplined method of attack and the bowlers carry it out ruthlessly. This can lead to periods during Test matches where both batsmen and bowlers are on the defensive. Test matches are a serious business, played for high stakes, and these periods are often highly absorbing for the connoisseur, but they do not make pretty watching. But such periods rarely last for long, as either the batsmen get on top of the bowling or, more commonly, a wicket falls and the West Indies go on the attack.

The West Indies are also often accused of being 'negative' because the majority of the balls delivered by their fast bowlers bounce too high to hit the stumps. If you accept the argument that the sole aim of bowlers is to hit the stumps then this criticism cannot be denied. But it is obviously not. The rules of cricket also allow batsmen to be dismissed if they hit a ball which is caught on the full toss. The West Indian quartet have simply taken a legitimate decision to concentrate on the second mode of dismissal. And, if truth be told, it is a decision that has been taken by most modern bowlers (faced with the difficulties of circumventing the modern lbw law and the improved defensive technique of the *average* first-class cricketer), as well as some of the giants of the past (W.G. Grace included). No intelligent bowler (unless he can command enormous swing or spin such as Waqar Younis or Shane Warne, George Hirst or Arthur Mailey) concentrates on trying to bowl out front line batsmen; the odds are too much stacked against him. He is much more likely to take an approach which extends his chance of getting a dismissal. The approach adopted by the quartet is an extreme one, but that does not make it negative or unfair.

As for opposition batsmen being restricted in the range of shots they can play, this is one charge to which the Windies fast bowlers would plead guilty. *It is their job to dismiss the opposing batsmen.* If they can best achieve this by keeping the ball away from front foot or off-side strokes then that is what they will do. It is up to the batsman, they would say, to make them change their game-plan. And, as Graham Gooch for one has shown, this is not impossible. Simply because an examination is difficult does not automatically mean that it is unfair.

9 | Setting the record straight

> I wonder if any team in any sport has been subjected to such an orchestrated campaign of defamation as the West Indies has had to endure for so long.
>
> Michael Holding

IN THE eyes of many, West Indian fast bowling is a cancer eating away at the heart of cricket. It is, say the critics, a brutal and simplistic corruption of a once honourable profession; it is an unacceptable reflection of our violent times; it is a boring, repetitive spectacle; it restricts the range of shots open to batsmen; it wastes time; it drives away the crowds and appeals only to the basest instincts of those who stay to watch. The sooner the West Indies fast bowling production line grinds to a halt the better.

What rubbish!

Whether or not the West Indies continue to produce world-class fast bowlers on a regular basis, it would be a travesty if the past 20 years were to be remembered for the negative images promoted by critics of the quartets. The skills of the West Indies pace quartets are one of the best-kept secrets in cricket. Despite their unapproached achievement in keeping their team at the top for 15 years, little has been written before on how and why they have been able to accomplish this. Imagine the millions of column inches and the hours of air-time that would have been devoted to an England or even an Australian side which had achieved the dominance the West Indies pace quartets have brought their side over the last 15 years. Roberts, Holding, Garner, Marshall, Bishop, Daniel, Clarke, Croft, Ambrose and Walsh were and are great bowlers. Imagine the endless eulogies if England had produced Tyson, Snow, Statham, Trueman, Loader, Bowes, Voce, Farnes, Larwood and Willis all in the last 20 years. Surely it would have been a 'Golden Age', not a 'reign of terror'.

The West Indian pace men mastered the art of fast bowling, one of cricket's most demanding disciplines. They allied their talent with an individual and collective intelligence to win hundreds of games, many against the odds. Contrary to popular opinion, the Windies did not steamroller over all opposition. Countless times, they found themselves staring defeat in the face, either in a match or a series. Usually, it was the fast bowlers and their ability to raise their game that snatched a draw or, in many cases, a victory for the Caribbean side. The challenge they posed for batsmen meant that any long innings played against them often assumed the mantle of greatness: Dennis Amiss's 203 at The Oval in August 1976; Graham Gooch's 153 and David Gower's 154 not out at Sabina Park in April 1981; Kim Hughes's 100 not out at Melbourne in December 1981; Sunil Gavaskar's 236 not out at Madras, December 1983; Allan Border's 98 not out and 100 not out in Trinidad, March 1984; Graeme Fowler's 106 at Lord's in June 1984; Kapil Dev's 109 in Madras, February 1988; Dean Jones's 216 at Adelaide, February 1989; Mark Waugh's 139 in St John's in 1991; Gooch's 154 not out at Headingley in 1991; Andrew Hudson's 163 at Bridgetown in April 1992 – these were all memorable largely because of the quality of the bowling they had to overcome.

There were also brilliant heroic knocks by Allan Lamb, Robin Smith, Salim Malik, Mohinder Amarnath and Dilip Vengsarkar. Try to compile a similarly lengthy list of 'great' innings played against England, Australia or any other Test-playing nation during the last 20 years. Not so easy, is it?

It is not unreasonable to suggest that around half of the greatest innings played in Test cricket during the 1980s were in games involving the West Indies.

The world's batsmen soon grew to realize that the pace quartet was the ultimate test; no batsman could be considered truly great by his peers unless he had scored a century against the West Indies. They were and remain the benchmark for modern Test cricket.

It is a point rarely recognized by those who grew up watching cricket in the 1940s and 1950s, like many of the English game's leading commentators. This was a point brought home during England's 1994 tour of the West Indies. At Sabina Park in Kingston, Jamaica on the third evening of the first Test, Courtney Walsh unleashed an aggressive and lightening-fast assault on the English top order batsmen. Four wickets went down, two of them to Walsh, including that of England captain Mike Atherton who battled heroically for two hours to score just 28 runs. Walsh bowled plenty of short balls, some of which struck the batsmen on the body. *Wisden Cricket Monthly* editor David Frith said that Atherton had been 'brutalized' by Walsh. However, the English captain himself described the session as one of the most exciting he had ever played in. The pride in his performance was plain.

'To me that was Test cricket at its best. Two or three fast bowlers steaming in, and a game to be saved on a pitch you had to watch. I was devastated to get out. But I knew I could go home and look in the mirror, knowing I'd given of my best. It wasn't good enough – they got me out – but it was the most testing two hours I'd had against fast bowling in my life.'

Atherton was finally defeated when, in Walsh's 12th over, the fast bowler switched to round the wicket and had the England captain caught at short leg. The temperature was over 80 degrees, but Atherton reckoned that Walsh got quicker with every over. As the fast bowler returned to his fielding position on the boundary between overs, the crowd were keeping Walsh fired up with cries of 'Encore! Encore!'

Atherton's respect for Walsh was total. 'I'd have been furious with myself if I'd been 30 or 40 not out on that pitch and got myself out to a crap shot after being in two hours. But I have to give credit to the bowler. He changed his line and got his wicket. I hated getting out, but I knew I'd done my best.'

Alec Stewart, Atherton's vice-captain, was equally positive. 'It was great Test cricket,' he said. 'Walshy bowled brilliantly: quick and short at the batsman.'

Beyond the boundary, the West Indies pace quartet provides a focus for racial and national pride. For a people whose ancestry is founded in slavery, cricket allowed them finally to throw off their shackles and has also enabled them to resist the onset of American economic imperialism. However much the USA may view the tiny nations that make up the West Indies as a global backwater, the people of the islands need not feel second-rate. They know that the West Indies has established itself as the most successful exponent of one of the English-speaking world's most sophisticated games. As Tony Cozier says: 'We are not underdeveloped or third world in cricket.'

The reasons that the West Indies have had to suffer the 'orchestrated campaign of defamation' that Holding speaks of are numerous. The very fact that the West Indies pace quartet, despite their success, have received such little recognition is enough to suggest that their critics are motivated by more than a natural disappointment as England or Australia lose another series.

What rankles with many of the critics is the way in which the West Indies, while winning match after match, have dismissed some of the supposed eternal truths of Test cricket (that every side must have a spinner for example). By the very nature of the game in England and Australia (where most of the game's financial and therefore administrative power lies), those in a position of influence and access to the media tend to be highly conservative in their views. They see the extent of the Windies' unprecedented dominance as overshadowing the cricket of the 1940s and 1950s, the period during which they first came into contact with the game either as players or spectators and the one they have the most personal investment in. This nostalgia also means that they react strongly to a dominant West Indian side in particular. In their minds, the West Indies side should be full of brilliant but flawed players, as it was in their youth. Consistency, whether in results, in the production of fast bowlers or in a disciplined approach to the game, offends their patronizing view of what West Indian cricket should be.

But there are more worrying motives behind the criticism of the Windies pace quartet. The fact that the Caribbean side's success has been based on four 'big, black men' hurling hard objects at (mostly) white men is a

godsend to those who would increase racial distrust. Anybody with a working pair of ears, who has spent more than an hour in most of the clubs and
pavilion bars with the older generation who exercise an unhealthy and dis-
proportionate influence over international cricket, would know that the
stereotypes of black men (and women) are kept alive in their conversations.
A desire to return to the status quo which operated in the 1950s is not
restricted to the world of sport; it was also the time of the master–servant
relationship which saw English-educated gentlemen picking a white man,
almost regardless of his right to hold down a place in the side, as captain for
the West Indies team as late as 1959.

Critics constantly use words such as 'good' and 'evil' when referring to
the relative merits of the 'English' and 'West Indian' way of playing cricket
– just consider some of the examples given earlier in the book. There is also
the consistent use of words and phrases normally connected with inner-city
street crime in the description of games involving a West Indies team. Just
prior to England's 1994 tour of the Caribbean, *The Sunday Times* carried an
article on its sports pages (with the headline: 'Cricket, lovely cricket gets a
chance at long last') proclaiming: 'There is no need now for West Indians
to play the game at the limits of legality, ugliness and violence ... Helmets
and body armour alone have saved the game from death at the crease.'

A bouncer bowled by an Australian bowler will be 'nasty'; the same delivery from a West Indian quick will be 'ugly' or 'vicious'. A containing spell
by the same Australian bowler will be described as valuable to his side; a
similar performance by a West Indian quick will be described in terms of
'deprivation', both of the batsmen's ability to score or of the spectators'
enjoyment.

Interestingly, many of the fiercest critics of the West Indies pace quartet
have 'come to terms' with the fact that much of their success is motivated
by racial pride. 'All right,' they seem to be saying, 'You've made your point.
Now can we have our game back.' They completely overlook the fact that
the West Indies have changed the game for ever and that the part of the
game now characterized by the Caribbean temperament is becoming the
international game's dominant hegemony – witness the post-wicket celebrations of almost any modern Test side and compare them to the embar-
rassed handshakes of 20 years ago.

And despite the torrent of abuse directed at the West Indies pace quartets, they remain the envy of the cricketing world. As we saw in Chapter 8,
other Test sides have not slavishly copied the idea of a pace quartet, but
that should not disguise the fact that, from Melbourne to Manchester,
Christchurch to Cape Town, what most cricket supporters want their team
to possess is a successful fast-bowling attack. This desire is nothing new, in
fact it is as old as Test cricket itself. Even in India, the supposed spiritual
home of spin bowling, the constant cry is for a pace bowler to avenge
defeats inflicted by Lillee, Willis and Marshall. As Mihir Bose says in *A*

Maidan View, 'Ever since India made its entry onto the international cricket scene, it has been obsessed by the need for fast bowlers. Opponents repeatedly humbled India through pace, particularly Hall, Gilchrist and Trueman. Every defeat increased the Indian obsession for an avenging fire. The great Hindu goddess of strength is Kali and for almost 50 years Indians sought a Kali on the cricket field.'

During the 1960s and 1970s, a string of West Indian fast bowlers (Gilchrist, Stayers, King and Watson) were employed by the Indian cricketing authorities to 'find a fast bowler'. Just prior to the arrival of Kapil Dev the search reached an hysterical intensity, as Bose explains: 'The Indian press regularly carried stories of "lost" fast bowlers. Harrowing tales were told of how a promising fast bowler had been ruined by the misdeeds of the Indian Board. Even in the heyday of the great spinners, the Indian Board was criticised for not including a bowler who aspired to be quick. Sporting displays of fear are never pleasant and for Indians all the victories won by their spinners did not compensate for the terrible shame and humiliation inflicted on their batsmen by opposing fast bowlers.'

The desire to produce a fast bowler stems from the sheer uninhibited excitement that they can produce and the way in which they can sweep away an opposing side. As unlikely a champion as Robin Marlar was caught up in the fervour created by Devon Malcolm's nine for 57 for England against South Africa at The Oval in 1994: 'When a fast bowler is firing, there is nothing more thrilling in our sporting life. Not least because the perform-ance and sheer excitement of it continues for over after over, hour after hour.' That praise comes from a man who rarely saw fit to write about the West Indies quartet in such glowing terms and indeed often criticized them for relying on a bowling tactic which saw fast bowlers operating for 'over after over, hour after hour'.

So if everybody wants fast bowlers, why can't everybody produce them in any great numbers or with any consistency? In other words, why can't they do what the West Indies have done? In the early 1990s, we have seen the South Africans attempt to copy the West Indian approach to Test match bowling. In Allan Donald and Craig Matthews, they have two highly proficient quick bowlers, but while South Africa have achieved some success by using four pace men their record is still far behind that of today's West Indies team which is itself weaker than other Caribbean sides of the past 15 years.

It is not simply a case of picking four fast bowlers and rotating them until they dismiss the opposition. In their first Test after their readmittance to the world stage, South Africa pitted their pace quartet against the Windies version. Despite only having to score 201 runs for victory in their fourth innings and reaching 123 for 2 they lost by 52 runs. The South Africans have much of the talent, but they have yet to learn the discipline which allows a team to come back from the dead or hold on to victory: witness the three drawn series against Australia (home and away) and England. In all three series, their fast bowlers won the first match of the three-game rubber, but then could not maintain a consistently high level of performance.

As we have seen, the birth of the West Indies pace quartet was a response to many developments: political, cultural, financial and physical. Clive Lloyd was also fortunate to be able to tap into a natural resource of fast-bowling talent created generally by the tradition of West Indies quick bowling, and more specifically by the inspirational performances of Hall and Griffith. Lloyd was surrounded by young quicks like Roberts, Holding and Croft, and, as Michael Manley has pointed out, simply ignored spin bowling as a feature of his side because there was no worthy successor to Lance Gibbs. Since then, of course, a whole generation of West Indians has had only the best fast bowlers to emulate. It stands to reason that for every one of the pace quartet, there are more than a dozen attempting to model themselves on their hero. As a recent example Curtly Ambrose's success has led to at least two 'Ambrose clones' appearing in Red Stripe cricket.

And if emulation gains the ultimate of a West Indies Test place for a young pace-man, he is then instilled with a sense of the inheritance handed down by older fast bowlers. Once in the Test side, there are few of the petty rivalries and jealousies that reduce the effectiveness of many international sides. Once picked, the young West Indian fast bowler knows that, as long as he continues to make the most of his talent, he will be picked consistently. This creates a confidence in which secrets of swing, seam and other tactics designed to dismiss the world's best batsmen are freely traded.

During Viv Richards's captaincy, he followed Lloyd's tradition of open discussion in the dressing room: 'I wanted it to be like a debate and thought this would be a good thing for the general spirit of the team. I wanted each individual to make his point and be understood by the rest of the guys. We always study the opposition together, in extreme detail. We examine the weak points and plan how to expose them. I want each person in my team to know exactly what his job is, exactly what is expected of him and how that job relates to the other players.

'Some teams insist on building some kind of atmosphere of intimidation, so that the newcomers have to fight to gain respect. We have never believed in that. We like to nurture young talent. We try to gain their trust. We involve them in crucial decisions, we make them feel important and they seem to return that with total commitment.'

Also, as Michael Manley stated, Lloyd 'did more than employ four fast bowlers. He trained and moulded his players into the most awesome fielding side in history.' The athleticism of the West Indies players as a whole, and the fast bowlers in particular, is no accident despite their advantage of being (as Dennis Waight pointed out) 'loose-limbed' with an abundance of fast-twitch fibres. Their physical superiority owes more to the immense amount of effort put in by Waight and the bowlers themselves which has not assured immunity from injury but has ensured that, if they do break down, it won't be for long (Bishop excepted).

Equally, all the fast bowlers bar none realized they had to be disciplined and work hard to develop their craft, not least because of the unsympathetic conditions they faced in the Caribbean. Sir Colin Cowdrey has suggested that fast bowling is not a 'science', while spin bowling is. With respect this is nonsense. Bowling fast is not an easy career path to choose. At its best, quick bowling has to be a marriage between extreme physical fitness and cunning technique. Simply being able to bowl a cricket ball at 90 m.p.h. does not guarantee you an extended run in the West Indian Test team – just ask Patrick Patterson. Only by developing techniques of swing and seam, yorkers and, yes, bouncers, with the result that there is barely a wasted ball, have the West Indies bowlers come to dominate world cricket. No less a judge than Michael Holding says fast bowlers can be assessed not by the numbers of wickets taken but by the number of bad balls bowled. You won't find many of those from any member of the West Indies foursome. Again the bigots among the critics of the West Indian pace quartet find it unbearably galling that the greatest understanding of bowling craft will not now be found at Headingley or Lord's, but in Barbados or Jamaica.

The reason the West Indies have not received due praise for their outstanding record over the past two decades is largely due to the fact that they have gone on winning for too long. True, the highly regarded Australian sides of the 1930s also had an unbeaten record which lasted more than a decade but the relatively few Tests played, compared to the 1980s and 1990s, meant that their dominance was not perceived to be as overbearing. Almost every year for the past 15 years, the West Indies have been somewhere in the world winning a Test series. This, of course, makes their unbeaten record all the more remarkable but it also means that their critics cannot escape being constantly reminded of the Windies' superiority and many dislike seeing their sporting rivals enjoying consistent high-profile success. There is little possibility of opponents retreating into the fantasy that 'If we were playing them this year, we'd beat them.'

The same factor also colours the view of the individual fast bowlers and the pace quartet as a whole. Lindwall and Miller, McDonald and Gregory, Hall and Griffith, were on show in England and elsewhere in the cricketing world much less regularly than the West Indies pace quartet, all of whom also play English county cricket of course. It is hard to form the same romantic view that is attached to many of the most fearsome fast bowlers from before Packer cricket when, as is the case with the West Indians, a pace man is returning year after year to sweep away your national or county side.

In the view of most sports commentators, great sides are not usually meant to overstay their welcome: be it Liverpool Football Club, Wales's rugby union team, the Harlem Globetrotters – the West Indies cricket team. Series against the West Indies are often described in negative terms because they are one-sided, as if the Caribbean team were somehow acting unfairly in winning match after match. In England particularly, prolonged success is always treated with suspicion as Ian Botham will gladly tell you.

Another myth often heard when the West Indies are in town is that the use of four fast bowlers produces a joyless spectacle for the crowds as batsmen wage a grim battle against the quicks. But compare the average Test match crowd for a game in which the West Indies are taking part against a match involving any other Test side. In the Caribbean and in England, particularly because of the number of West Indians in the crowd, but also elsewhere, the dramatic way in which the Caribbean side play the game, either batting or bowling, tends to rouse the crowd to a state of high emotion. As Michael Holding states: 'The West Indies have had fast bowlers for donkeys' years but everybody wants to see us play. They wouldn't be asking us to play that often if we weren't attracting the crowds – and we haven't been taking spinners. Everybody wants to play the West Indies in their own countries because they know we attract the crowds. All sold out.'

The West Indies 1994–5 world tour involved trips to India, then New Zealand, back home to the Caribbean for a series against Australia and finally to England for an unprecedented six-Test tour. India, despite their recent spin-inspired success, and youthful and highly talented batting line-up, could not achieve a single invitation to play Test cricket overseas during the same period.

And it is not only the size of the crowd that the West Indies pull, but its nature. Bob Willis, England's former captain and pace spearhead, believes: 'Your average waiter in Barbados knows more about cricket than the average professional English cricketer.' The level of enthusiasm and knowledge displayed by West Indies supporters is infectious. The shouts of support for their team are soon matched by cries of encouragement for their rivals. Debates start across the terraces and although they often concern the bowling of bouncers they almost never touch upon the issue of over-rates.

In 1933, England played the West Indies at Old Trafford. The game was notable for some hostile bowling from Constantine and Martindale, and a fiercely determined century by England captain Douglas Jardine. It was the first exhibition of 'Bodyline' in England and although the wicket meant that it did not pose the same dangers to the batsman's health as in Australia the previous winter, as good a player of fast bowling as Wally Hammond found the pace too hot. And the crowd reaction? Well, according to the *Daily Herald*, they loved it. 'The crowd enjoyed it all. Far from being shocked, they were hugely entertained. And that is what 50,000 people paid good money for.' This was a generation of cricket-watchers brought up on Tate and Freeman, and here they were cheering a dramatic, no-holds barred contest between the West Indian fast bowlers and the English batsmen.

Fast bowling has always been the greatest crowd-pleaser. The intensity of action when a fast bowler is operating raises the pulse-rate in spectator and batsman alike. Even the most aggressive century from a Test batsman is likely to take at least a couple of hours. The drama of crashing, attacking shots will be punctuated by regular defence and undermined if the batsman loses the strike. A threatening spell of spin bowling is difficult for all but the most experienced spectator to appreciate fully with the naked eye. All most can see from the ring is a flurry of pads and bat as the ball turns past the edge. Fast bowlers operate under none of these disadvantages. They are theatre actors compared to the spin-bowling screen stars. They do not require the close-up to catch the crowd's attention. Everything they do – the run-up, the whirling bowling action, the leaping delivery, the reactions they provoke from the batsman and the diving catches by the slip cordon – happens on a grand scale. Fast bowlers 'project'. And although the connoisseurs may carp, it is a fact that the majority of paying spectators would prefer to see almost any fast bowler operate instead of all but the most deadly spinners such as Abdul Qadir, Derek Underwood and, especially, Shane Warne, the spinner with the fast bowlers' attitude and approach to the game.

The possibility of being bored at a Test match involving the West Indies appears to be a problem only for the professional commentator.

And what of the players themselves? Well, have the critics asked themselves why West Indian cricketers who are brought up on undiluted pace are among the most positive and 'happiest' players in the game? Some non-West Indian players have claimed that playing against relentless pace can be a numbing experience, but that is not what the West Indies' most successful opponent believes. Graham Gooch dismisses any thought of the West Indian quartet as 'boring'. As far as he is concerned, they are 'classic professionals' and he adds, 'People want to watch the best, don't they? Well, they are the best. Why is anyone complaining?'

If there were dozens of Lance Gibbs and Sonny Ramadhins languishing in Red Stripe cricket, then the critics would have some cause for complaint, but why should the West Indies play a second-rate spinner – reducing their chances of winning and providing less of a spectacle for the crowds – to pander to some spurious idea of a balanced attack?

The original idea of a balanced attack was not to fulfil some aesthetic ideal, but to give a team the best chance of winning a cricket match by being able to take advantage of the prevailing conditions such as the state of the pitch and the weaknesses of the opposition. In the early part of the century, where uncovered pitches and run-ups made it difficult for fast bowlers to operate, English county sides would regularly play three or four spinners and, before the legalization of overarm bowling, captains would take advantage of the rough wickets of the day to pack their sides with fast bowlers. Each was responding to the conditions of the time. The West Indies, by consistently playing four fast bowlers, are truer to the spirit of the game as it was devised as a competitive contest than Raymond Illingworth's knee-jerk call for a balanced side when he took over as England's chairman of selectors. In any case, Illingworth quickly realized that this was a trite point and soon reverted to the tactic which teams have followed for most of the game's history: picking the right bowlers for the right conditions, which in the 1990s usually means three fast or fast-medium bowlers and only one spinner.

The rise of the West Indies pace quartet has little to do with the demise of the spinner. The blame, as is usually the case, should be laid at the door of the cricket administrators whose support for the invidious lbw law, promotion of one-day cricket, covered pitches, failure to outlaw heavy bats and many other crimes against the art of slow bowling are the real causes. As usual, though, they encourage the search for scapegoats elsewhere and if, as usual, the blame is pinned to a group of individuals from a different country, a different class or with a different coloured skin they are unlikely to raise any protest.

The West Indies in fact are to be applauded for ignoring the illogical and historically nonsensical calls for a 'balanced' attack. They have consistently stuck to the policy of picking their best bowlers regardless of their type and therefore presenting to the paying spectator the greatest amount of cricketing talent they can muster in 11 players. It is that quality which people go to see at a Test match, not some poor shadow of a mythical sporting ideal.

Without that approach, the game loses its seriousness and relevance as a contest at the highest level. For most spectators, as long as they are confident that they are seeing the best sides the two can field, they will be content. Tacitly they acknowledge that, while they may see an hour's less play from a side featuring four world-class fast bowlers, they will enjoy more quality cricket from the West Indies in five hours than they would get from many other Test teams during an entire five-day match.

Tony Cozier believes that: 'Those who come to watch Test cricket – or Shield or county cricket for that matter – do not enter the gate expecting a guaranteed number of overs in the day or a guaranteed number of runs or a guaranteed number of wickets. If they do, they should be paying to see a one-day match instead, when each team is allotted a certain number of overs and a result is certain. Test cricket is the game at its highest level and must be kept that way.

'As soon as legislators find themselves influenced into making changes to a structure which has stood the test of over 100 years then we are in trouble. As soon as the run-ups of all but three bowlers are restricted, as has been suggested; as soon as captains are forced into the artificiality of using the spinners, not because they are worthy of it but because they satisfy a mandatory over-rate, that is when spectators will feel they are being cheated.'

As we saw in Chapter 8, most of the criticism targeted at the West Indies fast bowlers centres around allegations of intimidation, although the facts show that for Test players facing the West Indies pace quartet, batting is not the highly dangerous activity many claim it to be. Most of those taking part in the game today seem to believe that the existing regulations, allowing umpires to step in when they believe a batsman is likely to be injured, are adequate. If the umpires are failing to make the necessary interventions, a claim with which the most respected of Test umpires, Dickie Bird, disagrees, then that surely is a matter for them and can hardly be blamed on the fast bowlers, fired up and trying to do their best for their national side. Is it not also significant that you hear few complaints from captains of teams playing the Windies claiming that an umpire should have stepped in to protect one of their batsmen from short-pitched deliveries?

Most professional cricketers believe that the problem lies not with short-pitched bowling by the pace quartet, but with the uneven wickets on which they sometimes operate, both inside and outside the Caribbean. A batsman's reaction to a short-pitched delivery is governed by how quickly his mind can deal with the 'data' (the bounce and direction of the ball). The great majority of injuries are caused when the data become 'confused', for example by uneven bounce, and a batsman does not have sufficient time to select the right course of action. As Andy Lloyd and Michael Holding believe, it is the uneven pitches which should be the first concern of the international game's administrators rather than the fast bowlers. Yet there has been no concerted effort equal to that recently introduced initiative in English county cricket which threatens sides preparing unfit pitches with a swingeing penalty. Steps along these lines should be taken urgently by the International Cricket Council. If it proves, as it may do, impossible to produce consistently true pitches, then the game's administrators, if they are still concerned about the potential physical threat of short-pitched bowling, might need to take even more radical measures. It should not be beyond the ability of manufacturers of artificial pitches, with sufficient funds for research, to produce a pitch which, while giving help to the seam and spin bowler, remains true in bounce throughout a five-day match. Research of this sort is already under way by manufacturers of artificial running tracks and most hockey is now played on artificial surfaces.

And if they don't like that idea, what about making sure that the ball itself cannot inflict as much damage as the traditional cricket ball? Former ICC chairman Sir Colin Cowdrey has pointed out that the cricket ball was developed when round-arm, let alone overarm, bowling was illegal. In this area, the game has out-evolved the equipment with which it is played. Again, surely cricket ball manufacturers could develop a ball which would behave like the traditional ball but, at the worst, would inflict only a bad bruise. This would not stop a West Indian fast bowler from bowling at high pace – many of them learnt to bowl skilfully with soft balls on hard, wet sand – but would reduce the number of injuries they would cause. The most innovative players have always forced changes in the game's laws and practices. The legalization of overarm bowling produced an improvement in the protective equipment available to batsmen. Now that fast bowling has once again evolved into its next stage with the arrival of the pace quartet, action should be taken to allow the rest of the game to catch up. It is not change which is unnatural and against the spirit of cricket, but a stubborn clinging to the status quo. It is not as if the game would be reacting rashly to a passing fad; after all, fielding a high-quality pace quartet has been the most successful method of winning Test matches for nearly 20 years.

But will this debate become academic over the next five years? *Is* the West Indies' fast bowling production line grinding to a halt? This question has been asked regularly from the early 1980s onwards and by those inside the Caribbean as well as elsewhere in the world. However, time and again, the Caribbean has produced another high-class fast bowler in good time to ensure that the pace quartet remains at or close to full strength. The initial impetus was provided by the mid-1970s crop of Roberts, Holding, Daniel, Garner, Croft and Clarke. The reinforcements arrived on average once every four years: Marshall in 1980; Walsh in 1984; Ambrose in 1988; Bishop in 1989. And to fill the gaps there has been a steady stream of good quality 'support' bowlers from Winston Davis to Kenny Benjamin.

But there must be growing concern in the Caribbean that no obvious replacement for Ambrose, Walsh or Bishop has emerged since 1989. Bishop's injuries, which have been unusually difficult to cure for a West Indian fast bowler, have only added to the problem. There is no shortage of would-be contenders for a place in the pace quartet. As well as Kenny Benjamin there are Cameron Cuffy, Anderson Cummins, Barrington Browne, Franklyn Rose, Ottis Gibson, Vasbert Drakes and Linden Joseph. But, significantly, at least three if not more of these bowlers are fast-medium rather than truly quick, reflecting perhaps the increasing slowness of West Indian wickets. Many are also not in the full flush of youth, suggesting that the Windies' selectors are having to reconsider players they may have initially passed over.

Perversely, the end of the pace quartet might finally mean that they receive the recognition for their phenomenal achievements over the past 20 years. In their absence, most would realize just how spoiled cricket followers in the past two decades have been in witnessing such an explosion of fast-bowling talent. Perhaps with hindsight the critics might appreciate the effort it took to weld them into a team and keep that team playing at an unprecedented level of success for 18 years.

The very length of time that the Windies have been successful has counted against them, meaning that many have taken their achievements for granted. However, it would be a tragedy if the members of the quartet and their three inspirational captains were only to be awarded their true place in cricket history once they had faded from the game. They should be celebrated *now* as the very pinnacle of one of cricket's most demanding and glorious arts, as well as a powerful demonstration of the skills, spirit and intelligence of their countrymen and women.

Celebrate them because, once they are gone, the world of sport will be a poorer place. Future generations will envy us our good fortune to have seen the pace quartets in action and wonder why their success was treated by so many in such a petty and contemptuous manner. History will judge that it was the administrators and commentators who have betrayed the game of cricket; not Roberts, not Holding, not Lloyd, not Richards.

10 | Biographical notes and playing records

'The greatest concentration of fast bowling talent ever.'

West Indies fast bowlers 1974–94

The players are listed in chronological order of their Test débuts.

Anderson Montgomery Everton Roberts: Born 29 January 1951, Urlings Village, Antigua. *Teams:* Leeward Islands, Hampshire, New South Wales, Leicestershire. *Test début:* Third Test v. England, Barbados, March 1974. *Last Test:* Sixth Test v. India, Madras, December 1983. *Best bowling in Tests:* 7 for 54, Second Test v. Australia, Perth, December 1975. *Height:* 6 ft 1 in. One of *Wisden*'s Five Cricketers of the Year in 1975.

Andy Roberts was the trailblazer for the West Indian quartet. Regarded as mean, aggressive, moody and immensely strong, he became the second West Indian bowler after Sobers to pass 200 Test wickets.

Clive Lloyd believed that Roberts deceived batsmen because he did not have that long a run-up, but still got plenty of pace and power into his deliveries. But Roberts was even cleverer than that, often softening a batsman up with one or even two slower balls before really letting one fly. He was, as many have said, 'the master of the throat ball'.

Roberts varied his pace with consummate skill without any change in body movement, making him acutely difficult to deal with. Although he was a highly intelligent user of the new ball, his short deliveries with the old ball were often more effective. He had two types of bouncer, with the one that skidded off the pitch being the more dangerous. This was produced by Roberts holding the ball across the seam, making sure that it did not pitch as usual on the raised part of the ball. Such a delivery would bounce lower than a normal delivery, while still maintaining the same pace, causing it to skid through at an awkward height.

Greg Chappell said of Roberts: 'He had real mean eyes. Subsequently I found him a hell of a nice bloke, but bowling he did a good job of making you think he was a Black Power man.' Michael Holding adds: 'Andy was the one who took us beyond bowling just fast. He had an incredible cricket brain and was instrumental in many of my successes.' Malcolm Marshall agrees: 'No one thought more about the game and his part in it than Andy Roberts.'

Michael Anthony Holding: Born 16 February 1954, Half Way Tree, Kingston, Jamaica. *Teams:* Jamaica, Lancashire, Derbyshire, Tasmania. *Test début:* First Test v. Australia, Brisbane, November 1975. *Last Test:* Fifth Test v. England, Antigua, April 1986. *Best bowling in Tests:* 8 for 92, Fifth Test v. England, Kennington Oval, August 1976. *Height:* 6 ft 3 in. Took 185 Test wickets during the 1980s, the eighth highest tally. One of *Wisden's* Five Cricketers of the Year in 1977.

Michael Holding was a prince among fast bowlers. His nickname of 'Whispering Death' was a testament to the smoothness and grace of his run-up – many have claimed that the umpire couldn't hear him approach the wicket.

Holding began as understudy to Andy Roberts and by the end of his career many regarded him as the fastest bowler in cricket history. Although capable of bowling swing and seam, he tended to rely on pure pace rather than movement in the air or off the wicket to dismiss batsmen.

Clayton Goodwin said of Holding: 'Holding provided an unprecedented blend of skill, artistry, devastation and technical perfection.' Sunil Gavaskar was less complimentary, claiming – after the Indian tour to the West Indies in 1975–6 – that: 'Short-pitched bowling at that speed is barbaric.' Holding claimed Gavaskar's wicket 11 times in Tests.

Wayne Wendell Daniel: Born 16 January 1956, St Philip, Barbados. *Teams:* Barbados, Middlesex, Western Australia. *Test début:* Fourth Test v. India, Jamaica, April 1976. *Last Test:* Second Test v. Australia, Trinidad, March 1984. *Best bowling in Tests:* 5 for 39, Third Test v. India, Ahmedabad, November 1983. *Height:* 6 ft 1 in.

Wayne Daniel was selected as a raw 19-year-old for the West Indies' 1976 tour to England alongside Roberts, Holding, Holder and Julien. Following the tour, Daniel played his first season for Middlesex in 1977 and finished third in the national averages with 71 wickets.

It has been suggested that there was no love lost between Lloyd and Daniel, but both deny this. However, West Indian selectors were occasionally bemused by Daniel's reluctance to use the bouncer.

Colin Everton Hunte Croft: Born 15 March 1953, Lancaster Village, Demerara, British Guiana. *Teams:* Guyana, Lancashire. *Test début:* First Test v. Pakistan, Barbados, February 1977. *Last Test:* Third Test v. Australia, Adelaide, January 1982. *Best bowling in Tests:* 8 for 29, Second Test v. Pakistan, Trinidad, March 1977. *Height:* 6 ft 6 in. Took 33 wickets during his first Test series – at the time equalling Lance Gibbs's West Indies record.

Colin Croft had played only one first-class game before being called up to the Test squad. He was not the most accurate of the pace quartet, bowling very wide in the crease and sending down frequent short-pitched deliveries. He ran in seemingly from mid-off and often bowled around the wicket. Largely ineffective as a county cricketer with Lancashire, he performed at his best in Tests with a superlative bowler at the other end.

Croft was the member of the quartet most likely to deliver the completely unplayable ball. Of Guyana's only great fast bowler, Michael Holding says: 'Croft – the most uncompromising cricketer I ever met, a hard, hard man. I only disagreed with Colin on one thing. If he hit someone he'd stare at them. That was wrong: the first thing you do is go and help and make sure he's okay.'

Croft joined the 'rebel' tour of West Indians to South Africa in 1983.

Joel Garner: Born 16 December 1952, Christchurch, Barbados. *Teams:* Barbados, Somerset, South Australia. *Test début:* First Test v. Parkistan, Barbados, February 1977. *Last Test:* Third Test v. New Zealand, Christchurch, March 1987. *Best bowling in Tests:* 6 for 56, Third Test v. New Zealand, March 1980. *Height:* 6 ft 8 in. Took 212 wickets during the 1980s, the seventh highest tally. One of *Wisden's* Five Cricketers of the Year in 1980.

Michael Manley described Joel Garner as 'an intelligent giant of a man'. He claimed that Garner 'knew how to use his height, to get more lift, without resorting to the explicit bouncer, than almost any bowler who ever lived'. He was also renowned for delivering an unplayable, toe-crunching yorker.

Greg Chappell explained the difficulties of having to deal with Garner: 'Your brain picks up the length of the ball by the angle it leaves the bowler's hand. Everything from Joel looked like it was going to be short yet he kept hitting me on the foot.' Geoff Boycott underlined the frustration that many batsmen felt when facing Garner, claiming that: 'They should cut him off at the knees to make him bowl at a normal height.'

Michael Holding was sure of Garner's greatness: 'Awesome with the new ball, unforgiving with his accuracy, impossible in his height … The Bird [Garner's nickname was Big Bird] could have taken more wickets than anyone, but he liked his nightlife just a little too much.'

Sylvester Theophilus Clarke: Born 11 December 1954, Lead Vale, Christchurch, Barbados. *Teams:* Barbados, Surrey, Transvaal. *Test début:* Third Test v. Australia, Guyana, March 1978. *Last Test:* Second Test v. Australia, Sydney, January 1982. *Best bowling in Tests:* 5 for 126, Second Test v. India, Bangalore, December 1978. *Height:* 6 ft 1 in.

Norbert Phillip: Born 12 June 1948, Bioche, Dominica. *Teams:* Windward Islands, Essex. *Test début:* Third Test v. Australia, Guyana, March 1978. *Last Test:* Sixth Test v. India, Kanpur, February 1979. *Best bowling in Tests:* 4 for

48, Fourth Test v. India, Madras, January 1978. *Height:* 6 ft 2 in.

Malcolm Denzil Marshall: Born 18 April 1958, Pine, Bridgetown, Barbados. *Teams:* Barbados, Hampshire, Natal. *Test début:* Second Test v. India, Bangalore, December 1978. *Last Test:* Fifth Test v. England, Kennington Oval, August 1991. *Best bowling in Tests:* 7 for 22, Third Test v. England, Manchester, July 1988. *Height:* 5 ft 10.5 in. *Weight:* 12 st 8 lb. Holds the record for the number of Test wickets taken by a West Indian. Took 35 wickets at 12.65 during the 1988 series against England, a West Indian record. Took 323 Test wickets in the 1980s, a world record. One of *Wisden's* Five Cricketers of the Year in 1982.

Malcolm Marshall's self-professed motto is 'keep smiling and live day by day', a sharp contrast to the batsmen facing him, who often felt they were living (in cricket terms at least) 'ball by ball'. Marshall was only ever really depressed by various captains' failure to take his aspirations as a genuine all-rounder seriously.

He claims that his most memorable day's play in Test cricket was during the 1988 Old Trafford Test against England. From 15 overs and 4 balls, he took 7 wickets for just 22 runs to win the game for the Windies. He remembers that 'as the last wicket fell, down came the rain'.

Marshall has criticized wickets in the West Indies for becoming slow. In the 1988 Red Stripe competition, he hinted that he would take early retirement if the pitches continued to be unsympathetic to fast bowlers. In that season and for that reason, Marshall turned to leg-spin for a brief spell and took three wickets in the final innings of a game against the Windward Islands. He still finished that Caribbean season with 27 wickets at 17.26 apiece!

Throughout his time as a Test bowler, Marshall was renowned for his great stamina. In the latter stages of his career he often bowled with two fingers each on either-side of the seam and his thumb curled into the palm of his hand. This, Marshall claimed, gave him greater powers of movement, but all those bowlers who attempted to emulate him found the ball almost impossible to control using this grip.

Mark Nicholas, Marshall's captain at Hampshire, claims that: 'Malcolm can bowl everything from inswing to outswing, cutters to lightning speed at your head. He only intimidates people when he knows they have a weakness for it.' Fred Trueman adds: 'One always wonders with Malcolm Marshall where the pace comes from, but to me he is in the top flight of fast bowling.' Imran Khan believes: 'Even if Kapil Dev gets 1000 wickets, he can never compare to Marshall.'

Winston Walter Davis: Born 18 September 1958, Kingston, St Vincent. *Teams:* Windward Islands, Glamorgan, Northamptonshire. *Test début:* Fifth

Test v. India, Antigua, April 1983. *Last Test:* Fourth Test v. India, Madras, January 1988. *Best bowling in Tests:* 4 for 19, Fourth Test v. New Zealand, Jamaica, May 1985.

Eldine Ashworth Elderfield Baptiste: Born 12 March 1960, Liberta, Antigua. *Teams:* Kent, Leeward Islands, Northamptonshire. *Test début:* First Test v. India, Kanpur, October 1983. *Last Test:* Fifth Test v. England, Antigua, April 1990. *Best bowling in Tests:* 3 for 31, Fourth Test v. England, Manchester, July 1984. *Height:* 5 ft 11 in. *Weight:* 12 st.

Milton Aster Small: Born 12 February 1964, St Philip, Barbados. *Team:* Barbados. *Test début:* Second Test v. Australia, Trinidad, March 1984. *Last Test:* Second Test v. England, Lord's, June 1984. *Best bowling in Tests:* 3 for 40, Second Test v. England, Lord's, June 1984.

Courtney Andrew Walsh: Born 30 October 1962, Kingston, Jamaica. *Teams:* Jamaica, Gloucestershire. *Test début:* First Test v. Australia, Perth, November 1984. *Best bowling in Tests:* 6 for 62, Fourth Test v. India, Jamaica, April 1989. *Height:* 6 ft 5.5 in. *Weight:* 14 st 7 lb. Took a hat-trick v. Australia, First Test v. Australia, Brisbane, November 1988. Only specialist bowler to captain the West Indies. One of *Wisden's* Five Cricketers of the Year in 1986.

Since his début in 1984, Courtney Walsh has only ever been absent from the West Indies team for a significant period when he was omitted from the 1992 World Cup squad. This, he says, was a 'blessing in disguise' as it gave him his first real break from international cricket in eight years.

Walsh believes that his best spell in Tests was the one of 11 overs, 7 maidens, 8 runs and 4 wickets during the last innings of the Windies' inaugural Test against South Africa at the Kensington Oval in 1992. 'That morning of my life was the best as far as Test cricket is concerned.'

Walsh has been seen from the outside as the workhorse of the Windies attack, bowling fairly long spells in the hottest and most humid conditions. However, that underplays his exceptional ability to bowl unplayable deliveries. Because of his height, he can exploit bounce on the flattest of pitches and his stock ball to the right-hander is one which cuts in, usually from just short of a length. He is more than capable of bowling a fine inswinging yorker. Walsh also varies his pace greatly, making it very difficult for the batsmen to pick up the length of each delivery. His is not a smooth action, as there is much whirling of arms and legs on delivery, again making the ball difficult to spot.

In common with other Windies fast bowlers, Walsh pushes himself to the limits – and sometimes through the pain barrier – for the sake of his team. He is an absolute dream with the old ball. His diplomatic nature made him an ideal captain at Gloucestershire.

Michael Holding says of Walsh: 'Most people don't give Courtney too much credit but if you look back and see the amount of work he does and the wickets that he takes, you come to appreciate his value.'

Balfour Patrick Patterson: Born 15 September 1961, Portland, Jamaica. *Teams:* Jamaica, Lancashire. *Test début:* First Test v. England, Jamaica, February 1986. *Last Test:* First Test v. Australia, Brisbane, November 1992. *Best bowling in Tests:* 5 for 24, First Test v. India, Delhi, November 1987. *Height:* 6 ft 2.5 in.

On the poorly prepared wickets of his début series against England, Patterson was often unplayable. Seemingly always smiling, this belied his aggressive streak.

His time with Lancashire improved his technique and direction. Many reckoned him to be quicker at his peak than Holding. The great Jamaican bowler himself has declared of Patterson in 1986 that: 'I don't believe any man ever bowled faster and certainly not more dangerously.'

Anthony Hollis Gray: Born 23 May 1963, Port-of-Spain, Trinidad. *Teams:* Trinidad, Surrey. *Test début:* First Test v. Parkistan, Faisalabad, October 1986. *Last Test:* Third Test v. India, Christchurch, March 1987. *Best bowling in Tests:* 4 for 39, First Test v. Pakistan, Faisalabad, October 1986. *Height:* 6 ft 7 in.

Winston Keithroy Matthew Benjamin: Born 31 December 1964, St John's, Antigua. *Teams:* Leeward Islands, Leicestershire, Hampshire. *Test début:* First Test v. India, Delhi, November 1987. *Best bowling in Tests:* 4 for 46, only Test v. Sri Lanka, Moratuwa, December 1993. *Height:* 6 ft 3 in. 'Temperamental but very talented', according to Michael Holding.

Curtly Elconn Lynwall Ambrose: Born 21 September 1963, Swetes Village, Antigua. *Teams:* Leeward Islands, Northamptonshire. *Test début:* First Test v. Pakistan, Guyana, April 1988. *Best bowling in Tests:* 8 for 45, Fourth Test v. England, Barbados, April 1990. *Height:* 6 ft 7 in. *Weight:* 14 st 4 lb. One of *Wisden's* Five Cricketers of the Year in 1991.

In his first full Red Stripe season of 1988, Ambrose took 35 wickets at an average of 15.5. He generates steep lift, has an exceptionally good yorker and is never far away from the next wicket-taking delivery. Remarkably, he was called once for throwing in a match against Trinidad and Tobago by Test umpire Clyde Cummerbatch, but his action is in fact high and clean. He bowls a vicious leg-cutter, hates conceding runs and losing at anything.

Ambrose tends to regard bowling more as hard work than as pleasure and he has complained of Test cricket ennui. His disciplined approach provides the key to his achievements. 'I like bowling fast, but there is little point bowling fast when the wickets are so slow', he claims.

According to Terry Alderman: 'Like Garner he uses his height to full advantage but he's even more difficult to play because he angles it in like Colin Croft.' Peter Roebuck adds: 'Once he is on a roll, he can destroy everything in his way.'

Ian Raphael Bishop: Born 24 October 1967, Port-of-Spain, Trinidad. *Teams:* Trinidad, Derbyshire. *Test début:* First Test v. India, Guyana, March 1989. *Best bowling in Tests:* 6 for 40, Fifth Test v. Australia, Perth, January 1993. *Height:* 6 ft 5.5 in. *Weight:* 15 st 10 lb.

Ian Bishop was called up for the 1988 tour to England after only a handful of games for Trinidad & Tobago – for whom he had just taken 19 wickets to top the Red Stripe averages. With Ambrose, he formed a formidable new ball partnership but has not played Test cricket since April 1993 because of a stress fracture of the lower vertebra. A devout 'born again' Christian, he is 'real quick' with a superb action and a good temperament.

Ezra Alphonse Moseley: Born 5 January 1958, Christchurch, Barbados. *Teams:* Barbados, Glamorgan. *Test début:* Third Test v. England, Trinidad, March 1990. *Last Test:* Fourth Test v. England, Barbados, April 1990. *Best bowling in Tests:* 2 for 70, Third Test v. England, Trinidad, March 1990.

Ian Basil Alston Allen: Born 6 October 1965, St Vincent. *Team:* Windward Islands. *Test début:* Second Test v. England, Lord's, June 1991. *Last Test:* Third Test v. England, Trent Bridge, July 1991. *Best bowling in Tests:* 2 for 69, Third Test v. England, Nottingham, July 1991.

Kenneth Charlie Griffith Benjamin: Born 8 April 1967, Antigua. *Teams:* Leeward Islands, Worcestershire. *Test début:* Only Test v. South Africa, Barbados, April 1992. *Best bowling in Tests:* 6 for 66, First Test v. England, Jamaica, February 1994. *Height:* 6 ft 1 in.

Kenny Benjamin made his Test début in the West Indies' historic first Test against South Africa at Kensington Oval. Susceptible to breakdown, he has suffered from a series of niggling injury problems. He has a 'rollicking run-up' and usually bowls a fullish length. He can skid the ball in, as well as seam it off the wicket.

He vehemently dislikes his middle names (Charlie Griffith after the Bajan fast bowler), fearing that most people will think it is an affectation. Michael Holding says that Benjamin 'is strong and, although he doesn't have a great deal of pace, he can move the ball around'. Jimmy Adams adds that: 'He hits the deck very hard, and is difficult to play off the back foot because of his sharp in-ducker.'

Anderson Cleophas Cummins: Born 7 May 1966, Packer's Valley, Barbados. *Teams:* Barbados, Durham. *Test début:* Fifth Test v. Australia, Perth, January 1993. *Best bowling in Tests:* 4 for 54, Third Test v. Pakistan, Antigua, May 1993.

West Indian fast bowlers: Test cricket records 1974–94*

	M	Balls	Runs	Wkts	Av	5 wi	10 wm	BPW	R/100 b	Ovs/ Test
M.D. Marshall	81	17584	7876	376	20.94	22	4	46.77	44.79	36
C.A. Walsh	65	13197	5824	222	26.23	6	1	59.45	44.13	34
M.A. Holding	60	12739	5896	249	23.67	13	2	51.16	46.28	36
J. Garner	58	13169	5433	259	20.98	7	0	50.08	41.26	38
C.E.L. Ambrose	50	11809	4616	219	21.08	11	3	53.92	51.89	39
A.M.E. Roberts	47	11136	5174	202	25.61	11	2	55.13	46.46	39
B.P. Patterson	28	4829	2875	93	30.91	5	0	51.92	59.54	29
C.E.H. Croft	27	6165	2913	125	23.20	3	0	49.32	47.25	38
I.R. Bishop	18	3918	1698	83	20.45	5	0	47.20	43.33	36
W.K.M. Benjamin	16	2882	1251	51	24.53	0	0	56.51	43.41	30
W.W. Davis	15	2773	1472	45	32.71	0	0	61.62	53.08	31
S.T. Clarke	11	2477	1171	42	27.88	1	0	58.98	47.27	38
W.W. Daniel	10	1754	910	36	25.27	1	0	48.72	51.88	29
E.A.E. Baptiste	10	1326	537	16	35.18	0	0	82.87	42.76	23
N. Phillip	9	1820	1041	28	37.17	0	0	65.00	57.20	34
K.C.G. Benjamin	7	1403	728	26	28.00	1	0	53.96	51.89	33
A.H. Gray	5	888	377	22	17.13	0	0	40.36	42.45	30
A.C. Cummins	3	270	144	5	28.80	0	0	54.00	53.33	15
M.A. Small	2	270	153	4	38.25	0	0	67.50	56.66	23
I.B.A. Allen	2	282	180	5	36.00	0	0	56.40	63.83	24
E.A. Moseley	2	522	261	6	43.50	0	0	87.00	50.00	44

*Ranked by number of Test appearances

For comparison

Wickets taken

Modern fast bowlers

Kapil Dev (I)	432	Imran Khan (P)	362
R.J. Hadlee (NZ)	431	D.K. Lillee (A)	355
I.T. Botham (E)	383	R.G.D. Willis (E)	325
M.D. Marshall (WI)	**376**	**J. Garner (WI)**	**259**

M.A. Holding (WI)	**249**		A.M.E. Roberts (WI)	202
C.J. McDermott (A)	231		J.R. Thomson (A)	200
C.A. Walsh (WI)	**222**		G.F. Lawson (A)	180
Wasim Akram (P)	222		Waqar Younis (P)	166
C.E.L. Ambrose (WI)	**219**		G.R. Dilley (E)	138
M.G. Hughes (A)	212		C.E.H. Croft (WI)	125

All-time fast bowlers

Kapil Dev (I)	432		**M.A. Holding (WI)**	**249**
R.J. Hadlee (NZ)	431		G.D. McKenzie (A)	246
I.T. Botham (E)	383		C.J. McDermott (A)	231
M.D. Marshall (WI)	**376**		R.R. Lindwall (A)	228
Imran Khan (P)	362		**C.A. Walsh (WI)**	**222**
D.K. Lillee (A)	355		Wasim Akram (P)	222
R.G.D. Willis (E)	325		**C.E.L. Ambrose (WI)**	**219**
F.S. Trueman (E)	307		M.G. Hughes (A)	212
J. Garner (WI)	**259**		**A.M.E. Roberts (WI)**	**202**
J.B. Statham (E)	252		J.A. Snow (E)	202

Bowling average

Modern fast bowlers

18.98	Waqar Younis (P)		23.92	D.K. Lillee (A)
20.45	**I.R. Bishop (WI)**		24.63	B.A. Reid (A)
20.94	**M.D. Marshall (WI)**		25.20	R.G.D. Willis (E)
20.98	**J. Garner (WI)**		**25.61**	**A.M.E. Roberts (WI)**
21.08	**C.E.L Ambrose (WI)**		**26.23**	**C.A. Walsh (WI)**
22.29	R.J. Hadlee (NZ)		28.00	J.R. Thomson (A)
22.81	Imran Khan (P)		28.38	M.G. Hughes (A)
23.30	**C.E.H. Croft (WI)**		28.40	I.T. Botham (E)
23.43	Wasim Akram (P)		28.47	R.M. Hogg (A)
23.67	**M.A. Holding (WI)**		28.98	C.J. McDermott (A)

All-time fast bowlers

18.41	F.R. Spofforth (A)		22.97	K.R. Miller (A)
18.56	F.H. Tyson (E)		23.03	R.R. Lindwall (A)
18.98	Waqar Younis (P)		22.81	Imran Khan (P)
20.45	**I.R. Bishop (WI)**		**23.30**	**C.E.H. Croft (WI)**
20.94	**M.D. Marshall (WI)**		23.43	Wasim Akram (P)
20.98	**J. Garner (WI)**		**23.67**	**M.A. Holding (WI)**
21.08	**C.E.L. Ambrose (WI)**		23.91	W.A. Johnston (A)
21.10	N.A.T. Adcock (SA)		23.92	D.K. Lillee (A)
21.57	F.S. Trueman (E)		24.18	P.M. Pollock (SA)
22.29	R.J. Hadlee (NZ)		24.63	B.A. Reid (A)

Strike rate (BPW)

Modern fast bowlers

36.64	Waqar Younis (P)	53.41	R.G.D. Willis (E)
46.77	**M.D. Marshall (WI)**	53.75	Imran Khan (P)
47.20	**I.R. Bishop (WI)**	**53.92**	**C.E.L. Ambrose (WI)**
49.32	**C.E.H. Croft (WI)**	54.12	Wasim Akram (P)
50.08	**J. Garner (WI)**	**55.13**	**A.M.E. Roberts (WI)**
50.85	R.J. Hadlee (NZ)	55.26	B.A. Reid (A)
51.16	**M.A. Holding (WI)**	56.96	I.T. Botham (E)
51.92	**B.P. Patterson (WI)**	57.95	M.J. Hughes (A)
52.02	D.K. Lillee (A)	58.00	C.J. McDermott (A)
52.68	J.R. Thomson (A)	59.36	G.R. Dilley (E)

All-time fast bowlers

36.64	Waqar Younis (P)	**51.16**	**M.A. Holding (WI)**
44.52	F.R. Spofforth (A)	**51.92**	**B.P. Patterson (WI)**
45.42	F.H. Tyson (E)	52.02	D.K. Lillee (A)
46.77	**M.D. Marshall (WI)**	52.68	J.R. Thomson (A)
47.20	**I.R. Bishop (WI)**	53.25	A. Cotter (A)
49.32	**C.E.H. Croft (WI)**	53.41	R.G.D. Willis (E)
49.44	F.S. Trueman (E)	53.75	Imran Khan (P)
50.08	**J. Garner (WI)**	**53.92**	**C.E.L. Ambrose (WI)**
50.85	R.J. Hadlee (NZ)	54.12	Wasim Akram (P)
51.10	T. Richardson (E)	54.15	G.O.B. Allen (E)

Economy rate (runs per 100 balls)

Modern fast bowlers

39.09	**C.E.L. Ambrose (WI)**	45.99	D.K. Lillee (A)
41.26	**J. Garner (WI)**	**46.28**	**M.A. Holding (WI)**
42.44	Imran Khan (P)	46.38	Kapil Dev (I)
43.31	Wasim Akram (P)	**46.46**	**A.M.E. Roberts (WI)**
43.33	**I.R. Bishop (WI)**	47.19	R.G.D. Willis (E)
43.85	R.J. Hadlee (NZ)	**47.25**	**C.E.H. Croft (WI)**
44.13	**C.A. Walsh (WI)**	48.98	M.J. Hughes (A)
44.59	B.A. Reid (A)	49.48	G.F. Lawson (A)
44.79	**M.D. Marshall (WI)**	49.86	I.T. Botham (E)
45.89	R.M. Hogg (A)	49.96	C.J. McDermott (A)

All-time fast bowlers

34.35	N.A.T. Adcock (SA)	**39.09**	**C.E.L. Ambrose (WI)**
34.63	W.A. Johnston (A)	39.88	V.A. Holder (WI)
37.34	K.R. Miller (A)	40.88	F.H. Tyson (E)
38.47	R.R. Lindwall (A)	**41.26**	**J. Garner (WI)**
39.00	J.B. Statham (E)	41.36	F.R. Spofforth (A)

41.45	G.D. McKenzie (A)
42.44	Imran Khan (P)
42.97	W. Voce (E)
43.02	P.M. Pollock (SA)
43.31	Wasim Akram (P)

43.33	**I.R. Bishop (WI)**
43.65	F.S. Trueman (E)
43.85	R.J. Hadlee (NZ)
44.13	**C.A. Walsh (WI)**
44.58	H. Larwood (E)

Work rate (overs per Test)

Modern fast bowlers

44 overs
D.K. Lillee (A)

42 overs
R.J. Hadlee (NZ)

40 overs
G.F. Lawson (A)

39 overs
A.M.E. Roberts (WI)
C.E.L. Ambrose (WI)
B.A. Reid (A)
C.J. McDermott (A)
M.J. Hughes (A)

38 overs
J. Garner (WI)
C.E.H. Croft (WI)
Wasim Akram (P)

37 overs
D.E. Malcolm (E)
Imran Khan (P)

36 overs
M.A. Holding (WI)
M.D. Marshall (WI)
I.R. Bishop (WI)
I.T. Botham (E)

35 overs
Waqar Younis (P)
Kapil Dev (I)

34 overs
C.A. Walsh (WI)
J.R. Thomson (A)

All-time fast bowlers

54 overs
T. Richardson (E)

49 overs
G.D. McKenzie (A)

46 overs
W.A. Johnston (A)

44 overs
D.K. Lillee (A)

42 overs
R.J. Hadlee (NZ)

41 overs
J.A. Snow (E)
N.A.T. Adcock (SA)

40 overs
G.F. Lawson (A)

39 overs
A.M.E. Roberts (WI)
C.E.L. Ambrose (WI)
B.A. Reid (A)
C.J. McDermott (A)
M.J. Hughes (A)
H. Larwood (E)
W. Voce (E)
J.M. Gregory (A)
F.R. Spofforth (A)
P.M. Pollock (SA)

38 overs
J. Garner (WI)
C.E.H. Croft (WI)
Wasim Akram (P)
F.S. Trueman (E)
J.B. Statham (E)
V.A. Holder (WI)

The quartets

The West Indies fielded 37 different pace quartets during the period 1979 to 1994. Seven played five or more Tests together. Those quartets were:

14 Tests = Marshall, Ambrose, Walsh and Patterson
11 Tests = Roberts, Holding, Croft and Garner
 6 Tests = Roberts, Holding, Marshall and Garner
 6 Tests = Holding, Marshall, Garner and Baptiste
 6 Tests = Marshall, Ambrose, Walsh and Bishop
 5 Tests = Marshall, Ambrose, Walsh and W. Benjamin
 5 Tests = Ambrose, Walsh, W. Benjamin and K. Benjamin

The records of the two most commonly used quartets are:

M.D. Marshall, C.E.L. Ambrose, C.A. Walsh and B.P. Patterson (June 1988–August 1991)
14 Tests: Won 7, Lost 3, Drew 4

3 games v. England 1988
4 games v. Australia 1988–9
5 games v. Australia 1990–1
3 games v. England 1991

	Overs	Mdns	Runs	Wkts	Average	5 wi	10 wm
M.D. Marshall	494.4	86	1324	63	21.02	1	0
C.E.L. Ambrose	605.1	142	1489	65	22.91	2	0
C.A. Walsh	525	103	1367	44	31.07	0	0
B.P. Patterson	435.3	63	1474	47	31.36	3	0
Overall					**25.82**	**6**	**0**

	BPW	Runs/100 balls	% of overs bowled*
M.D. Marshall	47.11	44.61	24
C.E.L. Ambrose	55.86	41.01	29
C.A. Walsh	71.68	43.34	26
B.P. Patterson	55.60	56.41	21
Overall	**56.47**	**45.72**	

*pace quartet only

A.M.E. Roberts, M.A. Holding, C.E.H. Croft and J. Garner (December 1979–February 1982)

11 Tests: Won 4, Lost 1, Drew 6

3 games v. Australia 1979–80
2 games v. New Zealand 1979–80
1 game v. England 1980
3 games v. England 1980–1
2 games v. Australia 1981–2

	Overs	Mdns	Runs	Wkts	Average	5 wi	10 wm
J. Garner	437.5	135	916	47	19.49	2	0
M.A. Holding	388.3	99	1049	51	20.57	4	1
C.E.H. Croft	419.3	71	1188	46	25.83	2	0
A.M.E. Roberts	395	91	995	28	35.54	0	0
Overall					24.12	8	1

	BPW	Runs/100 balls	% of overs bowled*
J. Garner	55.89	34.87	27
M.A. Holding	45.71	45.00	23
C.E.H. Croft	54.72	47.20	26
A.M.E. Roberts	84.64	41.98	24
Overall	**57.24**	**42.13**	

*pace quartet only

Bibliography

Bailey, Trevor and Trueman, Fred: *From Larwood to Lillee*, MacDonald Queen Anne Press, 1984

Bose, Mihir: *A Maidan View, the Magic of Indian Cricket*, George Allen & Unwin, 1986

Caro, Andrew: *With a Straight Bat*, The Sales Machine Ltd, 1979

Constantine, Learie N.: *Cricket in the Sun*, Stanley Paul

Cotter, Gerry: *England versus West Indies, a History of the Tests and Other Matches*, The Crowood Press, 1991

Eagar, Patrick and Ross, Allan: *West Indian Summer*, Hodder & Stoughton, 1988

Figueroa, John: *West Indies in England, the Great Post-War Tours*, Kingswood Press, 1991

Francis, Tony: *The Zen of Cricket, Learning from Positive Thought*, Stanley Paul, 1992

Frith, David: *The Fast Men*, Corgi, 1984

Ganong, W.F.: *Review of Medical Physiology*, 13th edn, Appleton & Lange, Norwalk, Connecticut/San Mateo, California, 1987

Garner, Joel: *Big Bird Flying High*, Weidenfeld & Nicolson, 1988

Gover, Alf: *The Long Run*, Pelham, 1991

Holding, Michael with Cozier, Tony: *Whispering Death*, André Deutsch, 1993

Khan, Imran: *All Round View*, Chatto & Windus, 1988

James, C.L.R.: *Beyond a Boundary*, Stanley Paul, 1963

James, C.L.R.: *Cricket*, Allison & Busby, 1986

McDonald, Trevor: *Clive Lloyd, the Authorised Biography*, Granada Publishing, 1985

McDonald, Trevor: *Viv Richards, the Authorised Biography*, Pelham, 1984

McFarline, Peter: *A Game Divided*, Marlin Books, 1978

McGregor, Adrian: *Greg Chappell*, Fontana, 1986

Manley, Michael: *A History of West Indian Cricket*, André Deutsch and Pan Books, 1988

Marshall, Malcolm: *Marshall Arts*, Queen Anne Press, 1987

Murphy, Patrick: *Declarations*, Ringpress Books, 1989

Richards, Viv: *Hitting Across the Line*, Headline, 1991

Sobers, Sir Garfield with Scovell, Brian: *Sobers – Twenty Years at the Top*, Pan Books, 1989

Stollmeyer, Jeff: *Everything Under the Sun*, Stanley Paul, 1983

Thomson, Jeff and Frith, David: *Thommo*, Angus & Robertson, 1980

Journals and magazines

The Cricketer
Cricket Life International
Daily Telegraph
The Guardian
The Independent
Johnny Miller 96 Not Out
News of the World
Sticky Wicket
The Sunday Times
Third Man
Wisden Cricketers Almanack
Wisden Cricket Monthly

Video

Playing Cricket, the West Indies Way (Apex Film & Video Services Ltd, 18 Ripon Road, Kingston 5, Jamaica)

Index

Aamer Malik 73
Abdul Qadir 187
Adams, Jimmy 74, 112, 137
Alderman, Terry 65, 142, 148
Allen, David 32
Allen 'Gubby' 18, 21
Allen, Ian 198
Alexander, Gerry 30
Ali, Inshan 46, 47
Amarnath, Mohinder 48, 175, 180
Ambrose, Curtly 15, 56, 59, 70, 71, 72, 73, 74, 75, 76, 79, 80, 83, 84, 89, 90, 96, 97, 98, 99, 100, 101, 112, 114, 117, 119, 124, 128, 136, 137, 141, 145, 146, 147, 148, 153, 154, 162, 165, 173, 177, 179, 184, 190, 197
Ames, Les 19, 23
Amiss, Dennis 50, 52, 180
Archer, Ron 29
Arlott, John 44, 107
Asif Iqbal 51
Atherton, Michael 96, 98, 99, 100, 143, 152, 180, 181
Atkinson, Denis 28
Austin, Richard 51, 53
Azad, K. 67
Azharuddin, Mohammad 133, 138

Bailey, Robert 138, 142
Bailey, Trevor 35
Bairstow, David 131
Baptiste, Eldine 65, 66, 68, 69, 71, 72, 114, 196
Barlow, Eddie 51, 173
Barnett, Kim 142
Barrington, Ken 35
Bedi, Bishan 37, 46, 48
Benaud, Richie 33, 34, 169
Benjamin, Kenny 15, 74, 75, 76, 153, 190, 198
Benjamin, Winston 15, 70, 71, 75, 114, 117, 118, 119, 138, 153, 154, 197
Bicknell, Martin 176
Binny, R.M.H. 175
Bird, Dickie 169, 177

Bishop, Ian 15, 72, 73, 74, 75, 81, 86, 87, 153, 154, 179, 185, 190, 198
Boock, S.L. 62
Boon, David 73, 132, 141, 148
Border, Allan 15, 65, 73, 131, 132, 133, 148, 176, 180
Botham, Ian 22, 84, 130, 131, 138, 140, 164
Bowes, William 18, 21, 157, 179
Boyce, Keith 36, 37, 38, 39
Boycott, Geoff 63, 80, 92, 93, 96, 134, 144, 145, 146
Bradman, Sir Donald 13, 18, 19, 22, 24, 116, 126, 130, 157, 168, 174
Brearley, Mike 51
Broad, Chris 117, 130, 142
Browne, Barrington 190
Butts, Clyde 70

Caddick, Andy 89, 98, 99, 176
Cairns, Lance 62
Camacho, Steve 116
Capel, David 142
Caro, Andrew 55
Chanderpaul, Shivnarine 97
Chandrasekhar, B.S. 46, 48
Chappell, Greg 15, 40, 43, 51, 55, 60, 92, 126, 130
Chappell, Ian 40, 45, 51, 61, 92, 155, 156, 168, 169
Christiani, Robert 21
Clarke, Sylvester 15, 63, 64, 65, 107, 116, 160, 163, 179, 190, 194
Close, Brian 32, 49, 119
Coney, Jeremy 110
Constantine, Sir Learie 17, 18, 19, 20, 21, 22, 23, 24, 25, 26, 186
Contractor, Nari 34
Cowdrey, Chris 136
Cowdrey, Colin 32, 35, 185, 189
Cozier, Tony 42, 56, 57, 78, 84, 95, 105, 112, 171, 181, 188
Cranston, Ken 25
Croft, Colin 15, 50, 51, 53, 58, 59, 60, 61, 62, 63, 64, 65, 72, 80, 93, 94, 102, 105, 107, 114,

173, 176, 177, 179, 184, 190, 193
Crowe, Jeff 128
Cuffy, Cameron 190
Cummins, Anderson 75, 111, 153, 190, 198
Curtis, Tim 117–20, 129, 136, 137, 138, 143, 162, 163, 166

Daniel, Wayne 15, 46, 47, 49, 50, 65, 66, 68, 160, 163, 165, 179, 190, 193
Davidson, Alan 33
Davis, Winston 15, 65, 66, 68, 70, 80, 190, 195
DeFreitas, Phillip 146, 165, 175
Dewdney, Tom 28, 29
Dexter, Ted 35, 129
Dilley, Graham 131, 137
Donald, Allan 183
Dowe, Uton 36, 38
Drakes, Vasbert 190
Dujon, Jeff 69, 72, 73, 102, 109, 112, 113, 114, 148, 162, 166
Dyson, John 128

Edgar, Bruce 62
Edrich, John 35
Edwards, Richard 36, 37
Edwards, Ross 51
Emburey, John 131, 135–6, 137, 165, 166

Fagg, Arthur 34
Farnes, Ken 18, 21, 179
Ferguson, Wilfred 27
Fingleton, Jack 13
Foster, Neil 137
Fowler, Graeme 180
Francis, George 17, 18, 19, 20
Fraser, Angus 99, 106, 165
Fredericks, Roy 40, 51, 54
Frith, David 149–51, 152, 155, 166, 180

Gaekwad, A.D. 47, 48, 130
Garner, Joel 15, 50, 51, 53, 54, 55, 58, 59, 60, 61, 62, 63, 64, 65, 68, 69, 70, 72, 78, 80, 83, 84, 87, 93, 95, 100, 101, 102,

105, 110, 113–14, 123, 133, 140, 160, 163, 165, 173, 175, 179, 190, 194

Gatting, Mike 59, 63, 116, 130, 134, 142, 144, 146, 158, 163-4

Gavaskar, Sunil 38, 46, 47, 48, 66, 125, 126, 130, 180

Gibbs, Lance 37, 38, 51, 184, 187

Gibson, Ottis 190

Gilchrist, Roy 28, 29, 30, 183

Gilmour, Gary 40, 46, 51

Goddard, Jerry 27, 28

Gomes, Larry 114, 115, 137

Gomez, Gerry 26, 27, 28

Gooch, Graham 63, 74, 92, 117, 118, 125, 128, 132, 134, 136, 139–7, 162, 165, 178, 180, 187

Gover, Alfred 80, 87

Gower, David 63, 106, 130, 132, 133, 134, 136, 139, 142, 143, 180

Grace, W.G. 178

Grant, George 24

Graveney, David 154

Gray, Tony 15, 68, 124, 197

Greenidge, Gordon 40, 46, 51, 62, 67, 72, 73, 74, 83, 104, 105, 112, 114, 148

Greig, Tony 49, 50, 51, 142

Griffith, Charlie 31, 32, 33, 34, 35, 36, 87, 89, 90, 184, 185

Griffith, Herman 17, 18, 19, 20, 21

Hadlee, Sir Richard 61, 62, 110, 123, 125, 130

Hall, Wes 29, 30, 31, 32, 33, 34, 35, 36, 80, 89, 90, 105, 110, 183, 184, 185

Hammond, Wally 19, 21, 22, 24, 186

Hanif Mohammad 29

Harper, Roger 69, 70, 109

Hayes, Frank 36, 59

Haynes, Desmond 51, 53, 62, 73, 112, 113, 125, 130, 148

Headley, George 20

Hearne, Jack 24

Hector, Tim, editor of *The Outlet* 43, 44

Hendren, Patsy 19, 21, 23, 24

Hewetson, Edward 23

Hick, Graeme 98, 99, 128–29, 165

Hirst, George 161, 178

Hirwani, N.D. 70

Hobbs, Sir Jack 20, 21, 23

Hogg, Rodney 60

Holder, Vanburn 36, 37, 38, 39,

42, 43, 45, 46, 48, 49, 50, 90, 101, 162

Holding, Michael 15, 40, 41, 43, 44, 46, 47, 48, 49, 50, 51, 53, 58, 59, 60, 61, 62, 63, 64, 65, 66, 68, 69, 70, 72, 77, 78, 79, 80, 81, 82, 83, 84, 85, 86, 87, 89, 90, 92, 93, 94, 95, 96, 99, 101, 102, 105, 108, 112, 113, 114, 123, 129, 130, 133, 134, 158, 159, 161, 162, 163, 164, 172, 173, 175, 176, 177, 179, 181, 184, 185, 186, 189, 190, 191, 193

Holford, David 46, 47, 51

Hookes, David 51

Hooper, Carl 73, 114, 137, 153

Howarth, Geoff 62, 128

Hudson, Andrew 180

Hughes, Kim 60, 61, 64, 65, 180

Hughes, Merv 73, 84, 148

Hulme, Joe 24

Hussein, Nasser 142, 143

Hutton, Sir Leonard 13, 25, 26

Hutton, Richard 150–1

Hylton, Leslie 17, 18, 19, 21, 22

Igglesden, Alan 89

Ilott, Mark 176

Illingworth, Ray 188

Imran Khan 15, 50, 51, 70, 72, 73, 79, 82, 89, 90, 93, 94, 95, 100, 104, 116, 124, 125, 152, 154, 170, 171

Jackman, Robin 131

James, C.L.R. 20, 22, 30, 31, 35, 77, 95, 103, 104

Jardine, Douglas 23, 24, 157, 186

Javed Miandad 50, 130, 131, 132, 138

John, George 17, 19, 20

Johnson, Hines 25, 26, 27, 28

Johnston, Bill 13, 26

Jones, Dean 73, 148, 180

Jones, Prior 25, 26, 27, 28

Joseph, Linden 190

Julien, Bernard 36, 38, 39, 40, 46, 48, 51

Jumadeen, R.R. 46, 47

Kallicharran, Alvin 46, 51, 53, 107, 109

Kanhai, Rohan 44

Kapil Dev 66, 84, 124, 125, 126, 175, 180, 183

King, Collis 51, 62, 183

King, Frank 28, 29

King, Lester 31

Kirmani, Syed 48

Kirsten, Peter 74

Knott, Alan 51

Laird, Bruce 60, 121, 128

Laker, Jim 27

Lamb, Allan 131, 132, 136, 141, 142, 180

Langer, Julian 75

Lara, Brian 56, 73, 75, 90, 98, 112

Larkins, Wayne 127, 142, 143

Larwood, Harold 18, 23, 24, 157, 179

Lawrence, David 89, 175

Lawry, Bill 36

Lewis, Chris 98, 99, 159

Leyland, Maurice 19, 21

Lillee, Dennis 40, 41, 42, 44, 46, 49, 51, 60, 64, 65, 77, 82, 101, 102, 142, 159, 182

Lindwall, Ray 13, 26, 29, 185

Lloyd, Andy 164, 189

Lloyd, Clive 39, 40, 41, 42, 43, 44, 45, 46, 47, 48, 49, 50, 51, 54, 55, 56, 57, 77, 78, 90, 94, 103, 104, 105, 106, 107, 108, 109, 110, 111, 112, 114, 169, 171, 172, 173, 184, 191

Loader, Peter 179

Logie, Gus 73, 112

Lord, David 53

McCabe, Stan 19

McCormick, E.L. 18

McDermott, Craig 73, 75, 88, 89, 148, 175

McMillan, Brian 176

McMorris, Easton 32

Madan Lal 48, 66, 175

Mailey, Arthur 178

Majid Khan 51

Malcolm, Devon 89, 165, 166, 167, 175, 183

Mallett, Ashley 40

Maninder Singh 67, 175

Manley, Michael 21, 82, 104, 107, 152, 184

Marlar, Robin 183

Marsh, Geoff 73, 148

Marsh, Rodney 51, 60, 65, 71, 168, 169

Marshall, Malcolm 15, 54, 58, 63, 64, 66, 68, 69, 70, 71, 72, 74, 79, 80, 81, 83, 86, 88, 93, 95, 101, 102, 112, 114, 115, 117, 118, 119, 123, 124, 125, 126, 131, 133, 134, 136, 138, 139, 140, 141, 144, 146, 147, 148, 154, 156, 160, 162, 163, 164, 173, 177, 176, 177, 179,

182, 190, 195
Martindale, Manny 17, 18, 19, 21, 24, 26, 186
Masood Anwar 73
Matthews, Craig 183
May, Tim 75, 174
Miller, Keith 13, 26, 29, 185
Moody, Tom 130, 133
Morris, Hugh 162
Moseley, Ezra 72, 116, 198
Moxon, Martyn 117, 143
Mudassar Nazar 130
Murray, David 98, 166
Murray, Deryck 51, 53, 65, 113, 166
Mushtaq Mohammad 50, 51

Navjot Singh 126
Nicholas, Mark 95
Norrie, David (*News of the World*) 152

Oldfield, Wally 24

Packer, Kerry 42, 51, 52, 53, 54, 56
Padmore, Albert 46, 47
Parker, John 62
Pascoe, Len 160
Patterson, Patrick 15, 68, 69, 70, 71, 73, 140, 141, 146, 148, 154, 162, 166, 173, 185, 197
Phillip, Norbert 194
Pollock, Graeme 51, 116
Pollock, Peter 173
Prasanna, E.A.S. 37, 46
Pringle, Derek 136, 145, 146
Procter, Mike 51, 173

Rae, Allan, President of the West Indies Cricket Board of Control 53, 107, 108
Ramadhin, Sonny 26, 28, 110, 187
Ramiz Raja 73, 130
Ramnarino, Didanth 56
Ramprakash, Mark 98, 99, 128, 143, 145
Redpath, Ian 51
Reid, Bruce 148
Reiffel, Paul 176
Richards, Barry 51, 116, 126
Richards, Jack 136
Richards, Vivian 13, 41, 42, 44, 45, 46, 49, 50, 51, 53, 54, 55, 65, 67, 73, 78, 84, 90, 94, 104, 105, 108, 109, 110, 111, 112, 113, 114, 125, 126, 129, 137, 140, 148, 149, 158, 159, 160,

167, 168, 184, 191
Richardson, Richie 44, 69, 72, 73, 74, 97, 98, 100, 111, 112, 115–16
Ritchie, Greg 130
Roberts, Andy 15, 39, 41, 46, 47, 49, 51, 53, 54, 58, 60, 61, 62, 63, 64, 65, 66, 70, 72, 80, 82, 87, 92, 94, 102, 105, 162, 173, 175, 177, 179, 184, 190, 191, 192
Robertson, Jack 25
Robinson, Tim 142
Roebuck, Peter 97, 111, 112, 131
Root, Fred 161
Rose, Franklyn 190
Rowe, Lawrence 46, 50, 51, 54, 62, 107, 108
Russell, Jack 98, 99, 101, 145
Rutherford, Ken 123, 130

Salim Malik 73, 124, 180
Salisbury, Ian 98, 99
Sandham, Andrew 23
Sandhu, B.S. 130, 175
Sarfraz Nawaz 124
Sealey, Edmund 83
Shackleton, Derek 32
Shastri, Ravi 67
Shepherd, John 36, 37
Shillingford, Grayson 36, 37, 38
Shoaib Mohammad 73
Simmons, Phil 97, 98
Simpson, Bobby 34, 53, 88
Small, Milton 68, 196
Smith, Collie 29
Smith, David 127
Smith, Robin 98, 99, 134, 136, 138, 141, 142, 145, 164, 180
Snow, John 51, 156, 179
Sobers, Sir Garfield 26, 28, 29, 30, 34, 35, 38, 44, 87, 89, 95, 104
Stackpole, Keith 41
Statham, Brian 175, 179
Stayers, Charlie 31, 183
Steele, David 142
Stewart, Alec 98, 99, 128, 142, 143, 144, 181
Stewart, Mickey 142
Such, Peter 165
Sutcliffe, Herbert 23
Swaranjit Singh 30

Tarilton, Percy 23
Tavare, Chris 143
Taylor, Mark 73, 131, 133, 148
Thomson, Jeff 40, 41, 42, 44, 46, 49, 51, 60, 82, 93, 142, 156

Thorpe, Graham 98, 99
Titmus, Fred 32
Trim, John 25, 27, 28
Troup, G.B. 62
Trueman, Fred 32, 80, 92, 175, 179, 183
Turner, Glenn 37
Tyldesley, Ernest 20
Tyson, Frank 20, 175, 179

Umrigar, Polly 48
Underwood, Derek 51, 187

Valentine, Alfred 26, 28, 110
Venkataraghavan 37, 48
Vengsarkar, Dilip 124–5, 126, 180
Viswanath, G.R. 47, 48
Voce, Bill 18, 23, 24, 157, 179

Waight, Dennis 77–90, 96, 100, 107, 171, 184
Walker, Max 40, 46, 51
Wall, T.W. 18
Walsh, Courtney 15, 68, 70, 71, 72, 73, 74, 75, 76, 98, 101, 112, 114, 116, 117, 123, 124, 125, 140, 141, 146, 148, 154, 158, 162, 163, 166, 167, 173, 177, 179, 180, 181, 190, 196
Walters, Doug 36
Waqar Younis 72, 73, 75, 89, 124, 178
Warne, Shane 74, 174, 178, 187
Warner, Sir Pelham 26, 157
Wasim Akram 72, 73, 75, 89, 124
Watkin, Steve 146
Watson, Chester 31, 33, 183
Waugh, Mark 73, 130, 148, 180
Waugh, Steve 73, 74, 129, 148
Weekes, Everton 26
Wellham, Dirk 65
Wessels, Kepler 74, 128, 129
Williams, David 56
Williams, 'Foffie' 25, 26, 27, 28
Willey, Peter 127, 128, 129, 131
Willis, Bob 50, 82, 86, 93, 104, 159, 165, 179, 182, 186
Woodfull, W.M. 19
Woolmer, Bob 53
World Series Cricket 43, 51–6, 78, 92, 103, 107, 126, 167
Worrell, Sir Frank 26, 28, 30, 31, 43, 44, 56, 103, 104, 105
Wright, John 61
Wyatt, Bob 21

Yadav, N. 67

Zaheer Abbas 53